Dear Reader:

The book you are about to read is the latest bestseller from the St. Martin's True Crime Library, the imprint *The New York Times* calls "the leader in true crime!" Each month, we offer you a fascinating account of the latest, most sensational crime that has captured the national attention. St. Martin's is the publisher of John Glatt's riveting and horrifying SE-CRETS IN THE CELLAR, which shines a light on the man who shocked the world when it was revealed that he had kept his daughter locked in his hidden basement for 24 years. In the Edgar-nominated WRITTEN IN BLOOD, Diane Fanning looks at Michael Petersen, a Marine-turned-novelist found guilty of beating his wife to death and pushing her down the stairs of their home—only to reveal another similar death from his past. In the book you now hold, LOVE ME OR ELSE, Colin McEvoy and Lynn Olanoff detail an unusual case of love gone terribly wrong.

St. Martin's True Crime Library gives you the stories behind the headlines. Our authors take you right to the scene of the crime and into the minds of the most notorious murderers to show you what really makes them tick. St. Martin's True Crime Library paperbacks are better than the most terrifying thriller, because it's all true! The next time you want a crackling good read, make sure it's got the St. Martin's True Crime Library logo on the spine—you'll be up all night!

Charles E. Spicer, Jr.

Charles E. Spicer, Jr.
Executive Editor, St. Martin's True Crime Library

For Kathryn,

LOVE ME OR ELSE

The True Story of a Devoted Pastor,
a Fatal Jealousy, and the Murder That
Rocked a Small Town

Thank you for reading!

Colin McEvoy and Lynn Olanoff

St. Martin's Paperbacks

LOVE ME OR ELSE

Copyright © 2012 by Colin McEvoy and Lynn Olanoff.

All rights reserved.

For information address St. Martin's Press, 175 Fifth Avenue, New York, NY 10010.

EAN: 978-0-312-54082-1

Printed in the United States of America

St. Martin's Paperbacks edition / March 2012

St. Martin's Paperbacks are published by St. Martin's Press, 175 Fifth Avenue, New York, NY 10010.

10 9 8 7 6 5 4 3 2 1

ACKNOWLEDGMENTS

We are indebted to a great many people who have helped make our first book venture a rewarding and successful one.

First, we would like to thank everyone who took the time to be interviewed for this book, particularly Jim and Dorothy Smith for sharing memories of their beloved daughter Rhonda with us.

We are grateful to all of the editors and staff of *The Express-Times,* especially Eileen Holliday, Nick Falsone and Rudy Miller for assigning us to the stories, and Tom Quigley for his assistance with and interest in our project.

We very humbly thank writers Lou Michel, Michael Beebe and Chris Bohjalian for their advice on how to get started on the long road to getting published.

We are extremely grateful to our agent, Jake Elwell; to Yaniv Soha, Charles Spicer, April Osborn, David Stanford Burr and Jessica Preeg from St. Martin's Paperbacks; and to attorney Ellis Levine for his legal review. You all took what was a completely foreign process to us and made it a very simple and enjoyable one.

Thanks also go out to Jaccii Farris and Brad Rinehart at WFMZ-TV for their assistance in providing us with photos for this book.

Big thanks to Sarah Wojcik, Donald Carpenter, Rick Olanoff, John Gebhardt and Art McEvoy for reading through the various stages of our manuscript. And a special thank you to Sandy Weber, who knew for years and years that this book was coming.

Lastly, we would like to thank everyone in our families for all their support and enthusiasm along the way.

The information presented in this book is based on a review of hundreds of court and police documents, as well as interviews with most of the key individuals involved, including Jim and Dorothy Smith, Gregory Stumpo, Robert Egan, David Zellis, Greg Shreaves, Judy Zellner, Sue Brunner, Kimberly Triol, Rosalie Schnell, Gregg Dietz, Paul Rose, Michael Applebaum, Thomas Joachim and Mary Jane Fonder, who spoke to the authors during a three-hour prison interview. In cases where individuals were not available for interviews, information was provided by court testimony or other legal documents.

CHAPTER 1

The door shouldn't have been unlocked.

Judy Zellner slipped her key into the side door at Trinity Evangelical Lutheran Church, but the door fell open before she could turn it. She looked down at the doorknob, surprised and more than a little annoyed. *This door is always supposed to be locked, everybody in the church knows that. Even out here in rural Bucks County, Pennsylvania, the door has to be locked.*

Whoever's in here is going to get a piece of my mind, Judy thought, slipping the key back into her purse and stepping into the hallway. She was glad to get out of the cold on this winter day of January 23, 2008.

The door to the church office was shut, but through the large interior window Judy could see the light was on. She hadn't expected anybody to be there that Wednesday afternoon, when she came on her twice-weekly routine to clean the church. She glanced briefly through the window, but nobody was sitting behind the desk inside the small office. *Perhaps,* she thought, *Pastor Shreaves is upstairs somewhere.*

But first things first. Judy walked straight past the office, dropped her purse and coat onto the table in the narthex, and headed for the bathroom.

The sixty-year-old grandmother of six had been faithfully attending Trinity Evangelical Lutheran Church for the last twenty-six years. Even after she moved from nearby Wassergass to Allentown, the largest city in the Lehigh Valley region, she continued to call this church her own, and encouraged her three children to regularly attend with her. Judy's home in Allentown was twelve miles away, and she had to pass by several closer churches on her way to this one, but she never once considered going somewhere else. She loved her church family here at this small parish. She loved singing in the choir and being involved with everybody's lives.

The church sits along Route 212, a winding country road that serves as a major thoroughfare in Springfield Township. The town of about five thousand residents rests five miles southeast of the Allentown and Bethlehem metropolitan area, and about forty miles north of Philadelphia. Bucks County grows far more suburban as it borders Philadelphia on its southern end, but here in the northern end of the county, Springfield Township remains an example of the area's rural heritage.

At over thirty square miles, Springfield Township is the county's second largest municipality in terms of land area, and about half of it remains undeveloped, preserved as agricultural open space or completely vacant land. More than 44 percent of the township consists of heavy woodlands, and much of the land is characterized by large rocky hills cut by valley streams and creeks.

And that's just fine with the residents of Springfield Township. Most of the township's residents—98 percent of which are white—fall between ages forty-five and sixty-four, and are perfectly content to drive outside the area for goods, services, and places of employment if it means maintaining Springfield's rural character. In a survey, when asked what types of stores, businesses and professional services were needed most in the township, 51 percent responded, "none needed."

Judy passed the church office again on her way up to the pastor's office, where she found his door was locked. Judy was surprised. Since he joined the church nearly three years ago in March 2005, Pastor Gregory Shreaves was almost always here. Judy hadn't yet met the new secretary, Megan, who was hired a few days ago. *Maybe she's here somewhere,* she thought.

Judy grabbed her cleaning supplies from the closet down the hall and went back downstairs to the church office. Nobody was behind the desk, so Judy started walking toward the cubbyhole of file cabinets in the corner of the room.

"Megan?" Judy called, tilting her head to see if anybody was in the corner. "Megan, are you back there?"

As she passed the corner of the desk, Judy froze as something caught her eye. Crumpled behind the desk lay the body of a woman, her legs folded at the knees, her head and upper body curled forward, pointing toward the ceiling.

There was a great deal of blood. The woman's head was soaked in a crimson puddle, strands of her long brown hair flowing outward in all directions. Judy looked at the woman's chest and found it motionless. Then her eyes drifted to the wound on the right side of the woman's head.

Judy's thoughts immediately turned to her many hours spent watching *CSI: Crime Scene Investigation* on television. *Don't touch the body,* she thought.

She froze. What if the person who did this was still in the church? *Oh my God,* she thought. *Somebody could kill me.*

Judy grabbed the cordless phone sitting on the desk and ran outside. Fumbling with it, she dialed 911.

"911, where is the emergency?" an operator said.

Judy screamed into the phone: a primal, fearful sound that was impossible to decipher. The operator tried to calm her down and instructed her to stop screaming, calming Judy long enough to find out the address she was calling from.

"Okay, what's the problem?" the operator asked.

"There's a girl murdered in our office!" Judy said, her voice loud, nearly hysterical.

"There's a girl what?" the operator asked.

"Murdered!" Judy shouted back, breathing long, panicked breaths.

"Ma'am, listen, calm down," the operator said. "What do you mean? What's wrong with her?"

"She's lying behind the desk, full of blood!" Judy said, her voice growing higher, her breaths getting so heavy she started to gasp between phrases. "I'm the cleaning lady at the church . . . and I just got here. . . ."

"Is she awake and able to talk to you?"

"No, it looks like she's dead!" Judy said. "There's blood all over her head and around her head! Oh my God!"

"Okay. And ma'am, you don't want to go near her?" the operator asked.

"I don't know if somebody else is in there! It's a big church!"

After asking for Judy's name, the operator continued, "All right Judy. Just breathe for a sec, okay? Don't touch anything, okay?"

"I didn't, I didn't," Judy said, sobbing. She was starting to find it difficult to say anything at all. "I . . . I . . . ah . . ."

"Okay, where do you see the blood on her?" the operator asked.

"It's all over her!"

"All over her?"

"Yes, it's all over the floor!" Judy said, crying even harder. "She must be dead!"

"All right Judy, just try to calm down. I know it's not something pleasant to see. Does she look like she's breathing at all? Does she look pale? Does she look blue?"

"She looks blue," Judy responded. She explained that a new secretary was recently hired, but that Judy didn't know what she looks like, and didn't know if the woman inside the church is her or not.

"Okay, all right Judy, listen. We have someone on the way, okay?"

Matthew Compton and Michael Maguire were just finishing a late breakfast around 1 o'clock at the local diner, Vera's Country Cafe, when they received a call on their pager. "Possible expiration," the page read. An unresponsive female had been found in a puddle of blood.

The two paramedics with Upper Bucks Regional Emergency Medical Services rushed out to their ambulance, Maguire taking the wheel. Fortunately the church was just a tenth of a mile up the road.

Probably an elderly woman who took a spill and hit her head, Maguire thought. If this were the nearby city of Bethlehem, where he also worked as a paramedic, he might have been expecting something more serious, but little ever happens in Springfield Township. In his fourteen years as a paramedic, most of his calls from Upper Bucks have been limited to medical situations or traffic accidents from motorists unaccustomed to the winding country roads.

Back in the late 1980s, when Interstate 78 was expanded into the area, it was thought Springfield Township's vast open space would become subject to extensive growth and turn into a bedroom community of sorts for residents who traveled to New York City or Harrisburg. This prediction proved false. While neighboring towns like Richland, Milford, Williams, and Lower Saucon Townships all experienced significant growth, Springfield Township generally saw a few new single-family homes on a couple acres of land. In fact, it was the only municipality among its neighbors to actually see a decrease in its population.

So as its neighbors saw the rise of brand-new large-lot residential subdivisions, Springfield Township continued to maintain the character of an earlier time, with numerous farms, inns, historic villages, and even a covered bridge still intact. Perhaps the township's biggest claim to fame is the old home of Eric Knight, author of the 1940 book *Lassie Come-Home.* Knight wrote the book right there in Springfield, and his family dog, Toots, on whom the famous fictional collie was based, is buried on the property in what was the dog's favorite hill.

The ambulance pulled into the church parking lot, and Compton and Maguire stepped out and rushed toward the church. A gray-haired man wearing a blue sweater, alerted by the sirens, greeted them as they approached the door.

"Can I help you?" the man asked confusedly.

"Somebody called for an ambulance?" Maguire asked.

"No," the man shook his head. "I'm the only one here. Nobody called."

Maguire pulled out his pager and read off the call with the church address: "Trinity Evangelical Lutheran Church at 2170 Route 212."

"That's the other church," the man responded, pointing to a sign that read "Trinity United Church of Christ," at 1990 Route 212. "Happens all the time."

The other church was a half mile up the road, and Maguire and Compton pulled in just a few minutes later. As they arrived, Judy Zellner stood waving at the bottom of a small stairway leading up to the side door. "She's inside!"

The paramedics stepped inside with Judy in tow. She pointed toward the office and Maguire peered inside, but didn't see anything out of sorts. "Where?" he asked.

"She's behind the desk," Judy replied. "She has a lot of blood on her. I think she's dead. I don't know what happened."

As Maguire stepped further into the office, he saw the woman on the floor, and he could immediately hear that she was still breathing. The high-pitched gurgling reminded him of the sound of a brewing pot of coffee.

"She's still alive," Maguire said to Judy. "Stay in the hall."

It was immediately clear the woman had been shot. Most of the blood appeared to have come from the right side of her head, and Maguire spotted what appeared to be a bullet wound just above her ear. Compton felt for a pulse and found one, but the woman was otherwise nonresponsive. Maguire grabbed his radio and contacted Bucks County dispatch, calling for a state trooper to respond to the scene.

As Maguire finished the call, Compton pointed toward a shiny piece of metal on the floor that appeared to be a bullet fragment. A quick scan of the room turned up no weapons. Compton took off his ball cap and placed it over the bullet so police could quickly find it later.

When Compton went outside for a backboard, Maguire grabbed a black Magic Marker from atop the desk. He knew he had to move the woman, but he also wanted to leave the crime scene as intact as possible for police. After outlining the body on the floor, he and Compton lifted the woman and placed her onto the backboard.

As the two men lifted the board, the woman's head tilted to the side, facing Judy as she watched from the other side of the office window. Judy gasped at the blood-streaked face of a woman she had seen so many times before.

"Oh my God," Judy said. "That's my friend Rhonda!"

CHAPTER 2

State Trooper Kevin Hibson was the first officer on the scene, pulling into the church at 1:08 p.m. Springfield Township has its own police department, a modest force of a police chief and three officers. But when one of the officers isn't on duty, state police are called in.

Judy greeted Hibson at the church door and directed him to the office, where two paramedics in royal blue uniforms were hoisting a middle-aged woman onto a backboard. He immediately noted what appeared to be massive head trauma, the victim's long brown hair stained and matted with blood.

Maguire and Compton carried the backboard past Hibson and Judy, where they were met at the door by another state trooper, Andrew Mincer. Mincer grabbed hold of the board and helped them carry the woman down the small stairway to the waiting ambulance.

"She has a single, possibly double gunshot wound to the head," Compton informed Mincer.

The paramedics placed the woman into the back of the ambulance, then got to work, setting up an IV, starting up the heart monitor, and running a breathing tube into her mouth. As they worked, Trooper Louis Gober, a forensic service unit officer, pulled into the parking lot. Noticing the paramedics were busy attending to a woman, Gober grabbed his camera and headed inside the church to photograph the scene.

Standing just inside the entrance, Judy explained to Hibson what had happened. She described arriving at the church, checking out the pastor's office, finding the body in the downstairs office.

"It's Rhonda Smith," she said. The forty-two-year-old woman had been coming to the church with her mother for a couple years now. "We're pretty close friends."

Hibson directed Judy to wait outside with Trooper Mincer, then started searching the church along with Gober. The office sat on the bottom floor of a relatively modern two-story section of the church. The 12×12 foot room was stuffed with office equipment including file cabinets, a copy machine, and a tall stack of mailboxes for church officers, all centered around an L-shaped desk. Several laptop computers were found readily available, but whoever shot the woman was seemingly uninterested in taking them.

Upstairs, the police found a long hallway with about a dozen doors to various rooms used for Sunday School classes, storage, and teen gatherings. A door marked PASTOR'S STUDY was locked, but a glance through a vertical window revealed nobody was inside the tidy office. Back downstairs, the small hallway led to an older section of the church, including the wood-paneled narthex lined with bulletin boards of church announcements. The narthex had two sets of double doors, one of which led to a large multipurpose room filled with tables for dining, with a stage at the far end. The other double doors led to a high-ceilinged, mid-eighteenth-century-style sanctuary with rows of wooden pews affixed toward an altar.

The search proved to be fruitless. Nobody else was inside the building, and no weapon was found.

Ugh, Greg Stumpo thought to himself as his cell phone started to ring. *I can never have an uninterrupted lunch here.*

The forty-one-year-old state trooper dropped his napkin onto his plate and answered the phone. Wearing a neat suit and tie, Stumpo almost resembled a military officer, with his close-cropped haircut, strong jaw, and broad shoulders. His shy, almost sleepy eyes betrayed an extremely close attention to detail that helped him rise in the ranks from road patrol to the crime investigation unit. He was noted among his colleagues for his intelligence and thoroughness, which they considered so intense it was almost a fault.

Stumpo sat at a table across from Greg Langston, a former state police colleague now working as a detective with the Bucks County District Attorney's office. They were dining at Roman Delight, a casual Italian restaurant not far from Stumpo's headquarters at the state police barracks in Dublin, a borough in the middle of Bucks County. One time while eating here, he received a call about two sheriff's officers being shot and killed outside the area. The call sent him to Bradford County, way up in the northernmost part of the state, and kept him there for two full days.

Today's call was much closer to home. A woman had been shot at a church in Upper Bucks, about seventeen miles north. Stumpo was ordered to head to St. Luke's Hospital in nearby Quakertown, where the woman was being transported. Stumpo hung up, said a quick good-bye to Langston and rushed out to his car. Cases like this didn't come along too often in this part of Bucks County. In fact, in the past two decades, there had been only two homicides in Springfield Township.

Stumpo had been with the Dublin crime unit for just shy of ten years. In all that time, there had only ever been one homicide in his jurisdiction, the justified police shooting of a man who pointed a shotgun at two troopers in Upper Black Eddy. Stumpo wasn't heavily involved in that case, and although he was the senior officer out of three in the crime unit, he had never handled a homicide case himself. Throughout his eighteen years in law enforcement, Stumpo had repeatedly tried to take homicide investigation courses, but was never approved for one.

While en route, Stumpo got another call. The victim was being taken to St. Luke's Hospital in Fountain Hill instead. The larger hospital included a trauma center, Stumpo realized. The woman's injuries must be serious.

CHAPTER 3

Jim and Dorothy Smith looked at the answering machine as they entered their home, and were surprised to see no messages waiting for them. *Rhonda should have called by now,* Jim thought.

The couple, both seventy-two, had seen their daughter's green 1996 Plymouth Breeze in the parking lot of the church as they passed by on their way to nearby Quakertown for lunch. They had thought it was odd that her car was still there at 12:30 p.m., since she was only scheduled to work from 9 a.m. to noon.

"Let's stop, we'll take Rhonda along with us," Dorothy had said.

"No, let her work," Jim had replied, figuring Rhonda was trying to get in some overtime. "She only has one more day, we don't want to interfere."

It was Rhonda's third day working mornings filling in as the church secretary while Pastor Shreaves was away at a convention. It was kind of the pastor to reach out and provide their daughter with a little work, the Smiths thought. Her bipolar disorder, which Rhonda had struggled with for nearly twenty years, since her early twenties, had made finding and keeping work difficult for her lately.

Dorothy and Rhonda had been attending Trinity Evangelical for a little over two years now, and the church had been a bright spot in Rhonda's life ever since. The pastor had been welcoming and friendly to her, and she had made friends with several of the ladies in the congregation, some of whom she would get together with outside of church.

Jim looked up at the clock. It was just after 2 p.m. The Smiths took a different route back from the Red Robin restaurant in Quakertown, so they hadn't passed the church again on their way home, but they couldn't imagine Rhonda would still be working. Jim picked up the phone and dialed Rhonda at home, but got no answer.

He shrugged as he hung up the phone, and took off his coat as he sat beside Dorothy at the kitchen table. The couple had owned the Cape Cod–style house in Lower Saucon Township, just north of Springfield in adjacent Northampton County, for forty-seven years.

Jim had his income tax papers spread out atop the round table at the center of the kitchen, a small room with just a refrigerator and wall of cabinets above the sink. An open doorway led to the living room, which was equally packed with couches and plush arm chairs alongside several cabinets of Precious Moments statues intermingled with photos of the family, including Rhonda and her two older brothers, Gary and Perry.

The telephone rang, interrupting Jim from his paperwork. He picked up the phone, expecting to hear his daughter's voice, but was surprised to hear the voice of a different woman, who identified herself as a social worker from St. Luke's Hospital.

"Your daughter's been hurt," the woman said. "There was an accident down at the church." *That can't be,* Jim thought. *How can you get hurt working at a church office?*

"What did she do, fall and break something?" Jim asked.

"No," the woman said. "She's been shot."

"Shot?" Jim said, frozen in shock. Reflecting on the call later, Jim said he was surprised his weak heart didn't give out right there.

"Yes," the woman said.

"How is she?" Jim asked.

"She's not too good," the woman replied. "She's not going to make it. If you want to see her, you'd better get up here."

Jim felt numb as he hung up the phone. The cold and casual tone of the woman's voice delivering the worst news of Jim's life would haunt him for years to come.

"Come on," he said to Dorothy. "Rhon needs us."

Judy Zellner sat stiff as a board inside her husband's van, shaken and silenced by the memory of Rhonda's body. She could still see the position of her friend on the floor, her seemingly lifeless face as it turned toward her, the small beads of blood dripping from her hair to the church floor as the paramedics carried her outside.

Her husband, Les, sat quietly next to her in the van parked alongside the street outside the church parking lot, which was now blocked off by more than a dozen emergency vehicles. Judy stared with unfocused eyes at the glowing lights.

Judy met Rhonda on her first day at the church two years ago. It was always Judy's way to go up and say hello to the new visitors, and she and Rhonda hit it off from the beginning. Despite the almost twenty years between them—Judy would turn sixty-one next month—they started to get together outside of church once every two weeks or so, having lunch or just hanging out at Judy's house. Judy was still very active and somewhat younger looking with her blonde hair, and the two shared an interest in fashion and occasionally exchanged clothes. From the very beginning, Judy had the feeling Rhonda needed a friend, and she had wanted to be there for her.

As crestfallen as Judy felt sitting in the van, the tears just wouldn't come. She had been on Prozac since 1992, when she found her mother dead in her apartment. Judy had gone over one day to have lunch, but there was no answer at the door. She peered into one of the windows, and could see her mother half slumped off the couch. Judy still remembers the crookedness of the eyeglasses slipping off her mother's face. The coroner later declared she had died from a heart arrhythmia.

It was a memory that continued to haunt Judy, along with the untimely death of her twenty-year-old son, Ricky, in 2001. He had set up candles on the back deck when his friends were over, and had left them burning after his friends had gone. While Ricky slept in the house alone, the candles sparked a fire, quickly igniting the wooden deck and the cedar-sided house.

The authorities told Judy not to look at Ricky's body as they carried it from the house, but Judy couldn't help it. *How do you not look?* she thought to herself.

Her mother. Her son. And now Rhonda.

Her thoughts were interrupted when a uniformed state trooper tapped gently on the van window. Judy rolled the window down, and Trooper Anthony Rhodunda asked if he could speak to her for a few minutes.

The Smiths had also known hardship—the drive to St. Luke's wasn't the first time they had rushed to the hospital in fear of losing Rhonda.

Dorothy had started hemorrhaging about two months before Rhonda was due in 1966. When they arrived at St. Luke's Hospital in Fountain Hill on January 17, the doctors told them the umbilical cord was wrapped around the baby's neck and strangling her. Rhonda would have to be delivered right away, or they would lose her.

The caesarian-section operation went smoothly, and Rhonda was born weighing four pounds and nine ounces. Looking back, Jim could still remember how happy he felt, and how he dropped down to his knees and thanked God for his new baby daughter.

The next day, however, Jim got a call from the hospital with more bad news. Rhonda was experiencing heart and bowel problems, and would need operations to fix both. St. Luke's wasn't equipped to handle the surgeries, so they had scheduled an ambulance to take her to St. Christopher's Hospital for Children in Philadelphia the next morning.

Dorothy couldn't come along because she had developed inflammations in her legs. As the doctors loaded Rhonda and her incubator into the ambulance, Dorothy cried lightly in her wheelchair, asking Jim what was happening and why. Jim couldn't give her an answer, and simply stood there, dumbfounded. During the trip itself, however, he was in a constant state of panic.

As they drove down Route 309, Jim watched Rhonda's chest to make sure it was still going up and down, as he had seen it do in the nursery. As they moved closer to their destination, one of the nurses started rubbing the baby's chest, which frightened Jim even more. "If Rhonda is alive when we reach Philadelphia, she'll be okay," the nurse told him.

At that moment, Jim looked up and looming atop the ambulance, he saw an angel. In the decades to come, Jim knew that others didn't believe him when he told this story, but Jim remained convinced for the rest of his life that an angel was in the ambulance that day. And once he saw it, he knew Rhonda was going to be all right.

When they arrived, doctors examined Rhonda and found she didn't need the operations anymore. The heart murmur had cleared up, and the excitement of the ambulance ride had caused Rhonda to have a bowel movement.

And now, almost forty-two years later to the day, Jim and Dorothy felt that old panic again as they pulled into St. Luke's Hospital. Jim tried his best to stay hopeful, reflecting back to those first hours of Rhonda's life. *That girl's been a fighter since the day she was born,* he thought.

CHAPTER 4

Judy Zellner followed the two state troopers into the church sanctuary, a place that had brought her so much comfort every Sunday for twenty-six years. In front of her lay the two even rows of warm, maple-colored pews, surrounded by a sea of red carpet. Sunlight shined through the tall, narrow stained-glass windows, illuminating the second-floor balcony that held the sanctuary's extra seating. Judy's eyes went to one of the banners on the walls: REJOICE, THE LORD IS AT HAND, it read in white writing between candles on a purple background. It made her sad to think of such a horrible crime happening in the Lord's house.

Trooper Anthony Rhodunda motioned for Judy to sit in the first pew, and he and Trooper Richard Webb filed in after her. She recounted the sequence of events leading up to her discovery of Rhonda. Her arrival at the church, the unlocked door, the light in the office, her trip to the bathroom. Going upstairs to the pastor's office, gathering her cleaning supplies, going back downstairs into the office.

Judy explained that several parishioners had keys to the church, and she had one because she was the sexton. Although it was unusual for the church door to be unlocked, she told the troopers, she wasn't surprised to see the office light on. Pastor Shreaves often left the light on after leaving, and usually left a radio going, too. There was a green car in the parking lot, Judy recalled, but she hadn't recognized it and thought it may have belonged to the new church secretary.

Then she described the image she would never forget for the rest of her life: Rhonda, dying on the floor in the large pool of blood. The image was so vivid in her mind, she felt she could do a perfect sketch of the scene if asked.

Following her call to 911, Judy recalled how she screamed at car after car that passed the church, but no one stopped to help. When the ambulance arrived, she led the EMTs into the office and realized it was her friend, Rhonda, who had been shot.

Rhonda had been a member of the church for two years, Judy told the troopers, and her mother was also a member. Rhonda and Judy sang in the choir together. She knew about Rhonda's mental health issues, and described how Rhonda would sometimes call Judy when she was depressed. Judy took Rhonda's calls at any hour of the day.

"I think I would help her out, make her laugh," she said.

Rhonda had talked about killing herself in the past, Judy told the troopers. During one of her calls, Rhonda told Judy she was on her way home from a shooting range where she had thought about killing herself. They talked for about an hour, and Judy thought she had cheered her up, but the next day, she found out Rhonda had been hospitalized.

That was how it went, Judy said. There would be days and weeks she was fine, but every couple months she would fall into a deep, dark hole of depression.

Rhonda had had a boyfriend, Judy said, but they had broken up about two weeks ago. It was a mutual breakup, she said, and Rhonda seemed fine with it. Ray lived one hour south, and he had taken Rhonda to the movies and dinner on several occasions. But Judy didn't know much more about him.

She didn't know of any enemies or people who would have wanted to harm Rhonda either, she said. She didn't know why Rhonda was at the church and could only assume Pastor Shreaves had asked her to assist with secretarial duties. Nothing appeared to be missing from the church, and not much money is kept around as the Sunday collections are deposited in the bank weekly, she added.

When Judy had finished, Rhodunda asked her to again recall the specific moment she found Rhonda.

"Did you see a gun in the room?" he asked.

"No," Judy replied.

"Could you have kicked a gun when you came into the room?"

"No."

"Which would be more upsetting to you? If Rhonda killed herself or if someone did this to her?"

Judy paused for a moment. She decided it would be worse if Rhonda were killed because Judy herself often worked alone in the church.

"Did you help Rhonda do this to herself?"

Judy was shocked. That thought hadn't even crossed her mind.

"No. I would not do that."

Only a few more hours, Pastor Shreaves thought to himself. *Amen, hallelujah.*

It was the third and final day of his orientation conference in Malvern, Pennsylvania, a requirement for all new pastors, which Shreaves not-so-affectionately called the "baby pastor convention." For three days every year, all the new pastors in the Lutheran Theology Seminary would get together outside Philadelphia, talk about their successes and their challenges, attend presentations, talk to each other. The theme of this year's retreat was "Solid Word, Shaky Ground."

These conferences made sense for the twenty-something new pastors, but for the second-career types like Shreaves, it felt like the kind of college orientation they had long ago outgrown. This was the last year Shreaves had to attend the conference, and he was more than pleased to leave it behind.

Just a few years ago, Shreaves never would have expected to have been where he was today, surrounded by pastors-in-training, learning how to be a man of God. Just ten years ago, he was a golf pro working in a high-profile job out of

Philadelphia as director of section affairs for the Professional Golf Association. Even today, at age fifty-six, Shreaves still looked more like a golf pro than a pastor. Standing over six feet tall, lean, with a touch of blond in his graying hair, his striking bright blue eyes made him especially attractive for a man his age.

Shreaves had loved golf since he was eleven years old, when he hijacked a set of golf clubs his father received as a Christmas gift. Shreaves would hit balls out of his backyard and found he had a gift for the sport, and by age thirteen he was traveling all over the country to play the game. As an older teen, he was the runner-up in the USGA junior amateur golf championship.

But around 1999, Shreaves started to feel a pull toward a life of ministry. There was no major epiphany that led to this decision, except that one of his friends had noticed gifts in him that Shreaves hadn't seen himself. Shreaves treated his fellow man with respect and compassion, the friend said, traits that would serve him well in the job of pastor. This friend had been a drinker in his past and nearly killed himself in a car crash, but was saved by his Christian faith, and the vision he saw for Shreaves slowly started to grow on Shreaves himself.

Shreaves joined the Lutheran Theology Seminary in Philadelphia in January 2002 and graduated in the spring of 2005, in two-and-a-half years instead of the normal four. Shreaves liked to say this didn't happen because he was smart, but simply because he worked hard at it. He took classes in the summers and during his internships, and by March 2005 he was interviewing for the job of pastor of Trinity Evangelical Lutheran Church.

It was a place of worship with a strong sense of history. The Lenni Lenape Indians were the first inhabitants of what is now Springfield Township, and the first white man settled in the land in 1728. The Trinity church was established just twenty-three years later, making it one of the oldest churches in the area. A log building doubled as a church and a schoolhouse until 1763, when the first formal church building was

constructed on the same plot of land where the existing church
remains today, although it has undergone much growth and
several renovations since.

The congregation had been worshipping regularly there
"since before there was a United States of America,"
Shreaves was fond of saying. Many of the congregants were
descendants of the families buried in the graveyard behind
the church. It was the kind of place where even if you'd been
there for fifteen years, there was probably still somebody
who would consider you a "newcomer."

Immediately upon setting eyes on the place, Shreaves could
tell the church was a perfect fit for him, and he thought the
church council felt the same way. Shreaves loved the rural
atmosphere, and wanted to find a place where he could settle
and call home for a long time, which is exactly what the
congregation was looking for in a pastor.

The church had been without a full-time pastor for about
two years, and it was taking its toll on the congregation. The
church council's search committee felt Shreaves was just what
they were seeking: an energetic, outgoing person who would
reach out to the community and engage his congregation.

Shreaves sat through several interviews with the council
and preached at a few services. By the end of the month,
before he was even officially ordained, he was accepting the
job.

Now, three years later, Shreaves was in the room he had
been staying in throughout the conference, when someone
knocked on the door. He was told he had a call from Jim
Nilsen, a past council president from Trinity Evangelical.
Shreaves was surprised. Malvern was a good hour and a half
away from the church. What could Nilsen need that Shreaves
would be able to help him with from out here?

"You need to talk to the state police right away," Nilsen
said. "This police officer is going to be calling you." Shreaves
hung up the phone to wait for the call, so startled he hadn't
even thought to ask what the problem was. *Could it be a fire?*
he thought to himself.

A few long minutes later, he got the call from the state

police. As Shreaves listened to the news, his stomach sank. He realized the quiet life he envisioned for himself at his small parish had just been forever altered.

Oh my gosh, he thought. *My whole life's never going to be the same after this.*

Trooper Stumpo arrived at St. Luke's Hospital shortly before 2 p.m. Inside the trauma center he found Trooper Shawn Smith, another Dublin officer, holding two brown paper bags. Inside were the blood-stained clothes Rhonda Smith had been wearing when she was shot, the garments ragged from being cut off her body. The two troopers looked through the bags for any evidence besides the clothes themselves, but found nothing unusual. Smith summarized what the police knew so far and told him Rhonda was still alive, on life support, but that it was not looking good.

"You know, I guess if you don't solve one of these in forty-eight hours, it makes it more difficult," Smith said.

Stumpo grimaced. "Shawn, I don't need to hear that right now."

After bringing the clothes out to Stumpo's trunk, Smith led Stumpo into a private room inside the hospital, where Jim and Dorothy Smith sat talking to one of the hospital's social workers, Linda Watsula. They looked up from their conversation, both with tears in their eyes behind their glasses. Both appeared to be in their seventies, Jim balding with a white beard and mustache, and Dorothy with blonde curly hair. With his weathered brow, tense shoulders, and head slumped slightly forward, Jim looked as if he had a heavy weight on his shoulders.

Jim and Dorothy's eyes turned immediately to Trooper Smith, the only one of the pair in a state trooper's uniform. Stumpo, in his suit, took the opportunity to slide into a seat in the corner where he could observe for a bit.

Jim read the uniformed trooper's name tag and felt a small sense of comfort. *A fellow Smith,* he thought.

Trooper Smith asked the Smiths to run down their day so far. Jim said Rhonda had called around 8:15 that morning.

He asked how she was, and she responded that she was "Up and at 'em." This was a sign, Jim explained, that she was in a good mood. Whenever she was feeling depressed, she simply said, "I'm up."

Trooper Smith asked if Rhonda felt depressed often. Jim explained that Rhonda was bipolar, and had to take a number of medications to treat her disorder. Just last night, Jim said, Rhonda had been feeling down. She had come to the Smiths' house for dinner and to use their computer because she didn't have the Internet at her apartment. Jim said she sometimes e-mailed Pastor Shreaves, who had been helping her with some of her problems.

Everything seemed perfectly normal when they talked to Rhonda this morning, Jim said. She had asked if her parents could do her laundry for her, and they agreed. After Rhonda left for work, the Smiths took the five-minute drive to her apartment in Hellertown to get her clothes, which they took to a nearby laundromat.

After returning Rhonda's clothes to her apartment, Jim said he and Dorothy drove to Quakertown for lunch. They passed the church a little before 12:30 p.m. and saw Rhonda's car was still there. It was the only one in the lot, Jim said. They discussed stopping to take her to lunch, but decided against it.

Passing the church wasn't the most direct route to Quakertown, but Jim said he took the long way because he liked to eat after 1 o'clock, when most of the crowds were gone. They were going to go to Applebee's, but found it too crowded and decided to go to Red Robin instead. They took the direct way home on Route 309, so they didn't pass the church on their way back.

Stumpo watched the couple as they talked to Trooper Smith. He noticed that Jim appeared to be doing most of the talking, with Dorothy doing little more than nodding or correcting her husband on a few minor details every once in a while. The two were obviously distraught, but Rhonda was still alive, and Stumpo sensed they were still clinging to some hope, however faint, that their daughter might pull through this. He felt sympathy for them, but knew the questioning had to continue. Stumpo asked whether Rhonda was married or had a boyfriend.

Jim turned his head toward him and with a quizzical expression, asked, "Who are you?"

Stumpo suppressed a smile, amused by the man's candor. Stumpo introduced himself as a state trooper, and Jim told him Rhonda had been dating a man she met online from Philadelphia named Ray Finkel, but that he stopped calling a few weeks ago. She didn't have a boyfriend now, but had planned to go on a date tonight with a man named Greg, who she met at the Lehigh Valley Hospital Bipolar Support Group. She had also been going to a support group at Unity House, a center for people with mental disabilities, in Bethlehem.

Stumpo braced himself for the next question. "Did Rhonda own a gun?" Jim immediately shook his head no, she didn't. About five years ago, during one of her darker moments, Rhonda had once thought about shooting herself at a firing range, Jim said. But she decided it was too loud there, and she left. In June 2007, she talked about doing it again, and she was hospitalized. Rhonda had been in and out of hospitals in the past because of her bipolar problems, Jim said.

Stumpo asked if he could come by the house some time later and take their computer so the police could look through the e-mail messages for anything useful. Jim and Dorothy nodded. Stumpo thought it would also provide him another opportunity to continue talking with the Smiths about Rhonda, under calmer circumstances.

Jim walked a step closer to Trooper Smith and said, "I don't want them to find a gun."

Trooper Smith and Stumpo looked at each other. *What could he possibly mean?* Stumpo thought.

"But you know what I mean, right?" Jim added. "I want them to find a gun. Later. But not in the church. I don't want a gun found down there in that church, but I want a gun found."

Stumpo now understood: Jim didn't want a gun found at the church because that would mean Rhonda killed herself, and he couldn't stand the thought of his daughter committing suicide.

Jim leaned in a little closer to Trooper Smith and added, almost whispering, "And I also believe in the death penalty."

CHAPTER 5

Stumpo headed over to the church to share what he learned from the Smiths with the investigators. There was Rhonda's bipolar disease—definitely something to check into—and the fact she used Internet dating sites. There was also Jim's unusual statement to Trooper Smith. From the way he insisted he didn't want a gun found at the church, Jim seemed desperate to believe his daughter's death wasn't a suicide. Rhonda was a fighter, Jim had said. He was proud of her, and Stumpo could tell he would be bitterly disappointed if she gave up on life that way.

Police cars were still scattered throughout the church parking lot when Stumpo pulled in, but troopers had concluded the first part of their investigation and found nobody else inside, and no gun. Police dogs were going to be brought in for a more thorough search, and the forensic investigators still had many hours of work ahead of them. The Springfield Elementary School, located just a half mile away on Route 212, was in lockdown mode in response to the shooting. It would remain in lockdown for the next several days.

Outside the church, Stumpo met with Dublin station commander Sergeant Ed Murphy; Stumpo's department supervisor, Corporal Paul Romanic; Corporal Ron Garza, a crime scene supervisor from the Bethlehem barracks; and a couple other supervisors who were at the church. Trooper

Gregg Dietz, who worked with Stumpo in the Dublin bar-racks' crime investigation unit, reported he spoke with a man named Richard Hari, who lived directly across from the church and maintained an old schoolhouse building on his property. Hari, who wasn't an active member with the church but knew a lot of the congregants, told Dietz there were no school bus stops in the general area, but that garbage was collected between nine and eleven on Wednesday mornings. Hari did not see anything unusual or hear any gunshots that morning.

As Stumpo relayed his interview with the Smiths to his supervisors, they were especially interested to learn the Smiths had driven by the church that day. Jim's explanation about wanting to get to Quakertown after the lunch crowds made sense to Stumpo, but he admitted Jim's cryptic state-ment to Trooper Smith at the end of their interview raised some questions.

After some discussion, a theory developed: Was it possible that Rhonda committed suicide and that her parents stopped at the church on their way to lunch and found their daughter dead? Horrified by the thought of their daughter killing her-self, especially in a church, could they have removed the gun to make it look like it wasn't a suicide?

Stumpo didn't think Rhonda had killed herself, and the absence of a gun certainly pointed to homicide in his mind. But he also knew this early in an investigation that it would be foolish to rule anything out. And there was Rhonda's his-tory of depression to take into consideration, along with the fact that she had contemplated suicide in the past. His super-visors decided he should talk to the Smiths again and ask them more about their drive past the church earlier that day.

Stumpo and Garza returned to the hospital to talk to the Smiths. Stumpo was pleased to find Dorothy Smith standing alone outside Rhonda's room. He remembered how quiet Dorothy stayed during their earlier discussion, how she tim-idly stood back and let her husband do all the talking. If they were lying about not stopping, Stumpo knew it would be easier to break Dorothy than Jim.

After exchanging a few polite pleasantries, Stumpo delicately asked, "Mrs. Smith, are you sure you guys didn't stop at the church? During traumatic experiences like this, your mind can forget things."

Dorothy shook her head no. "No, no, no, we just went by," she insisted and began to tell the story again of their trip to Quakertown. Within moments, Jim Smith exited the bathroom and walked over to his wife's side. Stumpo asked him the same question, and he, too, insisted they did not stop at the church. Their stories were consistent with their previous recollections of their drive to and from lunch.

Stumpo had interviewed a lot of people during his almost two decades of police work. More often than not, he could tell when someone was lying, and he knew the Smiths were not. Looking into their eyes, he saw no signs of dishonesty. He saw only the pained expressions of two people who were losing their baby daughter.

Judy Zellner and her husband Les came straight to St. Luke's Hospital as soon as police allowed them to leave the church. The Smiths were waiting in a small room with their son Perry; their nineteen-year-old granddaughter Amber; Pastor Shreaves, just returned from Malvern; and Serena Sellers, a pastor from the bishop's office. They all looked distraught, especially Amber, who Judy knew was so close to Rhonda she was more than just a niece—she was practically her little sister.

After a few minutes, Dr. Marc Portner came out and gave them the news they'd been dreading. Rhonda was brain dead, he said. You may notice her body twitching, he said, but that's only because it hasn't gotten the full message from her brain. The doctors were keeping Rhonda on life support for the possibility the family might consider donating some of her organs.

Jim could still barely comprehend the news. But when the doctor asked about the organs, he lifted his chin and nodded with conviction. "I think that's the thing to do because that keeps Rhonda alive. Part of her is still alive."

And then, almost as if saying those words made him realize it was real, Jim recognized he had to let his daughter go. She would have to be taken off life support. He turned to Shreaves and said, "I hope this is the right thing I'm doing." The pastor nodded.

Jim and Dorothy started filling out the organ donation paperwork, but were interrupted by word that they wouldn't be permitted to donate Rhonda's organs because her body needed to remain intact for an autopsy the next day. They needed all her organs to prove she died of a gunshot wound, which would be relevant in a homicide case, the Smiths were told. The Smiths could still donate Rhonda's corneas and portions of her skin, if they wanted.

Jim couldn't help but feel disappointed. He had no intention of doing anything to harm the investigation, but his daughter had been taken away from him, and now the one chance for part of her to live on had been taken away as well. With no other option, they sadly agreed to the cornea and skin donation.

And with that, there was nothing else to do but say goodbye. The Smiths, Perry, Amber, Judy, Les, Shreaves, and Pastor Sellers entered Rhonda's room. Her head was wrapped with bandages and her right eye was red and swollen. Her tongue protruded from her mouth. (The unnerving sight would keep Amber from sleeping that night.)

It was a far cry from the Rhonda Smith they had all known and loved. The tall brunette had always had such an approachable quality about her, with her kind green eyes and a warm smile that always lit up her friendly face.

The group fanned out into a semicircle around Rhonda's bed and grasped hands. Pastor Sellers led the group in prayer. Jim felt the need to say something, but the only thought that came to his mind was an old gospel song his deeply religious mother used to sing.

"Take my hand, precious Lord, lead me home," he said.

Stumpo and Garza were on their way out of the hospital when they passed a man wearing a clerical collar. They glanced at one another wearing the same quizzical expressions. "You think this is the pastor?" Stumpo asked. Garza shrugged, and the two troopers doubled back.

"Excuse me, Pastor Shreaves?" Stumpo called out. The man turned and nodded. Stumpo identified himself and asked, "Do you have a minute?"

Shreaves agreed to be interviewed and the two investigators began asking him about his history with the church and his involvement with Rhonda. The pastor really hadn't known Rhonda all that well, certainly no more than any given parishoner in the church. He couldn't even remember when Rhonda first came to the church. However, Rhonda had come to him for counseling and advice on two or three occasions, and told him about a past relationship that included abuse and ended with Rhonda having an abortion. There had been a more recent boyfriend, the pastor said, a man from northeast Philadelphia who Rhonda met on the Internet. But the relationship had fizzled out when he no longer wanted to continue a long-distance relationship, Shreaves said.

Rhonda also had mentioned that she was dating a married man, Shreaves said, but never revealed his identity.

A lot of things to check into, Stumpo thought. The trooper noticed that Shreaves seemed a bit nervous: stuttering, his eyes darting back and forth, not making eye contact. It was a difficult situation, of course, as it would be for anybody.

Shreaves seemed like a nice guy to Stumpo, and he appeared to have been doing his part to help Rhonda during difficult times. But at this point, Stumpo couldn't tell if the nervousness was just part of the man's personality, or something more.

"Are there any guns in the church?" Stumpo asked.

Shreaves said he knew the church inside and out, and there weren't any.

CHAPTER 6

Steve Wysocki was still working at Haycock Elementary School when he got the news. The forty-five-year-old second-grade teacher had worked for the Quakertown Community School District for twenty-five years now, and had been Trinity Evangelical Lutheran Church's choir director and organist for about twelve years. The weekly choir practice was scheduled for later that day, and Steve planned to head straight to the church to start getting ready once his workday was over.

But then his wife called him with some horrible news: There had been a shooting inside the church, and Rhonda Smith was dead.

The news shook Steve to the core. He could hardly believe that something like this could happen in his own church. But he had to put that shock aside, at least for the moment. Under the circumstances, there was no way that night's choir practice could continue, and he had to let the choir members know what had happened.

Steve and his wife, Debbie, spent the hour between five and six o'clock calling each of the choir members to tell them the bad news and let them know the rehearsal had been canceled. Steve didn't relish the duty and, indeed, everybody he called was either horrified, in disbelief, or both. By now, some church members already knew something had happened, but they were not sure exactly what or to whom. Some falsely believed it was the new secretary, Megan, who had been shot, but by the evening word of what actually happened was starting to reach much of the congregation.

With his calls nearly complete, Steve dialed the number of Mary Jane Fonder who, at sixty-five years old, was one of the long-time congregants at the church.

Steve saved her for last among his calls, in part because Debbie had told him that Mary Jane called the previous week and left a message claiming she was quitting the choir for a while. Something seemed to have made Mary Jane upset, Debbie had told him, although it was unclear to them whether it was related to the church or something else altogether. Steve hoped to talk to her about this and find out what was on her mind.

The other reason he saved Mary Jane for last was because, quite frankly, the woman was a talker. She had a reputation among the other church members as being a bit of an oddball, and was well known for her tendency to ramble endlessly once you got into a conversation with her.

When Mary Jane answered, Steve braced himself and explained that Rhonda had been found shot inside the church, and that she hadn't made it. To his surprise, however, Mary Jane seemed neither shocked nor even particularly fazed by the news. In fact, rather than acknowledging it, she started talking about the various things she had been doing that day, which included a trip to the hairdresser followed by some shopping.

"Mary Jane," Steve said, dumbfounded. "Did you hear what I said? There's been a shooting."

Mary Jane continued talking, but again barely seemed to acknowledge what was said to her. Steve wondered if she was in some sort of shock, and whether Mary Jane's nonresponse was some sort of defense mechanism.

After listening politely for a few minutes as Mary Jane continued to talk, Steve finally interrupted and said, "Look, Mary Jane, as far as I know, Pastor Greg is with Rhonda now in the hospital. Please pray for Rhonda, okay?"

"Thanks, I will. Good-bye," Mary Jane said before hanging up.

It was around 7 o'clock when Judy finally got back to her Allentown home, a modestly sized house her father-in-law built. She sat down on the couch across from an impressive ten-foot fireplace that served as the centerpiece for the living room. Judy had messages from several of her fellow church members, but she didn't feel up to speaking to most of them at the moment. She was too exhausted, too shaken up. Nevertheless, she picked up the phone and dialed the one person she desperately wanted to see: her best friend, Sue Brunner, who had been attending Trinity Evangelical nearly as long as Judy had.

Sue came over as quickly as she could, and Judy told her everything that she had gone through that day, from the horrible discovery of Rhonda's crumpled body on the church office floor, to the moment they said good-bye to her at the hospital. Sixty-one-year-old Sue, like Judy, had blonde hair and looked younger than her age, having maintained an active and happy lifestyle. Now, however, both women were in a state of shock and disbelief that something like this could happen at their church. And then they asked themselves the inevitable question: Who could have done this?

Judy's mind went to the strange, unkempt man who had attended the Sunday service just three days ago. New people caught everybody's attention at their small church community, but this man struck Judy and other parishioners as particularly unusual. He told conflicting stories to everybody he spoke to, and Bob Gerstenberg had told Judy the man tried to steal a glass during communion.

Judy even heard that the stranger had said something like, "This would be a good place to rob." Sue agreed, the man had certainly been strange. Maybe he had returned to rob the church as he had suggested.

Les Zellner interrupted the two women's discussion. "I know who did it," he said.

For a few long moments, the room was completely silent,

as if Les's sudden proclamation had frozen time dead in its tracks.

"What?" Sue asked. "How could you know who did it?"

"I know who did it," he replied matter-of-factly. "It's Mary Jane Fonder."

"What are you talking about?" Sue asked, even more flabbergasted. Mary Jane Fonder had been her neighbor in Springfield Township for twenty years, and she had known Mary Jane's parents for another ten years prior to that. Sure, Mary Jane, was odd, everybody knew that. But in all the years Sue had known her, Mary Jane had never seemed at all violent.

But Les was on the church council, and he had heard a few things recently about Mary Jane Fonder. She had been hounding Pastor Shreaves in recent weeks, Les said. She'd been leaving long-winded, almost incoherent messages for him all the time and even started buying food for him and leaving it on his doorstep. It had gotten to the point where the pastor went to the church council and asked them to convince Mary Jane to stop.

"I think she was jealous of Rhonda," Les said.

Sue looked at him quizzically. She didn't believe it.

"Wow," Sue said to Les, with a laugh, "you need to be a detective."

CHAPTER 7

Three men close to Rhonda were of special interest to the police that day: the man she had recently broken up with, the guy she was supposed to see that night, and the man she had been in an abusive relationship with.

Troopers Rhodunda and Webb were assigned to interview Gregory Danisavich, the local man Rhonda had set a date with for that evening. They found him at his house in Coopersburg, a small town about ten minutes from the church.

"Is this in reference to Rhonda?" he asked, a bit frantic. "Is she okay?"

He was supposed to pick up Rhonda at her apartment at 6 o'clock that evening. After receiving no response from knocking on her door, he waited for fifteen minutes before heading back home. It was now 7:50 p.m. Danisavich said he was worried that he hadn't heard from Rhonda and had planned to call her later that night.

They had met at a Lehigh Valley Hospital bipolar support group three months ago, Danisavich told the troopers. They had gotten together outside of the group—as friends—for meals or movies, maybe five or ten times.

Rhonda was very depressed at times, and Danisavich said he would try to make her feel better by taking her places. Rhonda said she had been suicidal in the past, but never mentioned any specifics except one time she said she felt like driving off the road into a ditch, Danisavich said.

Rhonda had wanted to get a job, Danisavich said, but couldn't take full-time work because then she would be cut off from government assistance, which she relied on for her housing. She had gotten a job at the Giant grocery store in Hellertown, but she had to stop because she could not work as many hours as the store wanted without forfeiting the assistance.

As for men, Rhonda was still upset over the abortion she'd had years ago, Danisavich said. Recently, she had been dating a man named Ray whom she had met on Match.com but Danisavich said Ray stopped calling her about a month ago. Rhonda was upset about it, but she believed Ray had only wanted sex from her, anyway.

As for Danisavich, he and Rhonda had last talked Monday when he called to reschedule a dinner date from the previous Thursday. She seemed in good spirits when they talked.

Danisavich told the troopers he was home the entire day taking care of his mother, Linda, who was recovering from surgery. The only time he left the house was to get pizza for his mother around 5 o'clock. Linda Danisavich confirmed her son's alibi.

Meanwhile, Gregg Dietz and Patrick McGuire, two more state troopers from the Dublin barracks, were en route to Philadelphia to seek out Ray Finkel, Rhonda's most recent ex-boyfriend whose name had already come up several times in their investigation.

It turned out not to be such an easy task. When the troopers arrived at the address listed on his driver's license in suburban Horsham, they learned he no longer lived there. Finkel wasn't at the next apartment in northeast Philadelphia the troopers had been referred to, either. But with the help of Philadelphia police, Finkel was found at his parents' house and detained for the state troopers.

Dietz and McGuire placed him in the back of their unmarked car and told Finkel he wasn't under arrest and had no obligation to talk to them. Finkel agreed to answer the troopers' questions.

The troopers started off by inquiring what Finkel did earlier that day. Like usual, Finkel said he took a 6:11 a.m. train that arrived in Center City around 7:30 a.m. From the station at Eighth and Market Streets, Finkel said he walked the short distance to Public Buildings Services, where he worked as a financial analyst. He was there all day with his boss and another coworker except for a noontime meeting and then lunch at 1:30 p.m. The times could be verified with his building's swipe card system, he said, that clocked him in and out of the building.

Finkel had yet to ask the troopers what their questions were all about. This struck them as odd. Usually, sitting in the back of a police car, the first thing a person normally asks is why the police wanted to talk to them, Dietz thought.

Nevertheless, the man was cooperative. When Dietz told him they were inquiring about Rhonda Smith, Finkel replied without hesitation that she was a friend that he had met on the online dating site PlentyOfFish.com. They had met online around the second weekend of October and had their first in-person date the following Friday, Finkel said. They had gotten together a total of four times, three times in Hellertown and once in Philadelphia, he said. He had met her parents once and described them as nice but very religious, possibly Mennonite.

The two had last gotten together the second weekend in November, he said. He had broken off the relationship because of the distance, and she seemed to understand, said. They had talked a few times on the phone since December.

"Do you own any guns?" Dietz asked Finkel.

"No," he responded. "I'm Jewish and don't believe in owning guns."

"Do you know anyone that owns a gun?" Dietz asked. "How about your father?"

Finkel laughed. No, his father didn't own any guns, either.

"Do you have any questions?" Dietz asked.

"Yeah," Finkel responded. "Why are you asking me about Rhonda? I date a lot of different women."

The troopers informed Finkel of Rhonda's death and he was appropriately surprised, they thought. He appeared visibly upset, and asked if there was anything he could do to help. Finkel gave the police permission to search his car and trunk—a search that turned up nothing suspicious—and said he would find out the exact times he swiped in and out of work that day to prove he wasn't involved.

McGuire checked into those times himself the next day—as well as interviewing Finkel's boss and coworker—and determined Finkel's timeline checked out. He could not have been in Springfield Township when Rhonda was killed.

Dietz, meanwhile, learned of two other men police would have to check into from an interview with the director of a bipolar group Rhonda had recently joined in Bethlehem. Christie Shafer, who ran the group at Unity House, said two men at the facility had especially taken notice of Rhonda since she joined January 7. Eric Hanus had offered to perform Rhonda's orientation even though he didn't work there. Benjamin Claudio, both a group and staff member, also had shown interest in Rhonda. Both men were present during all three of Rhonda's visits to the facility: January 7, 16, and 17, Shafer said.

The day Rhonda died, Shafer had helped Hanus move some new items into the Unity House group home where he lived, she said. Hanus received a phone call around 1:30 or 2 o'clock and became very upset and left the house. Shafer said she thought it was odd, especially after learning Rhonda died that day.

Claudio also acted strange that morning when Shafer informed the staff about Rhonda's death, she said.

Trooper Stumpo followed up with Hanus, who said he had known Rhonda since 2001 when she lived in an apartment owned by his parents. They became friends and nearly dated, but never did. After Rhonda moved out of the apartment, in 2002, they lost touch until Hanus ran into her at McDonald's this past fall. Rhonda began calling him sporadically, including Christmas night, and Hanus recommended both the Unity House and another bipolar support group to her.

Rhonda seemed to enjoy Unity House, he said, but being as intelligent as she was, didn't seem to like to be around the less intelligent group members. Hanus said he had seen Rhonda talking to Ben, Unity House's van driver, whom he didn't like because Ben was a "ladies' man."

Stumpo asked Hanus where he was the day Rhonda died and Hanus hesitated. He said he believed he had lunch at Unity House, which ran from 11:45 a.m. to 12:45 p.m., but couldn't remember what he did in the morning. Unity House had a sign-in sheet, he said.

Stumpo asked Hanus if he had a gun or if he knew if Rhonda did. Hanus said he did not but said Rhonda had told him she once went to a gun range to practice. Rhonda had told him several times over the years that she had considered killing herself.

Dietz checked out the other man, Benjamin Claudio, with Bucks County Detective Mike Mosiniak. Claudio said he had met Rhonda at Unity House and that she was friendly and kind of attractive, but not his type. He said she did not flirt with him, or anyone else at Unity House that he was aware of. As Unity House's van driver, Claudio said he picked Rhonda up once and was scheduled to pick her up another time but she didn't show.

Claudio didn't have much of an alibi for the day Rhonda died. He was scheduled to work, but had called in sick because new medicine he took that day had made him groggy. The officers asked what kind of car Claudio drove—a blue Chevrolet Cavalier—and ended the interview.

Two days after their interview, Hanus called Stumpo to report he had talked to his mother last night, Rhonda's former landlord, and Rhonda had told her that she was considering dating a married man. Hanus didn't know the man's name, but said his mother might and gave her telephone number to Stumpo.

Stumpo tried to follow up with Hanus's mother, Carol, but she was sick the day he called. Her husband, Steve, said his wife had talked to him about Rhonda and how she was thinking of dating a married man but never mentioned his name. Carol Hanus had advised Rhonda against it, because she would still be alone and there was nothing to gain from such a situation, Steve Hanus said.

Steve and Carol Hanus had become close with Rhonda during the time she rented an apartment from them, and they considered her one of the family. She was a sweet kid and you couldn't be mad at her, Steve Hanus said.

Stumpo learned more about Rhonda's former emotionally abusive relationship from Ellen Mooney, the client services director at Turning Point of the Lehigh Valley, a domestic violence assistance organization. Rhonda had come to the group in 2005 for regular counseling about her boyfriend at that time.

The state police would learn more about him from Rhonda's own writings. As part of her therapy, Rhonda had written about a time in March 2004 that he had sex with her without her consent. They had been at her apartment, fooling around on her bed when he penetrated her without asking and without using a condom as he usually did.

Rhonda was very upset by the experience, even more so when she found out a couple of weeks later that she was pregnant. Being on lithium for her bipolar disorder, Rhonda knew the fetus would already be damaged. She decided to have an abortion, which would trouble her greatly for the rest of her life.

In 2006, Rhonda reported the incident to police, who forwarded the case on to the Northampton County District Attorney's Office. Police reports did not indicate why Rhonda waited two years to report the crime. Nonetheless, the office declined to prosecute on the grounds that proving it would be too difficult.

CHAPTER 8

Another State Trooper, Michael Trebendis Jr., visited the houses neighboring the church on Route 212, but the effort proved largely fruitless. Most of the residents had not been home at the time of the shooting, or hadn't seen or heard anything unusual. One man told Trebendis an older gentleman had stopped by his house about a week earlier and was asking questions about the church. The man, who drove a sports utility vehicle with a Christian-themed license plate, claimed he built models of churches. The neighbor told Trebendis he suggested the man talk to Pastor Shreaves. He never saw the man again after that.

One woman, Diane Mair, told the trooper she had heard what sounded like gunshots some time between 8 and 10 o'clock the morning of the shooting. Mair had thought she heard a single shot, while her husband, James, who was in a separate downstairs room at the time, thought he heard two shots. Neither thought anything of it at the time, and assumed it was hunters, who occasionally roamed the woods surrounding their home. Only later, after watching the news, did they start to suspect it came from the church.

Several troopers were assigned to stop eastbound and westbound traffic on Route 212 and ask motorists whether they had seen or heard anything unusual the day of the shooting. This, too, produced little of value. Some who were familiar with the church said they saw unfamiliar cars in the parking lot, but couldn't describe them. One driver, who lived on Pleasant Hollow Road less than a quarter mile from the church, told Trooper Donald Marsh she had heard a man screaming and arguing with someone else about two weeks prior to the shooting. She couldn't see anybody because it was dark, but she heard a male voice shout, "I'm going to fucking kill you!" Nothing further came of the matter in the following two weeks, but Marsh dutifully took note of the incident nevertheless.

Throughout those early days of the investigation, the police continued to hear more and more about the strange man who had visited the church during its January 20 service. Word of the stranger had even traveled outside the sphere of the church itself. During one vehicle stop outside the church, Corporal Kevin O'Brien spoke with a Deborah Scott Dawson, who served as the pastor for a different local church. She said one of the Trinity Evangelical members—a man named Bobby, she believed, who drove a bus for the Palisades School District—had told her about the strange man who seemingly came from out of nowhere to attend a service, and then was suddenly gone.

"He didn't give me a description, but said the guy looked kind of scary," Dawson said. "If you talk to the Trinity minister, I'm sure he'll know who the bus driver is."

Just five minutes later, O'Brien spoke to Pastor Shreaves at his home, a small ranch house right next to the church, on the opposite side of the parking lot that had been littered with emergency vehicles and police tape just days ago. Shreaves nodded when the trooper brought up the stranger and confirmed the bus driver Dawson spoke about—Bob Gerstenberg—was sitting in the same pew with the stranger.

"I remember the guy," Shreaves said. "It was only one week. I spoke to him after the service. I was watching him during the service, just because he was new. He fidgeted a bit, but didn't really have any contact with the church members. He sat by himself."

Rhonda Smith wasn't at church the week the stranger was

there, Shreaves said. He described the man as about 5 feet 10 inches tall, medium build, white, with long salt-and-pepper hair and a gray and white beard. He had wire frame glasses on and was wearing what Shreaves called "rugged casual" clothing. He wasn't dirty, Shreaves said (although the man's appearance was getting filthier and filthier as the gossip around the church continued to build).

Shreaves didn't think the stranger had anything to do with Rhonda's death, and he couldn't help but feel a bit of annoyance at his fellow parishioners, some of whom were so convinced of this man's guilt that they believed they had solved the case. *It's stupid,* Shreaves thought. *There's no way in hell it could be him. It doesn't make any sense. What motivation would this guy have to come in here and kill somebody out of the blue?*

Shreaves thought there were two options that were much more likely. One was that it was some sort of gang initiation; some young kids on a dare to rob the church that ended with a terrible, senseless killing. The idea stemmed from the previous shooting of another Trinity Evangelical member. Back in the fall of 2006, the man had pulled over at an Interstate 78 exit near Newark to answer his cell phone, when somebody shot him in the face. The bullet went clean through his jaw, but he survived. It was a dangerous neighborhood, and word was that the shooting was some sort of gang dare.

The other theory weighing on Shreaves's mind was that it was one of Rhonda's old flames that had tracked her down and killed her based on some old grudge. During the few instances Shreaves had provided counseling for Rhonda, the talk of her ex-boyfriends had given him the unsettling feeling that Rhonda had a darker side to her, as if she was living a second life outside her realm of family and friends at the church. Shreaves never got the feeling Rhonda was a danger to others in any way, just that she was living in a kind of world the pastor knew little about.

That possibility frightened Shreaves even more than the idea of some random gang-related shooting. *Maybe there's some boyfriend out there looking to kill me because they thought I was involved with Rhonda.* Even though he was no closer to Rhonda than most of his parishioners, and there was certainly nothing romantic between them, the thought had been weighing on the pastor, to the point that he could no longer sleep comfortably in his own house.

Shreaves expressed to the police, as well as his fellow congregants, that he thought the stranger had nothing to do with Rhonda's death, but the troopers investigated it anyway. Greg Langston spoke to Bob Gerstenberg, who said the stranger had told him he had just finished school and was trying to figure out what to do with his life. The man had told Gerstenberg he was from Oklahoma, but strangely, told other congregants he was from Illinois, and told yet others he was from Nebraska. However, when he left the church, he drove away in a white four-door car with an Iowa license plate.

The conflicting reports about where he was from were far from the last thing that made the church members suspicious of the man. The police spoke to several parishioners about the stranger, most of whom spoke of his unkempt appearance and generally unusual behavior. Dolores Keller, who sat behind him during church, said he didn't take a church bulletin like everyone else, but simply sat alone in the pew and looked around at the stained-glass windows, seemingly uninterested in the service itself. James Nilsen, one of the church council members, told police the stranger seemed to be taking in every detail of the church, and looked out of place.

Like many small congregations, the members of Trinity Evangelical tended to pay close attention to anyone new at their services. But this man in particular had stood out for reasons beyond his appearance. Like everyone else, the stranger took communion, where wine is administered to parishioners with a glass. But when he was finished, the man allegedly tried to pocket the glass. When Bob Gerstenberg confronted him, the man simply said he was planning to keep it as a souvenir. "We don't do that here," Gerstenberg had replied, and the man handed the glass over.

Even more unnerving was a statement the stranger made, seemingly out of the blue, to church member Eileen Catino.

The two were talking after the service ended when the man, glancing around at the details of the church building, suddenly said, "This would be a good place to rob." The enigmatic statement did much to fuel talk after the shooting among church members who felt the stranger was a prime suspect.

Nevertheless, police also gathered statements that seemed to contradict the portrait parishioners had painted of the man. Dolores Keller said he was very friendly to everyone he spoke to after the service, and Bob Gerstenberg's wife, Patricia, said she saw him put ten dollars into the offering plate.

Langston contacted the Pennsylvania Board of Probation and Parole in Allentown seeking information on all interstate parolees from Illinois, Iowa, Nebraska, and Oklahoma. It took five days to produce a list of the parolees, dating from August 2000 to present, but none of them proved relevant to the Rhonda Smith case. Langston also called the Bucks County Adult Probation Office to see if anyone had been transferred to or from one of those states. The only promising lead was that of a man from the Telford, Pennsylvania, area who traveled back and forth to Iowa on business. But he was on parole for drunk driving and had a suspended license, and no car.

Langston called the office of District Magistrate C. Robert Roth in Quakertown and asked about any criminal citations for men from any of the four states. The detective was told the citations could not be automatically searched by state and would have to be checked individually, which would entail browsing through hundreds and hundreds of files. The process took about four days, after which Langston was informed nobody met the stranger's description.

Langston hit another roadblock when he called a Bucks County non-profit organization that provides overnight rooms to the needy. He was told the office could not provide any information about their tenants without a name. The detective called the owners of several hotels and motels in the Quakertown and Bethlehem areas, none of which could produce any information about a man matching the stranger's description.

After more than a week of searching, the police were unable to find any information about the stranger. He was never seen or heard from again, and where he went after leaving Trinity Evangelical remained just as big a mystery as where he came from in the first place.

In death investigations, it's commonplace for police to run a background check on the victim, in addition to the suspects. In this case, finding out about Rhonda fell to Trooper William Ortiz.

A criminal history check on Rhonda came back empty, as did a search of gun records. Her driving record was nearly as sparse—she had been a passenger in a car crash in 1986, and in 2006, she was cited for driving without her headlights on, but was found not guilty.

Ortiz called police in Hellertown, a small town of about fifty-six hundred people where Rhonda was living in a small apartment building on Main Street. The dispatcher recognized Rhonda's name right away—she had called the department fairly regularly for mental health incidents. The dispatcher recalled one incident in particular from June 2007. Rhonda had called the police department saying she planned to go to a local gun range and kill herself. Ortiz asked for a copy of that report and any other incident reports the department had involving Rhonda.

Ortiz received the reports the next day, and police reports also were collected from neighboring Lower Saucon Township, where Rhonda had lived with her parents on-and-off. The reports showed two police interactions in 2001 and then almost a dozen calls over the last three years. The reports detailed an argument between Rhonda and her ex-boyfriend, three fights with her parents, and three threats of suicide. Ortiz found that Rhonda had been committed to the hospital twice, once in 2001 and once in 2007.

A check of the church's phone records also led police to

investigate further into Rhonda's past suicidal threats. The records showed a call had been made to the Northampton County Crisis Center the day Rhonda had died. The call at 10:11 a.m. had lasted a minute and eight seconds.

Trooper Raymond Judge was assigned to find out more about Rhonda's call to the crisis center. On January 30, he met with three center staff members and learned Rhonda had called the center four times in the week before she died.

The first had been January 18, when she called crying uncontrollably, saying she hadn't been sleeping and felt like a failure. Caseworkers Rafael Rodriguez and Sharon Santiago, who Trooper Judge met with, followed up on Rhonda's call with a home visit that day. Rhonda again spoke of feeling like a failure, and Sharon had suggested she enroll in Hope House, a five-day inpatient counseling program. Rhonda had said she wanted to put off any program until she had finished working at her church, Sharon said.

Rhonda called the center two days later, again crying and saying she couldn't get out of bed. Caseworker Jane Newman visited Rhonda that afternoon and suggested she sign up for an intensive care manager, a counselor that would meet with her on a regular basis. Rhonda seemed interested, but two days later, she called the center again, reporting that she was feeling anxious. That was the day before she died.

That brought police to the phone call Rhonda made to the crisis center the day she died. It turned out she had called to tell Rafael that she was feeling better, but he wasn't due in until that afternoon. Rhonda said she would call again later.

CHAPTER 9

The Smiths' phone had been ringing almost nonstop since Rhonda died. There were family and friends sending their condolences, reporters seeking comment, and several calls from people with unhelpful tips about Rhonda's death. Jim called them the "crackpots" and traced all of their numbers to turn over to the police.

Jim and Dorothy were both home when their phone rang around 5 o'clock on the afternoon of January 25.

"I'm calling from the Lehigh County coroner's office," the woman on the other line said. "Your daughter committed suicide and the coroner is going to announce it tomorrow."

"How do you know that?" Jim asked. "The police haven't told us that."

"I just wanted to put your mind at ease," the woman answered before hanging up.

Jim hit *69 on his telephone, took down the phone number that made the call, and turned it over to the police.

Trooper Dietz later verified the call did not come from the Lehigh County coroner's office. After getting a warrant, the police conducted a reverse trace and found the number belonged to Sarah Schmid, a Bethlehem woman who had gone to Unity House with Rhonda. Police visited Sarah, who admitted to making the call in an attempt to comfort Rhonda's family. After hearing her explanation, the authorities did not believe her to be suspicious or consider her a suspect.

It had been two days since Rhonda's death, and the police still didn't have a strong suspect. Nothing substantial was turning up on the stranger and Rhonda's ex-boyfriends were getting crossed off the list one by one.

Back at the Dublin barracks, while Stumpo and Dietz contemplated what to do next, Stumpo remembered one angle they had yet to cover: it had been mentioned to them that the previous church secretary may have left on bad terms. Asking Pastor Shreaves about the secretary also would give the officers a chance to pick his brain again. It was a strategy Stumpo had successfully used before in cases: go back to the victim's family or close friends and ask them to go over everything again. Usually something new pops up.

Stumpo and Dietz went over to the pastor's house, located next to the church, around 2:30 p.m. They asked him about the previous church secretary, who they learned was named Karen Loch. And yes, it had not been a happy parting. Loch had been fired last March because she hadn't been able to do the job, Shreaves said. Loch was angry over the firing, and Shreaves said he thought she hated him. But she had returned her key when she was fired and hadn't talked to the pastor since then, he said.

The troopers made a note of this information before continuing. The bitter departure was certainly something to follow up on.

"Is there anything else you can think of?" Stumpo asked. "It might not be anything to you but it might be very important to us."

Shreaves sat quietly for a good minute before speaking somewhat hesitantly.

"Well, there is this woman who just," he sighed, "bothers me. She calls me all the time."

"Well, who is she?" Stumpo asked.

Shreaves paused again. "Well I don't really want to say anything because it's just nothing," he said.

After some more prodding, the troopers got Shreaves to tell them about the woman, a church member named Mary Jane Fonder, who Shreaves believed was infatuated with him. Mary Jane had been calling his house three or four times a week and leaving long, disturbing messages.

"Disturbing?" Stumpo asked, his interest piqued.

"Yeah, like she would call and say her spirits weren't right today, and things like that. It was disturbing," Shreaves responded.

It wasn't the type of behavior Stumpo would describe as disturbing, but some of what Shreaves told him next was certainly noteworthy. Though Shreaves had put a block on Mary Jane's phone number, she still managed to get through to his line, possibly using her cell phone. Also, Mary Jane had entered his house once when he wasn't home to put food in his refrigerator. Shreaves had confronted Mary Jane about this unwanted behavior, and the pastor believed that angered her. He had not heard from her in weeks.

Shreaves said he had turned off his answering machine to avoid getting any messages from Mary Jane, but Stumpo asked if he'd be willing to turn it on again so they might be able to hear some of these messages. Shreaves said he didn't really want to, because he wanted to be done dealing with Mary Jane—but he would for the troopers.

As the two troopers left Shreaves's house, Dietz turned to Stumpo and asked, "What the heck was that?" Sure, this Mary Jane sounded a little unusual, but he didn't see why Shreaves appeared so rattled by her. He felt the pastor's reaction to her was downright bizarre.

"He's really that concerned about a sixty-five-year-old woman leaving him messages?" Dietz said.

The next day, Trooper Patrick McGuire and county Detective Gregory Langston interviewed Karen Loch at her home. While she agreed she left the church on bad terms, the reason she gave for her dismissal differed from Shreaves's explanation. Loch said Shreaves was a perfectionist, and if work was not done to his liking, he would be verbally abusive toward her. One time, he even threw a stack of papers at her, she said. Another time, she had to miss a meeting because of bad weather and Shreaves sent her a nasty e-mail.

Shreaves tried to get her to quit, Loch said, but she refused. She was later fired by church counsel President Deb Keller, who offered her a $700 severance check if she would sign a statement absolving Shreaves and the church of any wrongdoing. Loch said she refused the deal.

But despite her problems with Shreaves, Loch said she would never do anything to harm the church. She had a new job, at a church in nearby Quakertown. On the day Rhonda was killed, Loch said she was home alone in the morning before having lunch with a friend at Applebee's in Quakertown around 1:15 that afternoon.

CHAPTER 10

Rhonda Smith was the youngest of three children born to Dorothy and Francis "Jim" Smith. Her brothers were Gary and Perry, of whom Dorothy's mother would often say, "Why did you name them that? You're going to get them confused!" They spent their childhoods at the Lower Saucon Township home where Jim and Dorothy still lived more than four decades later. The house was purchased in 1961, five years before Rhonda was born.

Despite the close call at her birth that required an emergency trip to Philadelphia, Rhonda was far from a sickly child growing up. She never seemed to get ill, and throughout Rhonda's childhood, her parents couldn't even remember a time when she had to take headache medicine. She "grew like a weed," her mother liked to say, to the point that strangers would ask her to reach for items on the top shelves when she'd go out to the store.

Jim was proud of the courage his green-eyed little girl showed from even a young age. She was four years old when the family first took her to the Center Valley farm where Dorothy had grown up, and while some older children would recoil at the sight of the cows and other animals, Rhonda showed no fear or hesitation. Her nerve was no doubt strengthened from living with two older brothers, especially Perry, who as a middle child tended to tease his kid sister. But

Rhonda gave it right back to him, much to the secret amusement and pride of their parents. One day, when Perry came home with a bad report card and started offering up excuses, Rhonda called him out in front of their parents and said, "Oh, you were daydreaming in school and not listening to the teacher!"

But for all her strength, Rhonda was also a shy, reserved child. They had few neighbors and even fewer little girls her age in their rural Northampton County neighborhood; although she got along with her brothers, they tended to run off on their own to play boy games. As a result, Rhonda largely kept to herself, with her pet dogs and guinea pigs substituting for the companionship she lacked from other children. Even as she started to get older, she had few friends, and no boyfriends.

She was a good student, all As and Bs, but didn't get involved in many sports or extracurricular activities. Since her family couldn't afford any fancy vacations, she didn't get to travel much, instead going on fishing trips with her father to Roosevelt State Park near Allentown, or Lake Nockamixon, the largest lake in Bucks County. And, in the absence of friends her age, her mother became Rhonda's best friend. The two would often take shopping trips, do each other's makeup or hair, go ice-skating, or cook together. Rhonda would often say, "Mom, no restaurant could beat your cooking!"

Rhonda started coming out of her shell while attending Saucon Valley High School. She developed new interests like basket making, horseback riding, and, especially, acting in the school's theater department. Standing up in front of an audience was so contrary to her personality, but her parents thought it sparked something inside her, and served as a "turnaround" from her past shyness.

From the age of six, Rhonda wanted to be a teacher. She spoke about it so often, her father used to joke that it was all she ever talked about. And her enthusiasm for the career didn't dampen with time. In the years immediately after she graduated from high school in 1984, Rhonda worked in a number of jobs, ranging from newspaper typist to customer service representative for a phone company. But by 1986, she had saved enough money to enroll in Northampton Community College, making her the first in the family to attend college.

In 1988, Rhonda graduated from the community college with an associate's degree in secretarial science, and she moved on to Bloomsburg University in Bloomsburg, Pennsylvania, about two hours northwest of her home. She continued working throughout school, mostly as a cashier at Acme Markets, and paid her student loans all by herself, a source of great pride for her father. Rhonda started to travel like she never had in her youth, visiting cities like St. Louis and Las Vegas, and places like Niagara Falls and Mexico City. Within three years, she was student teaching and on track to graduate in December 1991 with her teaching certification in business education.

But in the months approaching her graduation date, signs started to emerge that something was dreadfully wrong with Rhonda Smith. With each passing day, she was increasingly losing her appetite, to the point that she was barely eating at all. Long periods of insomnia kept her awake at all hours of the night. She started to develop strong feelings of paranoia, growing convinced even her closest friends could not be trusted.

Between her grueling college schedule and the growing irrationality of her thoughts, Rhonda was dimly aware that she might need to take a break, to put her education on hold and take a semester off. But she couldn't. She told herself her teachers and colleagues would think less of her, but in reality, the pressure was coming completely from within. For Rhonda, failing to meet that December 15, 1991, graduation date would make her a failure, plain and simple.

But Rhonda's tortured feelings only grew worse as the weeks passed. She reached what she later described as her "total emotional breaking point" early one November morning, during the two-hour drive to Mansfield University to take her national teaching exam, one of the many tests required for her eventual certification. She was traveling on the high-way, a car swerved into the opposite lane in front of her, and Rhonda was convinced she was about to crash, thinking to herself, *I'm a goner!*

There was no crash, but Rhonda pulled over to the side of the road and broke down crying, believing for the first time that she would never be able to earn her teaching certifica-tion. Nevertheless, she forced herself to continue on to Man-sfield, and despite the panic she still felt from earlier in the day, she passed the exam.

Eventually, Rhonda's increasingly erratic behavior began to draw attention. One of her friends knocked on the door of her apartment to check on her one evening, but Rhonda, her paranoia increasing each day, was convinced it was some-body trying to break into her apartment. On another occa-sion, Rhonda called the police in tears, claiming somebody was trying to break in, but when they arrived it proved to be untrue.

Rhonda also started to believe there were hidden cameras in her apartment walls, filming her every move. One after-noon, Jim Smith was working at the Lehigh Valley Railroad when he received a call from his daughter.

"Dad," Rhonda said.

"Yeah?" Jim replied.

"You'd better call *A Current Affair*," she said, referring to the television newsmagazine program.

"For what?" Jim asked, completely baffled.

"You'd better get a hold of Maury Povich," Rhonda said, referring to the show's host. "You'd better call him, because they have cameras in my room. Watching me."

Jim was overwhelmed with feelings of fear, worry, and sympathy for his daughter. He had known she was under pressure, but the full extent of Rhonda's suffering had been a mystery to him until this phone call.

It's over, he thought sadly to himself. Rhonda was only a few short weeks away from her graduation date, but sud-denly, her longtime dream of becoming a teacher seemed nothing short of impossible.

"Rhonda," he said. "Pack your things and come on home."

"Yeah," his daughter's sad, weak voice replied. "'Cause I'm scared."

"Come on home," Jim said again.

But by now, Rhonda was in no state to drive, and others at the school had taken notice. Two of the university's psychiatrists convinced Rhonda to check into the Geisinger Medical Center, just fifteen minutes away from Bloomsburg University.

Rhonda eventually agreed to go, but upon arriving, her paranoia had reached dangerously high levels. She threw away all the contents of her purse before entering the hospital so nobody would know who she was. Upon entering, she ran to a payphone to call her father and, when security tried to restrain her, she screamed, "Rape!"

Rhonda was calmed after speaking with her parents, who assured her she needed to agree to a seventy-two-hour stay for her own health and safety. But the calmness was not to last. Later that day, when she was brought to her room and introduced to her roommate, Rhonda was convinced the black-haired, dark-eyed woman had "the eyes of the Devil."

During the night, Rhonda awoke to find her roommate sleeping peacefully, and fled to the bathroom to avoid looking at her. Staring into the mirror, Rhonda removed the tampon from her body and, after washing some of the blood from it, used it to draw a cross on her forehead, believing this would prevent evil spirits from harming her.

That next morning, the doctors discovered Rhonda alone and naked inside her room, shouting and threatening her roommate whenever she tried to come back inside, calling her a devil. Rhonda believed if she wasn't wearing her clothes, she could not be seen, and she pulled open all the drapes on the windows to allow as much sunlight as possible into the room to ward off the evil spirits.

Eventually, the doctors wrapped her in blankets and took her into isolation, which consisted of a room with only an uncovered mattress and a red call button in case she needed help. Rhonda was calmer, having been provided with antipsychotic medication, but she still felt evil spirits were all around her. During one instance in the bathroom, she smashed her head against the mirror, shattering it, and giving herself a permanent quarter-inch scar above the eyebrow. At the time, she felt as if a higher power was pushing her into the wall against her will.

Two days after Rhonda was first hospitalized, Jim, Dorothy, and Gary came down to see her. Her parents assumed she had suffered a nervous breakdown, that the stress of college had proven too much for her. It was only when they finally saw Rhonda for the first time that they realized the severity of the problem.

Rhonda sat there almost in a trance, barely able to speak or acknowledge her parents' presence. She stared straight ahead with a glassy, distant look to her eyes. It was those eyes that bothered Jim the most, causing him to break down and cry right there at the hospital, in despair that this had to happen to his daughter when she was so close to reaching her dream of becoming a teacher. Dorothy hugged Rhonda and grasped her hands, which felt cold to the touch.

It was November 21, 1991, when Rhonda Smith was diagnosed with bipolar disorder. What Rhonda had previously dismissed as "mood swings" were actually abrupt periods of mania and depression that were typical symptoms of the psychiatric diagnosis. The agitation, poor temper control, reckless behavior, lack of sleep: All of these symptoms of Rhonda's life for the past several months were symptoms of bipolar disorder.

It was difficult for Jim and Dorothy to believe, especially considering that Rhonda never caught so much as a fever or a cold growing up, but they soon learned it was common for the illness to strike in a person's early twenties. As hard as it was for them to accept, however, it was nearly impossible for Rhonda. She refused to believe the diagnosis at first, just as many people don't when they are first diagnosed with the disorder.

When December 15, 1991, came, Rhonda would indeed graduate from Bloomsburg University, but not with the teaching certification she had so desperately sought. Instead, her degree was in business administration, for which she had already earned enough credits long ago. Jim and Dorothy came out, took pictures with her, cheered her on—provided all the moral support their daughter could want. But in Rhonda's mind, she was a failure.

Rhonda struggled against the idea that she had bipolar disorder in those first months, still clinging to the hope of earning her certification. "I don't have bipolar," she would repeatedly insist. "I don't have bipolar, I don't have bipolar, I don't have bipolar." She tried three times to take the teaching certification test after she graduated, but whenever the time would come, the illness would take over. The best way she could think of to describe it to her family was to say that her "mind was racing." Her thoughts were so fast and so jumbled it was impossible to concentrate, and Rhonda would end up just sitting in place, almost comatose, just waiting for her racing mind to stop.

Some days, you could hardly tell there was anything wrong with Rhonda at all. She'd be laughing, smiling, joking; Jim would give her a call in the morning and his daughter's bubbly voice would reply, "Up and at 'em, Dad-e-o!" But other days, her mind would start racing again, and that starry-eyed look that had so saddened her parents at Geisinger Medical Center would return.

You could follow her mood swings by the fluctuation in her weight: When she was happy, she slimmed down, and when the illness took hold, she became heavier. By now, Rhonda was on medication, and she never returned to the rock bottom levels she reached in those darkest days at Bloomsburg and Geisinger. Nevertheless, she had to be hospitalized several times over the next few years. On some days, like the day she visited that shooting range, she considered ending it all altogether.

But as the years passed, Rhonda worked hard to build a life for herself. In the first few years after her diagnosis, her father had to help her manage her finances because, as Rhonda put it, she was "bouncing checks like a rubber ball."

She worked a number of jobs, again most often cashier work or customer service: jobs that allowed her to talk to people, which she enjoyed. Sometimes she would get down on herself, regretful that she wasn't teaching, and would say to her father, "Jeez, I'm not going nowhere."

Keeping a job for more than a few years was a challenge due to the illness, and so Rhonda was often in dire financial straits, but she insisted on living on her own and paying rent for her apartments herself, which made her family proud. She never lived more than five miles away from her parents and, although the illness sometimes led to fights, they were a source of strength for her. The Easter before she died, Rhonda wrote a four-page letter to her father, thanking him for inspiring her never to give up despite her illness. She also wrote a poem for her mother, which ended with, "I am very fortunate because she shows me the truth when all I see is black. My mother is the best gift of all."

It was the winter of 2005 when Rhonda and Dorothy first came to the Trinity Evangelical Lutheran Church. (Jim himself never joined them. When Rhonda would invite him, he'd shrug and reply, "I went when I was young.") They had gone to several other churches in the area, but still hadn't found one that really suited them. This congregation was fairly small, and most of its members were much older than Rhonda, but she and her mother both liked the place right away. They especially liked the music from the choir, and the friendly new pastor, who managed to keep his sermons funny and enjoyable while maintaining his strong spiritual convictions.

New attendees always created an atmosphere of excitement and curiosity around Trinity Evangelical, and this proved to be doubly the case for Rhonda Smith, who was attractive and didn't quite fit into the church's age demographic. From the morning of that first service, when Rhonda and Dorothy joined the church members for some after-service coffee and conversation, Rhonda immediately clicked with the congregation, particularly with longtime member Judy Zellner. Soon, Rhonda was singing in the choir, spending more and more time at the church, and joining the other ladies for shopping and other social engagements.

But her bipolar disorder proved to be a challenge for Rhonda even during these happy times, and soon she was having difficulties with her finances again. She confided these troubles to Pastor Gregory Shreaves who, although he didn't know Rhonda particularly well, provided her with counseling on a handful of occasions. The church had an informal network of congregants with stronger financial means than the others. It was Shreaves who, around the Christmas of 2007, decided to reach out to that network and see if they could help Rhonda out.

It wasn't much, maybe a couple thousand dollars in total, but the gifts they gave Rhonda allowed her to pay her rent, electric and phone bills. Rhonda was extremely grateful for the assistance from the church, which had already helped her overcome so many difficulties in her life. Rhonda asked Shreaves whether she could stand up at the next service and thank the congregation for their generosity, and he agreed. *This is what a church is,* he thought. *It's helping others and giving thanks.*

And so, during a Sunday morning service in January 2008, just weeks before her death, Rhonda stood up in front of the entire congregation and thanked them for their moral, spiritual, and financial assistance. She spoke about her bipolar disorder, how difficult her life could be, and how much she appreciated their understanding and support. She thanked them all, especially the pastor, and expressed how much better it made her feel to know she had friends she could truly count on.

"You helped me out," Rhonda put it simply. "I was sick, and you helped me."

Although clearly emotional, Rhonda remained stoic and dry eyed as she sat down following the announcement. But Judy Zellner's eyes swelled with tears of pride to see how far Rhonda had come in the two years since joining the church. As Judy looked around the church, she saw others had been moved to tears as well, while some were smiling and nodding in Rhonda's direction. One longtime congregant, Paul Rose, was impressed with Rhonda's courage. He believed Rhonda's life had changed for the better during her time at the church, and he felt joyful that she had been given that opportunity.

Amid all the happy and emotional expressions in the crowd, however, one woman sat motionless, staring straight ahead, with no visible reaction on her face.

It was Mary Jane Fonder.

CHAPTER 11

"How are you going to feel sitting in that pew alone?" Pastor Shreaves asked Dorothy Smith on a visit to the Smiths' house in the days after Rhonda died.

"She won't be alone," Jim Smith chimed in. "I'll sit with her."

Although he had never regularly attended the church, Jim Smith kept his word. He started going to church with his wife every week, starting with a memorial service at the nearby Trinity United Church of Christ the morning of Friday, January 25. Jim felt it was his responsibility to be there for his wife by taking Rhonda's place at her side in the pew.

More than sixty people went out to Trinity United that morning. It was a somber service where members of the community said prayers, sang songs, and silently reflected on the tragedy that had so shaken their spiritual home. Serena Sellers, the assistant to the bishop in the Evangelical Lutheran Church of America's Southeastern Pennsylvania Synod, spoke to the congregation about how their presence at the service proved how loved Rhonda was in the community.

"There are so many questions," she said at the service, according to a report in *The Intelligencer,* the local Bucks County newspaper. "But despite all the things we don't know, we know the truth of life. In the midst of all the suffering, the pain and sin, we know Jesus."

Sellers strongly urged the Trinity Evangelical Lutheran Church congregation not to let the murder deter them from coming together to worship, nor from welcoming strangers and new members into their midst.

"Somewhere, someone felt a need to do this," Sellers said. "But our prayers need to be strong enough that God will be stronger than sin."

Pastor Shreaves took a few moments to speak as well and echoed Serena's words.

"We are grieving the loss of a sister and disciple of Christ," he said. "There is disbelief, anger, and sadness. I invite the members of our tiny congregation down the road to affirm every emotion we feel."

Shreaves also pointed out that the theme of his recent pastors' retreat, where he was when he learned Rhonda died, was "Solid Word, Shaky Ground."

"How true we know both of these to be today," he said. "This death is not the final victory."

The service was hard for Jim and Dorothy, both of whom sat silently in the pew and tried, not always successfully, to hold back their tears. It was doubly hard on Jim, who was suspicious as well as mournful. He looked upon the other church members around him with an almost unexplainable feeling of mistrust and disdain. It wasn't that he suspected they hurt Rhonda, not really. But they were the ones closest to her in the days before she died, and he couldn't help but feel apprehensive about them.

Mostly, though, he just missed his daughter. After all that she had been through and survived in her life, Jim hated that her life had come to an end this way.

Leaving the church, Jim and Dorothy were approached by a reporter from *The Intelligencer,* who asked them whether they thought Rhonda's death was a homicide or a suicide. Jim's answer was instant and unequivocal.

"She did not do this to herself," he told the reporter. "She was brought up to believe in God. A self-murderer does not get into the kingdom of heaven."

"It's impossible," Dorothy agreed, then reflected on the horrific nature of the murder.

"Someone goes into a church and kills someone," she said, shaking her head. "I guess they don't like churches."

Others also spoke to the *Intelligencer* reporter as they were leaving the service that day. Roxanne Miller, a Hellertown resident, admitted she had not felt safe in her own home since Rhonda had died.

"For years, you'd never think of locking your door," she said, "and now it's come to that."

Bill Rex, a pastor at the St. Luke Evangelical Lutheran Church in Ferndale, Pennsylvania, shared an even more pessimistic view with the journalist. Rex felt it was only a matter of time before violence made its way to the rural Bucks County area. To reinforce his point, he cited the high school shootings in Columbine, Colorado, a quiet place where residents felt safe until the horrible massacre that killed thirteen people.

Rex also pointed out that, just three months ago, the local Palisades High School went on lockdown when an anonymous caller told the school two students were armed with guns. The warning turned out to be a false alarm, but it was enough to startle many local residents, including Rex.

"It's an infection," he told the *Intelligencer* reporter of the epidemic of violence he felt was sweeping across the country. "If it can go to Columbine, it can come here."

Other reactions were less extreme but spoken in a similar vein, including that of Paul Rose, who had been with the church for twelve years.

"You live in this part of the world to get away from all this," Rose later said. "Then this happens at our own church. It's not a sanctuary anymore."

Jim and Dorothy also attended the first Sunday service at Trinity Evangelical Lutheran Church since their daughter's death. And the tiny church was crowded like never before.

Just as so many people returned to church after the terrorist attacks of September 11, 2001, members of Trinity Evangelical showed up in force that first Sunday after the tragedy in their midst. There were even people who had never attended before, likely curious about what had happened there. While some attended just that Sunday, many would go on to become permanent members.

The church council had discussed blocking off the office hallway altogether, but the majority overruled the plan. *You can't hide what went on here,* Shreaves felt. Instead, everything was moved out of the office and into the choir room across the hall, which would serve as a temporary office for many months. The office door was locked and its large window into the hallway was covered with paper. And while the office had been cleaned, there still was a slight chemical smell from the cleaning agents themselves and the gunpowder residue.

To upgrade security, the church's locks were changed and they were kept locked once the services started. The Springfield police were asked to be onsite and the church also formed its own volunteer group to guard the doors. Mary Jane Fonder was among the volunteers.

A group from the Lutheran Disaster Response attended and talked with church members between the 8:00 and 10:30 a.m. services about any of their safety concerns.

Pastor Shreaves drew upon the theme of the conference he had just attended for his sermon. The conference had addressed how people tread on rocky soil amid God's firm foundation, and Shreaves spoke to how despite living on shifting soil, the foundation of God's presence is greater than any evil or fear we may have.

The church also distributed copies of *Amish Grace,* a book written about how the Amish community in Nickel Mines, Pennsylvania, had forgiven the gunman who killed five children and injured five others in a schoolhouse. The shooting had happened fairly recently, and Shreaves thought there could be parallels drawn between the two incidents.

Judy Zellner was particularly touched by the large turn-out. As she joined the church choir in the front of the sanctuary, Judy took a moment to acknowledge how much the crowd meant to her.

"I need you to be here, to get through this," she said.

CHAPTER 12

Pastor Shreaves didn't remember the first time he met Mary Jane Fonder. He had met so many people all at once when he first started at Trinity Evangelical that most of those initial greetings were a blur to him, and there was no reason for him to have thought of Mary Jane any differently than all the others. In short order he would come to be familiar with her in the same way the rest of the congregation was: an eccentric old lady who could get a bit annoying at times, but was otherwise harmless and had good intentions.

He hadn't gotten to know very much about Mary Jane in his first year at the church. Of course, she was a talker, and she had bent his ear a few times after Sunday services. And her physical appearance certainly left an impression. The wigs she wore reminded Shreaves of the divots from his golfing days, and whenever she laughed, Shreaves couldn't help but think that her belly shook like a bowl full of jelly much like that of Santa Claus.

The first time Shreaves spoke at length with Mary Jane was the day of the funeral for Sue Brunner's father in the summer of 2006. The service was in Feasterville, an area in southern Bucks County almost an hour away from the church. Due to the distance, not many people from Trinity Evangelical attended besides Shreaves and Judy Zellner. But Mary Jane Fonder was there, along with her brother Ed.

During a luncheon at the Buck Hotel after the funeral, Shreaves spotted Mary Jane and Ed wandering alone, looking for a table. The pastor admired them for coming so far to attend the funeral. He also appreciated that despite the oddball reputation Mary Jane had developed, the woman was usually in good spirits—she was often the first one to laugh about her own wigs or her other oddities. He knew that the congregation treated Mary Jane civilly, but he also knew she had few very close friends among them, and was seldom invited to dinners or social gatherings. Nevertheless, no one could question her love of the church and the community.

Shreaves decided it was time to reach out to the Fonders, and he called them over to sit with him. They chatted casually for the next ninety minutes or so, with Mary Jane herself doing most of the talking, of course. After a while, they started to discuss her artwork. She had a strong talent for painting and crocheting, among other mediums. To Shreaves, Mary Jane seemed a bit lonely, and since she was always eager to do more with the church, he thought of a way to get her more involved while utilizing her interests.

"Hey Mary Jane, why don't you come and do some work at the church?" Shreaves said. "How about you decorate the bulletin boards in the narthex for us?"

Mary Jane happily agreed, and before long she was visiting the church one or two mornings a week. Shreaves would let her into the church and help get her started, then leave her unsupervised to do the work. She worked on the bulletin board for several months, but after a while, Shreaves took over that job himself: It turned out for all her artistic abilities, she really made a mess out of the boards. Nevertheless, she continued coming to the church on weekday mornings and helping out in other small jobs, like updating the calendars or folding the newsletters.

Sometimes Shreaves would start chatting with her, but for the most part, he tried to steer clear. Once you gave her an opening, Mary Jane had a tendency to go on and on, to the point that it felt impossible to end the conversation at all. As a result, the two tended to only speak in passing from time to time while Mary Jane performed her duties.

But one day, in the fall of 2006, Mary Jane sought out Shreaves for a conversation. One that would forever change things between them.

Shreaves was working on his laptop computer atop the L-shaped desk in his office, a relatively small but welcoming room on the church's second floor. He heard Mary Jane coming up the stairs, but between her age and relatively poor physical fitness, it took quite a while before Mary Jane finally wandered through his door. It appeared she wanted to speak with him, so Shreaves invited her to take a seat in a maroon armchair at the opposite corner of the room next to a bookshelf and a couch.

It was the first time Mary Jane had sought him out for a one-on-one conversation. She launched into a long discussion mostly about herself, talking about her past, her family, her old home in Philadelphia, the various jobs she had worked over the years. She showed Shreaves old photos of her younger self that she carried in her wallet, and described ballet lessons she used to take as a young woman.

Shreaves was no counselor, and would normally refer his congregants to a professional after one or two conversations like this one if he felt they needed someone to talk to regularly. But he got the impression Mary Jane simply wanted to tell her story, a story that perhaps few people had ever really taken the time to listen to before.

Okay, just be a pastor, Shreaves thought to himself. *Just listen to her.*

An hour went by, and still Mary Jane continued talking. She talked about how pretty and talented she was back in her youth, about all the things she wanted to do with her life. She talked about moving to Springfield Township when her parents got sick, and how her life changed so much after that. Shreaves spent most of the time nodding and making short acknowledgments like "Yes" or "I understand." It struck him that Mary Jane seemed to be purging her feelings, almost like a confessional, and he tried to simply affirm what she was saying, without offering his own opinions or passing any judgments.

Then, out of nowhere, Mary Jane said the words that Shreaves would remember for the rest of his life: "You can't deny what's going on between us."

He was taken completely aback. Shreaves had never noticed Mary Jane express any kind of romantic interest toward him, and he had never expressed any toward her. His first reaction was to laugh, not a mean-spirited laugh but a surprised, awkward one, as if he could simply shrug the statement away.

"Mary Jane, there's no . . . no . . ." he started to say, but found that words failed him. "Let's . . . let's not go there. . . ."

Mary Jane immediately launched back into her conversation, changing the subject and talking as if nothing had happened. But Shreaves knew he couldn't just sit there and continue to listen.

"Mary Jane, we need to stop," he said. "I can't do this anymore."

The conversation over, Mary Jane simply stood up and left the room, not saying another word about her sudden outburst, but the words seemed to hang in the room even after she had gone. Shreaves was shocked. He tried to think back to whether he had ever given any indication that he was interested in her that way, but nothing came to mind. Maybe she got the wrong idea from the way he reached out to her back at the funeral, or from the way he listened to her discussing her past for the last hour.

Or maybe it was simply the fact that he was single, even though there was nearly a ten-year age difference between them. Shreaves knew some of the women in the church considered him attractive.

You've got to be kidding me, Shreaves thought to himself. *I mean, I'm no Robert Redford, but oh my God, what is she thinking?*

Upon later reflection, Shreaves would come to believe it really had nothing to do with him at all, but rather the position he held. He had learned about this in past seminars, where they referred to it as transference. Mary Jane probably wasn't interested in him, Shreaves reasoned, but rather what the office he held represented and its connection to God.

Nevertheless, the whole encounter deeply troubled Shreaves. He called Claire Burkat, a bishop with the Evangelical Lutheran Church of America's Southeastern Pennsylvania Synod, just to let her know that it happened. Shreaves wanted to make sure someone in an official capacity was aware of the comment, because who knew where something like this could lead? He also called a meeting of the church council just to make them aware of it. But he asked that the council not do anything about it just yet, hoping the whole matter would simply go away.

It didn't. In fact, only a few weeks after that conversation, Mary Jane started calling Shreaves's home on a regular basis. Most of the time, she called when he wasn't home and left long, rambling messages on his answering machine. She would talk about some random subject for four minutes until the message time ran out and the machine cut her off, then she'd call back and speak for another four minutes until it cut her off again. Sometimes, she would call every day for as many as five days in a row, leaving the same type of long-winded, stream-of-consciousness message each time.

Sometimes, Shreaves would answer and end up talking to Mary Jane for as long as he could stand it before finding some excuse to end the conversation. But after a while, he realized most of the times that she called, it was when she knew or suspected he would not be home. Shreaves quickly reasoned that she didn't necessarily want to talk to him at all, but just wanted to leave these long messages for him, so he stopped answering the phone and simply let the machine pick it up.

It went on that way for months and months. The volume of calls tended to fluctuate—one week she might only call once or twice, the next week almost every day—but they continued well into the winter of 2007. After a while, Shreaves couldn't take it anymore and decided to have a phone block preventing Mary Jane from calling his home number, a measure that caused him some semblance of guilt. But Mary Jane was hardly deterred by the effort: She simply started calling from her cell phone instead.

When it became clear that she was not going to stop, Shreaves played some of the messages for the church council and asked them to speak to Mary Jane about it. But, much to Shreaves's displeasure, they seemed reluctant to get involved. Some council members shrugged it off, insisting it would stop or simply saying something like, "We'll get to it," and never addressing it. Others just chalked it up to Mary Jane's generally unusual nature and insisted it was harmless.

Then, one week in the summertime, Shreaves noticed he had extra food in his freezer that he had not purchased. He usually left his door unlocked, and a few more times after that, new food would suddenly appear in his home, or a bag of groceries would be left on his front porch. At first, he didn't make any connection to Mary Jane at all, believing somebody else from the congregation had bought it for him. Then one day, when he answered one of Mary Jane's phone calls, she asked him if he needed any more food, and he realized she was coming into his house and dropping off groceries for him.

"No, Mary Jane," Shreaves said. "Just don't do that anymore."

But Mary Jane persisted, even after the pastor started locking his door. One day, she left yet another bag of groceries on his front porch, Shreaves decided the only way to make his point was to leave them there and not bring them inside. They sat in front of his house for about a week, and the food eventually spoiled.

Upon learning this, Mary Jane called and left yet another of her messages for Shreaves, but this time, her voice was lower and angrier, like that of a different person altogether. To Shreaves, it was an evil, almost demonic sounding voice.

"How can you do this?" Mary Jane angrily demanded. "Ungrateful! Somebody's trying to take care of you and you're snubbing them!"

To Shreaves, it was positively frightening. It had gotten to the point that Shreaves didn't feel comfortable considering himself Mary Jane's pastor. He would even pray that she stay in good health despite her physical problems, because he was not sure whether he could bring himself to visit her in the hospital if she did.

Oh this is great, he thought. *What have I gotten into here?*

But the whole situation finally came to a breaking point one Sunday, when Mary Jane called at around 10:30 at night. Not accustomed to calls at that hour, even from her, Shreaves worried that it must be some sort of emergency. But instead, he found it was yet again just Mary Jane, looking to leave another one of her messages.

Fed up, Shreaves yelled into the phone, "Mary Jane, don't call here anymore. In fact, I don't know if I can be your pastor. Maybe you need to find another church. I just can't pastor you."

At first, there was nothing but silence on the other end. Then, all of a sudden, Mary Jane launched into an angry tirade against the pastor, much as she did after he refused to accept her groceries. When reflecting back on the call later, Shreaves could not recall exactly what Mary Jane had said, but he remembered her voice perfectly. It was that same evil-sounding voice as the last time she became angry, except this time with a touch of nervousness and restlessness as well.

The calls became slightly less frequent after that, but Shreaves was deeply disturbed. It was as if Mary Jane had shed her persona and revealed a completely different, darker personality altogether.

CHAPTER 13

Stumpo and Dietz's recent interview with Pastor Shreaves gave them a lot to follow up on. Just as they had looked into Karen Loch, the disgruntled ex-secretary, they now had to check into Mary Jane Fonder, the parishioner who was apparently infatuated with the pastor.

Dietz and Bucks County Detective Mike Mosiniak went over to Mary Jane's house the day after meeting with Shreaves. Her small ranch home was also in Springfield Township, a short three miles or so from the church.

After pulling up to the house, Dietz knocked on the door and waited, but no answer came. There was a car in the driveway and Dietz believed he saw a light on inside the house. He knocked again, but again, no answer. Dietz and Mosiniak waited a little while longer, pacing around the front step and eventually walking around the house, checking whether anyone was in the backyard or at one of the windows.

After about ten minutes, Dietz took out one of his business cards and wrote a brief note asking Mary Jane to get in touch with them as soon as possible. After slipping it under the door, Dietz and Mosiniak started back toward their patrol car. But as soon as they reached it, the front door of the house suddenly opened, and out stepped Mary Jane's older brother, Ed Fonder.

A sixty-nine-year-old man of medium build and regular

height, with a balding head of white hair, Ed wore a pair of glasses and an almost entirely bland facial expression. He did not smile as he greeted the troopers, nor did he appear especially unhappy to meet them. Ed was a retired physics teacher and, the troopers believed, he looked the part.

The officers explained they were looking for Mary Jane because they were interviewing members of Trinity Evangelical Lutheran Church about Rhonda Smith's death. But Mary Jane was not home at the moment, according to Ed. He further explained that unlike his sister, he was not a member of Trinity Evangelical, and instead attended a parish in New Jersey where he previously lived.

Ed did not invite the men into the house. In fact, he stood in the doorway as if to block their view of the inside altogether. Dietz didn't get the impression he necessarily had anything to hide, but that he simply didn't like having outsiders at his home. From their brief conversation, it appeared to Dietz that Ed was an extremely intelligent man, but also extremely awkward and completely lacking in social skills.

The officers left a message asking Mary Jane to call Dietz regarding Rhonda's death.

Later, Stumpo checked the various records that state police have access to, including the Commonwealth Law Enforcement Assistance Network, the National Law Enforcement Telecommunications System, the National Crime Information Center, and a Pennsylvania gun ownership query. In his research, Stumpo stumbled across something intriguing. State records showed Mary Jane owned a gun, a .38-caliber Rossi revolver she bought in December 1994.

Mary Jane Fonder's name continued to come up as Stumpo proceeded with his investigation. On January 28, now five days after Rhonda's death, Stumpo received the phone records for the church office. He was surprised to note that on January 21, the Monday before Rhonda died, the church had received three calls from Mary Jane's home.

The first call came in at 11:07 a.m. and lasted just six seconds. The second call was at 11:10 and lasted for four minutes and twenty-two seconds. The third call was at 11:25 and ran two minutes and thirty-seven seconds.

Two days later, Stumpo received a report from Corporal Mark Garrett, one of the state police's local ballistics experts. Garrett had completed his bullet analysis in the case. He studied two bullets—the one in the church office ceiling and the one that lodged in Rhonda's brain. Garrett had determined the bullets were of the .38/.357 caliber class and that they could have been discharged from several makes of revolvers, including Rossi.

Holy cow, Stumpo thought. *Mary Jane Fonder is basically stalking the pastor, and she owns a Rossi. . . .*

Rhonda's funeral was held Monday, January 28, at the Heintzelman Funeral Home in Hellertown. It was located on the same street where Rhonda used to live, just up the road from the Smiths' house. The outpouring overwhelmed the Smiths, with more than 250 people attending the 1 o'clock service.

"Can you believe it? All these people?" Rhonda's brother Perry said to his father. "If it was me or you, we'd have about ten."

Trooper Richard Webb was sent to the funeral to watch out for white cars that could belong to the strange man who had stopped by the church the week before Rhonda's death. He was also supposed to check whether Mary Jane Fonder was among the mourners.

Webb noted eight white cars in the funeral home parking lot, but all belonged to either Smith's friends or Trinity church members. What he did not find, however, was Mary Jane's 1997 Ford Escort. She did not attend the funeral.

Rhonda was buried at the Union Cemetery in Hellertown. Some voiced concern about the idea of Rhonda being buried before it had been formally determined whether she killed herself or was murdered, but Paul Hoffman, Lehigh County's first deputy cororner, assured the public it was not unusual for a victim to be buried before the manner of death was determined.

"It's considered pending," Hoffman told *The Intelligencer.*

Leaving the funeral, a reporter from that newspaper approached Sandy Rehrig, the church council's secretary. Sandy reflected on how sad the church congregation still was, and how difficult Rhonda's death had been on the entire community.

"It's not only the church, it's the whole community," she said. "We're still just hoping and praying it gets resolved soon for the peace and closure of everyone. We really miss Rhonda."

The state police received Rhonda's autopsy report during the first week of the investigation. Dr. Sara Funke, an Allentown-based forensic pathologist who performs regular autopsies at St. Luke's Hospital in Fountain Hill, filed the report.

She recorded two gunshot wounds to Rhonda's head. The first was on her forehead, starting several inches above her eyes, just right of center and ending at her hairline. That bullet had traveled upward along Rhonda's forehead, splitting the skin and grazing the front of her skull. The first wound was nonfatal. The second one was not.

The other wound was just above her right ear, penetrating her skull with no exit wound. A copper jacket and lead projectile subsequently found in the lower left rear of Rhonda's brain indicated the bullet took a front-to-back and slightly left path, Funke noted.

There was no soot found on Rhonda's skin that would have been consistent with a gun being pressed to her skin. However, Funke said she could not rule out such contact without knowing what kind of gun was used.

Funke found stippling, or small, round gunpowder marks, on Rhonda's right hand and the right side of her face. The stippling indicated Rhonda was shot at an intermediate range, between three and four feet away, but Funke again noted she couldn't be sure of that without knowing the weapon used.

Funke ruled that Rhonda's cause of death was a gunshot wound to the head. The manner of death, however, was left as undetermined for now.

CHAPTER 14

About a week into the investigation, the state police brought in Corporal Bob Egan to assist Stumpo with the case. The twenty-four-year police veteran was part of the local criminal investigation assessment team, a group that worked on complicated homicide and cold cases. Still unsolved after more than a week, the investigation into Rhonda Smith's death was proving to be a complicated one, and if not solved soon, authorities feared it could find itself among those cold cases.

In terms of homicide experience, Egan was the antithesis of Stumpo. While Stumpo was now serving as the main investigator on his first homicide case, Egan had worked on seventy-five homicide cases and been the main investigator on fifteen of them. Starting out as a patrolman in Montgomery and Bucks Counties for the first decade of his career, Egan started working investigations at the Bethlehem barracks in 1993.

Among his cases was Charles Cullen, the male nurse who killed as many as forty patients over sixteen years while working at hospitals in Pennsylvania and New Jersey. Cullen was serving life in prison, where authorities were still trying to get information from him about all his victims. There was also the case of Bryan and David Freeman, two teenage skinheads who killed their parents in Salisbury Township, just outside of Allentown. The two brothers and their cousin, Nelson Birdwell III, were convicted and sentenced to life in prison for the slayings.

Only one of Egan's cases had gone unsolved—the murder of Charlotte Fimiano, a real estate agent found strangled to death in Lower Saucon Township. His other seventy-four cases were solved and closed.

Egan had been in Missouri, interviewing a suspect in a seemingly mob-related shooting on the Pennsylvania Turnpike, when he got the call about Rhonda Smith's death. Investigators explained there were still conflicting opinions about whether it was a suicide or a homicide, but they wanted him to join the investigation when he returned.

Egan joined the case on January 31, and was paired with Stumpo as one of the case's main investigators. Stumpo had briefly met Egan once or twice in the past, but mainly knew him by reputation from others who knew the detective from the Bethlehem barracks. From what he heard, Stumpo got the impression Egan was a fairly low-key guy who liked to stay out of the limelight.

And, upon first impression at least, Egan more than lived up to his quiet reputation. The balding, forty-seven-year-old man seemed to go out of his way to stay in the background. It didn't do much for Stumpo's confidence in the man, and he began to wonder whether Egan would be a help to him at all during the case.

"Don't mind me," Egan said as they climbed into Stumpo's car. "I'm just along for the ride."

"You're not going to offend me," Stumpo said. "If you're going to have anything to say, say it."

"No, no, I'm just along for the ride," Egan repeated.

Great, Stumpo thought to himself. *He isn't going to be helpful at all.*

But Stumpo would learn this was just Egan's way. He didn't say much, but his mind was always fixated on the case.

One of Egan's first duties was to attend a meeting with the various investigators and law enforcement officials working on the case. State police Lieutenant William Teper ran the meeting, which also included other state police supervisors, criminal investigators, and forensic services officers. Members of the Bucks County District Attorney's office also took part, including First Assistant District Attorney David Zellis, who had been assigned to oversee the case for the office.

The law enforcement officials remained split in their thoughts about the shooting. With Rhonda's history of depression, some still strongly believed she had committed suicide. They cited Rhonda's previous attempts to kill herself, especially her trip to the gun range.

One official pointed to statements Jim Smith had made to the media that his daughter would never commit suicide because she knew she would go to hell if she did. Jim had said her daughter was "brought up to believe in God" and that "a self-murderer does not get into the kingdom of heaven." This made some authorities wonder whether he was some sort of religious nut. It was pointed out that the Smiths had already admitted they drove right past the church the day Rhonda was killed. What if, as troopers had speculated early on, they found her body and, determined to protect their daughter's reputation from the stigma of suicide, removed the gun from the scene?

Those leaning toward homicide pointed out that Rhonda had not one, but two gunshot wounds. But that didn't convince some of the veteran law enforcement officials, who had seen suicides with more than one gunshot wound before, especially in cases like Rhonda's, where one wound was superficial.

The stippling noted in the autopsy report suggested Rhonda was shot from a distance of three or four feet. But that didn't convince all of the investigators, either. While the forensic pathologist had worked on many suspicious deaths in Lehigh County, Dr. Sara Funke was unknown to many in the primarily Bucks County–based group. Some didn't know whether to trust her findings.

Those supporting homicide went through the list of possible suspects. The boyfriends all had alibis, they said, and the investigation into the mysterious stranger was going no-where fast.

One official asked if they were getting anywhere with church members. The investigators brought up the fired church secretary and Mary Jane Fonder, a parishioner who was bothering the pastor.

The name sparked a memory in the mind of Mark Lauden-slager, the Springfield Township Police Department chief who had also been called in for the meeting. Laudenslager recalled that Mary Jane's elderly father, Edward Fonder, had gone missing back in 1993, while Laudenslager was still a patrolman on the force. Fonder was never found and was now presumed dead.

Back in 1993, Mary Jane had been considered the prime suspect in his disappearance.

Even with this new information about Mary Jane, how-ever, the police meeting concluded with a determination to keep investigating the Rhonda Smith case both as a possible homicide and a possible suicide.

CHAPTER 15

Mary Jane Fonder was born July 5, 1942, the youngest of two children of Edward and Alice Fonder, native Philadelphians.

During Mary Jane's childhood, her family, which included older brother Edward IV, lived in West Philadelphia, near the intersection of South 57th Street and Thomas Avenue. Edward Fonder III was a machinist at Messinger Bearings, a Philadelphia manufacturer, while Alice Fonder worked as a proofreader at Chilton Publishing Company in the neighborhood.

Mary Jane's younger years were happy ones. The highlights of her weeks were always the weekends. On Saturdays, she and her brother received their $2.50 allowances, and those mornings were like a party to them. On Sundays, Mary Jane and Ed would go to church before spending the afternoon at their grandmother's house, where they would play with their cousins and some of the neighborhood children.

But Mary Jane started having emotional problems at a young age. She had her first nervous breakdown when she was eight years old. Following the breakdown, her parents bought her a dog to lift her spirits, a treasured black dachshund, which she named Minnie Minerva.

Mary Jane's emotional problems resurfaced when she was sixteen, and this time, they were far worse. That year, her brother had moved to New York to attend Columbia University and Mary Jane missed him terribly. After he left, she felt she had no one to talk to in her life. She also was upset by the recent breakup from her first boyfriend, Jim Schnell.

At the time, Mary Jane was taking several accelerated classes at John Bartram High School, and her emotional problems starting taking a toll on her schoolwork. Her problems were affecting her physically, too. She became afraid of crowds, which made her feel like her skin was tightening up.

That year, she tried to commit suicide by overdosing on chloral hydrate, a sedative used to treat anxiety and insomnia. Her mother came home and rushed her to the hospital before any real damage was done.

Mary Jane was institutionalized at a mental hospital for a month following her suicide attempt. Mary Jane felt the hospital helped her get herself under control, but social interactions continued to be difficult for her. She dropped out of high school shortly after she left the hospital.

One respite in Mary Jane's life was her family's country home in Bucks County, which they had purchased back when Mary Jane was a child. All throughout Mary Jane's childhood, the family loved to take road trips. In fact, when Mary Jane was still a little girl, her father asked her and her brother to pick whether the family should buy a car or a television. For her the choice was easy: They went with the car, which allowed them to travel the area.

One of the family's favorite places to drive was Bucks County, some of the closest rural land to the urban Philadelphia. When Mary Jane was twelve, her family bought a small cabin on more than eleven acres of land in Springfield Township. Mary Jane's father so loved the new home that he dubbed it his "Garden of Eden."

The Fonder family would spend the weekend away at their cabin as often as they could, and they soon became close friends with the Schnell family who lived down the road. Mary Jane became very close with her ex-boyfriend Jim's younger sister, Roseanna, and even Jim's new girlfriend,

Rosalie, and she soon preferred life at the country home over her time spent in Philadelphia.

The Schnell and Fonder women would often play board games or crochet together, while Mary Jane's father regularly went off on his own to explore the property. At other times he was more social, and enjoyed entertaining the families on the piano or accordion.

But even life in the country wasn't always enjoyable for the Fonder family. Rosalie, who went on to marry Jim in 1965, remembers the family regularly quarreling, especially Mr. and Mrs. Fonder. The pair would routinely argue with each other over little things, and would sometimes pick on their children in the same way, too.

Back in Philadelphia, Mary Jane joined a ceramics studio to fill her days. She found she liked art, and she was good at it. Painting would continue to be one of her life's passions for many years.

Once she was old enough to work, Mary Jane found jobs in a wide variety of fields. One of her first was at Philadelphia's famed Wanamaker's department store, and then she worked in the knitting industry at several factories. She then became a cardpunch operator for J. P. Lippincott, a publishing company that manufactured Bibles and other religious works. Mary Jane worked there for eight-and-a-half years, one of the longest-held jobs of her life.

Mary Jane liked to work, and she especially liked living on her own, which she did for the first time in 1969, when she was twenty-six. Her parents' neighborhood was becoming increasingly crime ridden. One time she was mugged, and on another occasion she was chased and attacked. This finally encouraged her to get her own place.

As with her jobs, Mary Jane had a variety of apartments over the years, mostly in the northeastern section of the city. She had friends she would walk her dogs with, or who would join her to crochet and sew. She especially reveled in buying her first car, a Toyota her father helped her pick out.

Just as she took some time before living on her own, Mary Jane didn't start dating until later in life. She wasn't romantically interested in men until her late thirties, and even then she kept meeting men who weren't interested in a serious relationship.

She had two serious boyfriends, including a man named Joe, who was divorced with children and was significantly older than Mary Jane. When they met in 1979, she was thirty-six and he was already in his fifties. Mary Jane found him smart and funny, but he was out of work and living with his mother. They had talked of marrying, but it never happened.

Rosalie Schnell didn't think much of Joe from the beginning. She felt like he was taking advantage of Mary Jane: He regularly borrowed money from her, and generally made a bad impression on her during his visits to Bucks County.

"I don't like the man, I don't like the man at all," she told her husband.

"Well there must be something wrong with him, because you like everybody," Jim Schnell responded.

Mary Jane once lamented to Rosalie that she wished she could find someone to be happy with, the way Rosalie was happy with Jim. It was clear to Rosalie that Mary Jane was a very lonely woman.

Ed and Alice Fonder moved up to Springfield permanently in 1981, and Mary Jane followed in 1987 to take care of them. Both were having health problems, which increased as the years went by. In the spring of 1992, Alice Fonder was having such major circulation problems that her doctor recommended one of her legs be removed at the hip.

The surgery did not go well and Alice ended up in a coma. She remained in the hospital for four months following her surgery. Hospitals made Ed Fonder uncomfortable, but Mary Jane made sure to visit her mother every single day.

On September 7, 1992, Alice Fonder's breathing tube malfunctioned. Doctors believed either food got stuck in the tube, or that Alice herself damaged it while trying to pull it out. She died that day.

Ed Fonder was devastated by his wife's death, and he expressed his depression through anger and fussiness toward his caretaker, Mary Jane. He became more and more difficult to live with, and fighting became a regular occurrence between the two.

The tension came to a boiling point the following July, when two of Ed Fonder's elderly cousins visited from the Philadelphia area. They brought with them a cake to celebrate his birthday. But what they really came for was to give the family a hard time, Mary Jane claimed.

Shortly after they arrived, the cousins started talking about how terrible they felt the world was today. Before long, their criticisms were being directed squarely at Mary Jane, as they went on about how poorly she treated her father and how she never took him on any trips. The words deeply hurt Mary Jane, and both she and her brother felt her father was deeply affected by the visit as well.

"It was an unforgivable thing and it blew our family apart," Mary Jane's brother was quoted as telling *The Morning Call* newspaper in 1994.

After that visit, Ed Fonder just seemed different, according to Mary Jane. He didn't speak much to her anymore. Aside from the occasional nasty remark, he would just give her cold looks and ignore her for long periods of time.

Previously almost entirely confined to the house because of his physical difficulties, the eighty-year-old now started to walk more. At times he would walk without his cane up the back steps, something he previously couldn't do. He started spending more time outside, wandering around the twelve acres of woods on their property, Mary Jane later told police. Sometimes he'd wander a little too far, and Mary Jane claimed she'd have to catch up to him and bring him back.

Mary Jane said August 26, 1993, was a day like any other: She had gotten up that morning around 7 o'clock, came out to the kitchen, and set the table for breakfast for her father. She recalled that she went back into her bedroom to lie down a bit and, at one point, heard the front door open. She thought nothing of it, assuming her father had gone outside to get the newspaper as he often did.

Mary Jane said she dozed off for a bit after that. When

she got out of bed later, around 11 o'clock, she came out and found her father was gone. She stepped outside and found the newspaper still sitting on the ground in front of her house, her father nowhere to be seen. Mary Jane called out his name, but he did not respond and she couldn't find him anywhere. She called the police, as well as some of her Winding Road neighbors to ask for their help.

Jim and Rosalie Schnell came right over and stayed past midnight to help in the search. Neighbors Sue and John Brunner also came, bringing their own dog to help the police in the search of the large property. Sue had just been over to the Fonder house two days prior, and remembered there seemed to be a lot of tension between Mary Jane and her father, who were being gruff with each other and making snippy remarks.

The search lasted for hours, but it proved fruitless. Police dogs tracked Ed Fonder's scent down to the end of the driveway and just across the road, but nowhere else. Along with the Brunners' dog, the police walked most of the Fonder property with their bloodhounds, but they didn't find Ed's scent or any other clues elsewhere on the land.

Theories began to form about what could have happened. Mary Jane thought someone must have picked him up at the end of the driveway: a taxi driver, or perhaps one of the cousins who had just visited. Mary Jane also thought he could have returned to their old Philadelphia neighborhood or, since he had a strong interest in horticulture, had gone to the Fort Washington flower show that was being held around that time.

Through the course of their investigation, police discovered that Ed Fonder had been talking to a phone sex operator in the months before he disappeared. Maybe he had paid her to come and pick him up, some thought. But the theory was investigated and proved a dead end.

Rumors were spreading throughout Mary Jane's neighborhood. Some neighbors heard that the garbage man had made a comment while taking away the Fonders' trash that the garbage bags were unusually heavy and smelly. This led to talk that Ed's body was in the trash. The rumor kept

changing with time. Some said the garbage man had called
the police to report it, but nothing ever came of it. Others
said it was the garbage truck that struck Ed, and the trash
collectors had thrown his body away to cover it up.

There were several reports from people who thought they
saw Ed Fonder after his disappearance. People reported seeing him in Quakertown, Allentown, Philadelphia, and on a
bus to Atlantic City. But the authorities checked out every
sighting, and none of the leads panned out.

Rosalie Schnell would call Mary Jane whenever she
heard on the news that a dead body had been found in Philadelphia. None of those ended up being Ed Fonder, either.

In April 1994, nearly a year after his disappearance, Ed
Fonder's wallet was found in an Allentown mailbox, its contents still intact. That got people thinking: How could he be
surviving without any money, and without his medication,
which he had left behind at the house? He hadn't taken any
clothes or other personal items with him, either.

Ed Fonder's doctor told police the elderly man would
likely not live ten days without his medication, but Ed
Fonder IV theorized his father could be obtaining medication under a false name.

"The reason I believe my father is still alive is that he
doesn't get around well on foot, so if he died it would almost
have to be close to a road. He couldn't go cross-country on
his own," Ed Fonder IV told *The Morning Call* in February
1994.

On the one-year anniversary of her father's disappearance, Mary Jane took out an advertisement in the paper asking
her father to come home.

Mary Jane was very depressed during this period. Following her father's disappearance, Mary Jane started leaving
rambling messages on Jim and Rosalie Schnell's answering
machine, often about how she was afraid living alone on the
large, secluded property. She feared there were demons on
the property, and perhaps the Devil had taken her father.

Some started to suspect Mary Jane herself had a hand
in her father's disappearance. Some pointed to the smelly

garbage theory and speculated that Mary Jane had killed the old man herself. Others talked about an old well on the back of the Fonder property that Mary Jane allegedly didn't let the police go near. Maybe she had pushed him down into it, some people said.

John and Sue Brunner certainly had their suspicions. Mary Jane had always been friendly toward them, even overly gracious at times, showing up with gifts of food or other trinkets, but her explanation that he could have walked away didn't make sense to them. Ed Fonder wasn't very mobile in his later days, and the closest towns of Coopersburg, Hellertown, and Quakertown were all about ten miles away.

The Springfield Township police investigation was headed up by Kimberly Triol, a five-year officer and, as assistant chief, the second-in-command of the small department. Triol had interviewed Mary Jane several times, and started to grow suspicious from early on.

On the day that Mary Jane first reported her father missing, she told Triol he started wandering off the property right after the cousins visited. Mary Jane explained that on that very day, Ed Fonder had disappeared for about an hour and a half, and that she had called several family members looking for him before finding him in a field behind their property.

The story confused Triol. She asked Mary Jane why she didn't report him missing back then, and she shrugged and replied simply, "Because I found him." But Triol didn't understand why Mary Jane immediately reported her father missing the day he disappeared, but didn't do so even after ninety minutes the last time.

During that first interview, Triol noticed several items piled atop each other inside Mary Jane's house. The items—which included milk crates, oil cans, windshield wiper fluid, blankets, and an oil jacket—had obviously come from the trunk of a car. Mary Jane agreed to show Triol her trunk, which had been completely emptied.

Upon seeing it, Triol suspected Mary Jane had placed her father inside and taken him away.

In another early interview, Triol glanced into Mary Jane's bathroom and noticed a bucket filled with pinkish water, alongside towels and a mop. When Triol asked what it was, Mary Jane explained that her dog had gotten sick. Triol knew she should have investigated it further, but she suddenly became very nervous being in the house alone with Mary Jane. She let it go, something that bothered the officer for years to come.

During another interview, Triol discovered the corpse of a dog that had been wrapped in plastic and placed inside Mary Jane's freezer. When Triol asked what happened, Mary Jane simply explained it was her father's dog, and that it died. Later, after an autopsy, it was discovered that the dog had consumed some of Ed Fonder's diabetes medicine and died of poisoning.

Nevertheless, over the course of several interviews, Triol developed a positive rapport with Mary Jane, who called her "Officer Kim." Triol came over so often that Rosalie Schnell came to the rather bizarre conclusion that Triol was in love with Mary Jane.

Although Mary Jane enjoyed Triol's company, she seemed to never forget she was speaking with a cop. Once, after Triol asked her a question, Mary Jane said, "I watch all the cop shows, I know why you're asking me this. You're trying to trap me."

But the rapport they had fell apart after an interview at Mary Jane's home on November 29.

Mary Jane had made no secret of the fact that things changed between her and her father after the cousins' visit. They were fighting constantly after that point, so much so that Mary Jane contemplated suicide. She was taking a variety of pills to treat her depression, including several that Triol believed should not have been mixed.

At one point, Mary Jane startled Triol by, out of the blue, pulling out a Taser gun and showing it to the officer.

"Look what I bought," Mary Jane said, then flipped it on, creating a blue burst of electricity.

Triol felt threatened and attempted to end the interview.

But, just as the conversation appeared to be winding down, Mary Jane surprised her by returning to the topic of her missing father.

"Yeah, I don't think I did anything to my pop," Mary Jane said. "I swear to God I don't think I did."

Mary Jane stopped talking and looked away, then whispered, "Maybe the drugs did something. Maybe I don't remember."

Triol was shocked. She believed Mary Jane was on the verge of confessing to the murder of her father.

"Do you want to talk about the drugs during that time? That week?"

"Yes, we can," Mary Jane said. "Okay."

Triol became nervous that if Mary Jane confessed, and the officer had not read her her Miranda rights, that the confession would be inadmissible in court.

"Mary Jane, I need to go through with procedure and read you your Miranda warnings," Triol said.

"Okay," Mary Jane replied, but seemed suspicious. "Why? Are you going to try to get me to admit something? Like that black woman on TV?" Mary Jane added, referring to one of her police shows.

"No," Triol said, "I just want to talk about the drugs and that week, and I have to read you these warnings."

"Oh, okay," Mary Jane said. "You're investigating a crime and you're doing your job."

Triol read her the rights, but worried she might be better off with another witness present. She asked whether she would mind if the police chief, Robert Bell, came over to listen to their conversation. Mary Jane agreed, but seemed even more hesitant.

"Obviously, I don't have the funds to hire a lawyer," she said, before adding, "Oh, it's late."

Triol could feel the momentum of the interview fading away. "Do you want to do this some other time?"

"No, we can do it now," Mary Jane said, but a moment later, it was over.

"Well, it is late," she said. "Maybe tomorrow."

After that day, Mary Jane's cooperation with the police had come to an end. She hired a lawyer and insisted she never wanted to see Kimberly Triol again. She told reporters the police were flubbing the investigation into her missing father, and trying to make her confess to something she didn't do. She claimed, falsely, that she had thrown Triol out of the house and told her to never come back.

After that, the police knew they no longer had any need to be subtle. Chief Bell asked Mary Jane to take a lie detector test to prove she didn't hurt her father. Mary Jane refused. Bell spent the next five months trying to convince Mary Jane to take the test, but she wouldn't budge.

For his part, Mary Jane's brother Ed told *The Morning Call* that he felt the township police had bungled the case and now, in their embarrassment, were trying to pin it on the Fonders.

"I get the impression that they wanted to dump this. It wasn't one of their successful cases and they wanted to sweep it under the rug," Ed told the newspaper. Unlike his sister, he was never approached to take a lie detector test.

Additionally, the Fonder investigation took place at a tumultuous time for the Springfield Township Police Department. The police were often at odds with the board of supervisors, the township's governing body. Those tensions reached a boiling point in January 1994, when the supervisors voted not to reappoint Bell as police chief during their annual reorganization meeting. The reasons for this action never became public: Aside from one comment about problems with the police computer system, the supervisors never publicly addressed it except to say they had gotten several complaints about the chief. Bell stayed on as chief despite his lack of a reappointment, but morale in the township was low. The township eventually hired a private investigator to look into Bell's personal and professional activities. But, when the investigator turned up no evidence of misconduct, Bell was reappointed chief—a position he stayed in until 2003—and the matter was put to rest.

Nevertheless, Triol didn't feel the politics hindered the

investigation. She left the force in June 1994 for personal reasons, leaving Ed Fonder's disappearance the only unsolved case from her time on the department. Although the case was handed over to the other officers and kept open, Triol believed her departure hindered the investigation.

She felt guilty for leaving the case unsolved. Although she never knew Ed Fonder Sr., she felt as if she did, and felt that she failed to do right by him by discovering what happened to him.

"I carry it with me like a burden," Triol later said of the case. "I don't have closure on this at all. This is a part of me."

CHAPTER 16

Mary Jane Fonder lost many of the key people in her life between 1992 and 1993. In addition to her mother's death and her father's disappearance, Mary Jane's best friend, Roseanna Schnell, died in 1992.

After all those losses, Roseanna's brother Jim and his wife Rosalie became Mary Jane's closest friends. Though Mary Jane could get a little long winded and overbearing, the sweet-natured Rosalie was very tolerant of her, listening to every word of her sometimes-endless chatter. Even after Jim Schnell died in 2006, Mary Jane and Rosalie continued to get together for a meal or outing on a regular basis.

A few days after Rhonda Smith's death, Mary Jane telephoned Rosalie to say she was heading to Quakertown to go to the laundromat. Rosalie mentioned she had planned to go to Quakertown that day, too, to pick up a couple of items at the grocery store. The two women decided to go into town together, and made a day of it by stopping for lunch while Mary Jane's clothes were drying.

"How about that murder at your church?" Rosalie said over lunch. "Can you imagine?"

Rosalie had heard of Rhonda's death through a neighbor. She didn't attend Trinity Evangelical herself, but the entire Schnell family, including Jim, was buried in the church's cemetery. The church was only a couple miles away from her home, and it was hard for Rosalie to fathom a murder happening in her quiet township.

"Well, they don't know if it was a murder or a suicide," Mary Jane responded. "They don't really know what happened there."

"Well, I happened to see it on the news," Rosalie continued, "and they didn't say anything about a gun or a weapon or anything. She certainly couldn't have committed suicide and hid the weapon."

Mary Jane took a bite of her food before speaking again.

"Yeah, it's a shame," Mary Jane said. "Such a nice family and they don't know what happened."

"I'm sure they'll find out sooner or later what happened there," Rosalie concluded.

With the question of whether Rhonda's death was a homicide or a suicide still hanging in the air, Bob Egan decided the best way to get to the bottom of it was to meet Jim and Dorothy himself. The theory that Jim found Rhonda's body and cleaned up the scene so it wouldn't look like a suicide was a reasonable possibility, and certainly not an unprecedented one. But before one could make a leap like that, Egan felt, you had to know the person you're accusing, and he wanted to look them in their eyes for himself and see if they were lying.

So, about a week after the murder, Egan and Trooper Patrick McGuire visited the Smiths at their Lower Saucon Township home. They had already been interviewed several times by the police by then, and it would have been understandable for them to be a bit tired of the process, but Jim and Dorothy cordially invited them in and patiently answered all their questions. They recalled the details of that horrible day they lost their daughter: the phone call, their trip to the hospital, being told that their daughter was brain dead. They also reconfirmed, yes, they drove by the church that very morning, and almost went inside to invite Rhonda to lunch with them.

Egan asked whether the Smiths owned any guns. Jim told him he had some hunting rifles he had inherited when his brother died, but that he never used them. When Egan asked about handguns, Jim said he had given his only one away to his nephew, who lived in Vermont. Jim consented to a search of his home to confirm what guns were on the property.

Jim and Dorothy both spoke candidly about the challenges of raising Rhonda and dealing with her bipolar disorder. She was often out of work, didn't have much money, and they constantly had to help her, even when Rhonda was resistant.

"But she was our daughter," Jim said, "and we loved her."

Jim shared with the detective a four-page letter that Rhonda had written to him the previous Easter, which Jim now kept at the table next to his favorite living room chair and read repeatedly when he started to miss his daughter. Printed from the computer on paper with clouds in the background, it was labeled "My Gratitude List for my Father, Francis W. Smith, a/k/a/ Dad-E-O." Rhonda spoke of how thankful she was for the way Jim had taken care of her throughout the years, and helped her realize that she could overcome her mental illness and do anything she set her mind to.

"You taught me that my name, even as common as it is, means a lot and I should defend it at all costs, legally and financially, and I will for life!" the letter read in part. "You taught me even with my mental illness, I can do anything anybody else can do. I have this theme where when somebody tells me I can't do it, I prove I can.

"You instilled in me a belief in God through your actions. You forgave me for my mistakes, even when I couldn't forgive myself. You never bring them up, even when I insist on doing it. We are taught that God loves us and wants the best for us. Maybe I should learn to accept this from my earthly father! You taught all of us not to give up even when all the cards are dealt out. Sometimes I think it would be easier, but I still fight because I know I'm on a good team."

The letter ended, "You will always be my dad and I wanted

you to know these things that you taught me in 41 years. I love you! But sometimes, I still need a hug. Happy Easter! Love, Rhonda."

Egan left the house convinced that Jim and Dorothy were loving parents who had nothing to do with covering up Rhonda's suicide. Nothing they had said aroused his suspicions or led him to believe they were lying. Egan knew to wander into such a horrific scene as finding their daughter dead in a church would have been one of the most difficult things for a parent to see, and he did not believe they would have been able to conceal their emotions from the police if they had.

Afterward, police ran a check on guns owned by Jim Smith, and confirmed that what Jim told him was true: The only handgun registered to him was now owned by his nephew in Vermont, just as he had said. Later, authorities in Vermont checked out that gun, but it didn't match the one that killed Rhonda.

Additionally, Egan and Stumpo later checked out a security surveillance tape taken at the Red Robin restaurant where Jim and Dorothy ate the day Rhonda was killed. If the police theory about Jim finding Rhonda were true, then the Smiths would have already known their daughter was dead when this footage was shot. However, the tape revealed Jim and Dorothy showing no signs of strong emotions when they entered or exited the restaurant. Stumpo and Egan agreed that if they had just found the body of their dead daughter, there was no way they would have appeared so calm on the tape.

For Stumpo and Egan, there was no longer any doubt in their minds. The Smiths were completely innocent, and Rhonda Smith's death was no suicide. It was murder.

Looking further into Mary Jane's background, Stumpo and Egan learned through unemployment hearing records that she had been fired from a Denny's restaurant in 1994 for threatening a coworker. Her unemployment hearing in the case took place on December 13, 1994, a date that particularly stood out to the two troopers.

It was the same date Mary Jane first obtained her gun.

The officers were able to track down several of Mary Jane's former coworkers from Denny's in Center Valley. Kimberly Riedy remembered Mary Jane as a strange woman who took a lot of medications. She also recalled that Mary Jane would often complain about how mean her father was to her, but that she was very upset when he went missing.

She couldn't remember any specific threats Mary Jane ever made while at the restaurant, and it was clear to police that the topic made her uncomfortable.

"The whole subject sort of freaks me out," Kimberly said.

However, she pointed the officers in the direction of Diane Anderson, who had been the Denny's general manager at the time and was now living in California. A few days later, Stumpo and Egan contacted Anderson via telephone, and she seemed equally uncomfortable talking about Mary Jane.

"One day, she'd come in and she was perfectly fine," Diane said. "The next time, she was just a crazy woman. . . . It was like a switch you could click on and off. One minute, you're like, 'Oh, this older lady is a wonderful person,' and the next minute, you're looking at her like, 'What the hell are you talking about?'"

Mary Jane was a little unusual right from the very beginning, Diane recalled. Sometimes, she would show up to work with her wig backward and look just plain ridiculous. Having previously worked at a hairdressing salon, Diane repeatedly offered to style her wigs so Mary Jane could tell the front from the back and put them on correctly. But Mary Jane always politely refused, and continued coming to work with her hairpieces on backward.

But despite her oddities, Diane initially liked Mary Jane. She felt bad for the woman, who often spoke about how desperately she needed money and how difficult it was to take care of her aging father. Diane was happy that she was able to give Mary Jane the job at Denny's, feeling she was helping the woman in some small way.

But after Mary Jane's father disappeared, her oddities intensified—to a frightening degree.

It all started when Diane made a special type of lasagna and served it as part of the Denny's menu. Shortly afterward, a furious Mary Jane came storming into Diane's office, screaming that that lasagna was her recipe and that Diane had stolen it. To Diane's surprise, Mary Jane even went so far as to threaten to kill her.

"That was the beginning of the end there," Diane recalled.

Mary Jane's erratic behavior continued, as did the threats against Diane's life. Eventually, Diane called Mary Jane into the restaurant's back office and, with another manager present for protection, told Mary Jane they were firing her. As Diane expected, Mary Jane flipped out, once again threatening to shoot Diane with a gun and kill her. Diane and the other manager followed Mary Jane out to ensure she left the restaurant and, as they walked through the dining area, Mary Jane continued her tirade, yelling and screaming even in front of the customers.

"She's just not right in the head," Diane said.

When it came time for Mary Jane's unemployment hearing, Diane brought her husband along because she was afraid to be there alone, and parked three blocks away from the courthouse because she did not want Mary Jane to see what kind of car she was driving. Diane recalled that Mary Jane dressed well for the hearing and, at first, seemed to act relatively normal. But as the hearing escalated, Mary Jane became more and more worked up, her behavior becoming increasingly erratic.

By the end, when the board ruled against Mary Jane and denied her any unemployment compensation, she seemed to snap, lashing out at the board members and everybody in the room. She even made a bizarre accusation that all the men on the board were Diane's boyfriends and that was the only reason they were siding with her.

"It was just the craziest thing," Diane said. "She was just making these crazy accusations all over the place. It was horrible."

Although Mary Jane had gotten a gun earlier that day, she left it in her car and did not attempt to bring it into the courtroom. Diane never saw the weapon and had no idea Mary Jane obtained it that day until after the police spoke to her. The very thought of it chilled her to the bone.

"She was going to kill me with it," she was convinced.

The officers also got in touch with a third Denny's co-worker, Barry Schaller. Schaller was probably Mary Jane's closest friend at work; he drove her home from work when she had car problems and he also stayed in touch with her for a few years after she was fired.

Schaller also overheard Mary Jane threaten to shoot Diane Anderson, which he believes he reported to management. He knew Mary Jane owned a gun for self-protection, but he had never seen it.

Although they were friends, Schaller was convinced Mary Jane was involved in their father's disappearance, he told Egan. On one occasion, when Schaller was house-sitting for Mary Jane while she was at the hospital, he even searched the house looking for clues that might prove Mary Jane had killed her father. He said he also thought it was odd that around the time of her father's disappearance, Mary Jane had hired an out-of-town company to cut down trees on her property.

They remained friends through 1996 or 1997 when Schaller stopped hearing from Mary Jane, he said. The year before, Mary Jane had started to change, when he started dating a woman. Mary Jane was very jealous of the woman and called Schaller a ladies' man and a player. Schaller was surprised at how quickly Mary Jane could switch from one emotion to the next, seemingly at the drop of a hat.

"She's a Dr. Jekyll, Mr. Hyde," Schaller told Egan.

CHAPTER 17

The state police continued to interview as many church members as they could. And the more they talked to, it seemed, the more often Mary Jane Fonder came up.

Sue Brunner, Mary Jane's neighbor on Winding Road, told Trooper Raymond Judge about a conversation she had with Mary Jane just two days before Rhonda died. Sue was out walking her dog along the road when Mary Jane passed her in her car and stopped.

"I've decided I'm not going to come to choir anymore," Mary Jane said out her car window.

"Why?" Sue asked her.

"I don't know. I'm just too upset. I'm just too upset about things and I just can't do it," Mary Jane responded.

"Well that's a shame, Mary Jane, because church and choir are two things that you really love," Sue said. "I think you ought to really rethink this because I know how important those two things are to you."

It was far from the first time Sue had seen Mary Jane depressed in the twenty years she'd known her. She often talked about how things were bothering her and how she couldn't come to grips with her life. Mary Jane also on occasion flooded Sue's answering machine with messages all about the "bad vibes" she was feeling.

Mary Jane started discussing a new topic. Sue had missed

church services the day before, January 20, and Mary Jane told her about how Rhonda had stood up in front of the congregation to thank the group for helping her financially.

"Did you know that Rhonda had gotten help?" Mary Jane asked Sue.

"Yes I did," Sue replied. In fact, she had been among the group that made the financial contributions.

Looking upset, Mary Jane said good-bye and drove away.

The police also interviewed Mary Brunner, another Trinity parishioner, who bore no relation to Sue Brunner. Trooper Stumpo had heard that Mary Jane Fonder had told Mary Brunner to stay away from Pastor Shreaves, and Stumpo wanted to find out if that was true.

On February 2, Stumpo met with the sixty-six-year-old Mary Brunner and her husband, Gus, at their Springfield Township home. Stumpo asked whether Mary Jane Fonder had ever asked her to stay away from Pastor Shreaves. Mary Brunner thought about the question for a while before saying no, she could not recall that.

However, Mary did note that Mary Jane had been acting a bit odder than usual lately, especially with regards to Pastor Shreaves. Normally, Mary Jane seemed to really like the pastor, but lately had claimed she wanted nothing to do with him anymore. In recent weeks, she also seemed to get angry with Mary for helping the pastor with odds and ends around the church.

Normally Mary Jane helped Shreaves coordinate some of the Sunday services jobs, and when she was unavailable, Mary Jane would ask Mary to do it. But then, a few days later, Mary Jane would suddenly seem mad at Mary for doing the work, even though it was Mary Jane herself who approached her in the first place.

Mary also recalled a conversation she had with Mary Jane just a few days before Rhonda died. Mary Jane would sometimes stop in Mary's driveway to chat if she was driving by, and had done so on the Saturday morning of January 19.

Mary Jane told Mary she was feeling very depressed and had a bad feeling about the church choir. She made references to experiencing bad vibes and spirits, but that she loved the people at the choir. Mary Jane also offhandedly mentioned that Rhonda Smith was in choir now, and she had been at the last practice. Mary Jane told Mary Brunner she did not plan to go to choir practice for a while.

Also during the first week of February, Stumpo interviewed Pastor Shreaves's girlfriend, Aline Filippone. Aline, who lived in the Catskills region of New York, had come down to be with Shreaves following Rhonda's death and had attended services the first Sunday, where she came into contact with Mary Jane. Aline told Stumpo that Mary Jane peppered her with questions about how long she was staying and would not stop.

Also that week, Stumpo stopped at the Smiths' home to pick up the sympathy cards and the guest book from Rhonda's funeral. As police suspected, Mary Jane had not attended Rhonda's funeral, but she had sent flowers and a card to the Smiths. The card had contained a long and rambling message:

> "I am so grateful that so many of our church loved and got to know Rhonda so well. She was swell and so eager to help Pastor Greg. We all loved our pastor, as he was so kind to us all. . . . He always had a cheering committee. Many times, we took turns helping him, so many of us at different times. He helped so many of us. Judy Zellner and he were very kind to me, too, in 2006 when my world was falling apart. . . . I was, too, an avid admirer of his, always.
>
> "That's one wonderful church. Once again I was on my way. The pastor has been there for young and old alike. He has always had a nice way with women. He especially likes the little children. He loves to joke and laugh with people. TLC is a generally happy church.
>
> "That should have been me in the ground instead of Rhonda; many of us would gladly have been in her place. She had too much to live for.

"This never should have happened. Anyone could have been there that day, volunteering. Rhonda was always so nice to me. We all had such a good time at the Prime Timers," Mary Jane wrote, referring to the church's senior citizens group.

The police looked into the tree-cutting company Mary Jane had hired following her father's disappearance.

The tree cutter, Michael MacHukas, had filed both a criminal and civil complaint against Mary Jane for harassment. The police in Colebrookdale Township, where the MacHukases lived, no longer had information about the criminal complaint, but Bucks County court records showed the civil case was settled.

Although it had been fourteen years, MacHukas vividly remembered Mary Jane Fonder when Trooper Gregg Dietz called him asking about her. Mary Jane had hired MacHukas to cut timber on her property, but there was one area of the land Mary Jane would not let him near, claiming it was sacred.

"She wanted to be there every time," MacHukas later told a reporter from *The Intelligencer.* "She pointed out a sacred area and called one spot 'the hole from hell.'"

Mary Jane spoke openly to MacHukas and his wife, Cynthia, about her father's disappearance, even when it became clear the police suspected she had killed him. Cynthia recalled to *The Intelligencer* one time when a state police helicopter flew over the property. Mary Jane turned to her and said, "I guess they're trying to find where I buried the body," Cynthia later told the newspaper.

Then one day, Mary Jane inexplicably threw Michael MacHukas off her property, he told Dietz. Although he struggled to recall details after so much time, he said Mary Jane accused him of stealing something, possibly her father's tools. MacHukas denied it at the time, and continued to deny it to this day.

Then, MacHukas said, the threats started.

Mary Jane started calling him at his work and home,

threatening to "take him out," MacHukas told Dietz. She claimed to know where he lived and said she would "take out his wife and kids," claiming she "knows how to do it" and that she could "get away with it," MacHukas told Dietz.

Dietz also talked to MacHukas's wife, who verified the threatening phone calls. Cynthia MacHukas said she herself received several threatening calls from Mary Jane, saying things like, "I know where you are and I am watching you," and, "I know where you live and the spirits are going to get you," she told Dietz.

Cynthia told Dietz that one time, the MacHukases' young son picked up the phone when Mary Jane called and she asked him to hang up so she could leave a message on the answering machine. Mary Jane called three times in a row, leaving bizarre, rambling messages on their answering machine each time.

The MacHukases reported the calls to police, but they did not stop, Michael MacHukas said. She only finally stopped calling after the civil court judgments were settled.

CHAPTER 18

By now, Stumpo and Egan were desperate to interview Mary Jane Fonder. The tales of her odd behavior just kept piling up, and they needed to find out more about her gun.

Troopers Gregg Dietz and Pat McGuire had struck out when they tried to get her at her house a couple days prior to talking to the MacHukases. But the next day was Wednesday, and the troopers were sure they would find Mary Jane at the church's weekly choir practice.

Stumpo called Pastor Shreaves the next morning to find out whether Mary Jane was expected at choir practice that night. Shreaves confirmed she was, so Stumpo and Egan made plans to work a late night and head over to the evening choir practice. With Rhonda being a former member, they decided it would be worth their while to interview some other choir members while they were there as well.

The troopers arrived an hour early for the 7 o'clock practice. The choir director, Steve Wysocki, also was there early and had something for the troopers. Mary Jane had written a sympathy card to the entire church membership, as well as a separate card for Wysocki and his wife, and they both struck the choir director as odd.

Stumpo and Egan thanked Steve for showing them the cards and told him that they hoped to interview choir members in another room. Steve agreed to send members their

way as they arrived. The troopers set themselves up in a
second floor room typically used for the church's teen group.
The large rectangular room boasted sky-blue cinderblock
walls, dusty chalkboards, and second-hand couches and arm-
chairs. They seated themselves on folding chairs at a long
table and started reading through the cards Steve provided
them, starting with the one written for the entire church
congregation:

> *"To members of Trinity, especially the Trinity choir
> members, who loved Miss Rhonda so dearly. No words
> can convey how sad I am for you all.*
> *"Always sweet and nice when she spoke to me, I
> barely got to know her until I joined the Trinity choir
> around Christmas time. We all had such a good time
> singing together. I knew then that Rhonda had prob-
> lems, too, and you all were helping her.*

"I wish I could trade places with her now. And that she
could be alive instead of me," the card continued. "She did
not deserve such a terrible end. Nor her loved ones this catastrophe."

The card to the Wysockis was much of the same: "I was
wondering what you all did for Rhonda, I can't say one bad
thing about her. I did see though how sweet and very affectionate she was with everyone. No wonder she was so well
loved. When we spoke on many occasions, she appeared very
happy to see me or speak with me at those times.

"Yes, I knew Rhonda was ill that way," it continued. "Dis-
orders of the mind are terrible to deal with. In 2001, the same
with me. We were on suffering street big time. High doses
of medications . . . to balance our chemistry. Minds + bodies.
I can appreciate Rhonda's problems. . . .

"Last fall I had another health & chemistry problem.
Which needed attention I had no choice but to get rest &
deal with it. Everybody loves Pastor Greg . . . He has helped
plenty of us & has made many friends. These other ladies &
(Rhonda) were lucky to have had you <u>directing</u> their lives. I

worked with doctors & treatments outside the church—But always managed to get fixed up . . . "

The card ended with, "This freak & horrendous act on Rhonda, no Christian could have done such a thing. I regret that it happened in our church <u>or to her</u>, or anyone else that might have been in the office, that day. God help us all, Mary Jane Fonder."

The troopers' readings were interrupted when the door suddenly opened and Mary Jane Fonder entered the room. Much to the troopers' delight, she was the first choir member to arrive for practice, and thus their first interview. They recognized the short, heavyset woman from her driver's license photo. She wore a big, almost goofy grin on her chubby round face, and her skin was pale and wrinkled. A large pair of wide-rimmed glasses was perched on her nose, and what was obviously a large brown wig sat atop her head.

"You know, I've been meaning to call you guys, I've been meaning to," she said as she walked toward the table. "I knew you were at the house, I've been meaning to call. I was hoping I'd run into you at the church."

Stumpo and Egan were taken aback. Before even introducing herself, she was already talking a mile a minute.

"There's something I have to tell you, I haven't told anyone else this," she continued. "I just have to tell you, I spoke to Rhonda the Monday before she was murdered."

That certainly got the troopers' attention. They were anxious to hear more, but first had to interrupt Mary Jane so they could actually identify themselves. Once they got her settled at the table, however, they didn't have to wait long until she was talking again.

Mary Jane proceeded to explain she had called the church Monday looking for the new church directory and was surprised when Rhonda answered the phone. Rhonda informed her, Mary Jane said, that she was filling in as secretary at the church office while Pastor Shreaves was away at a conference. They talked for about ten minutes, and Rhonda volunteered to look around the office for the new directory but was unable to find one. Mary Jane said she told her not to worry and that Rhonda took down a message for Pastor Shreaves that she had called.

They also talked about how Mary Jane was not getting along with her brother and was tired of living with him. Mary Jane claimed Rhonda told her about an apartment next to hers that was vacant. The next day, Mary Jane went to go check out the apartment. While on her way to Hellertown, she drove past the church in the morning and saw Rhonda's car in the parking lot. There weren't any other cars in the parking lot and nothing else seemed odd. After checking out the apartment, Mary Jane said she had lunch at the local McDonald's.

Mary Jane suddenly stopped talking and turned to look Stumpo directly in the eye.

"It's a wig," she blurted out.

"Excuse me?" he asked.

"You're looking at my hair," she said. "It's a wig."

"I wasn't looking at your hair," Stumpo said. "I was just looking at you."

After a brief pause, the troopers moved on from the bizarre little exchange as if it never took place.

"So," Stumpo started, "Did you tell Rhonda about checking out the apartment?"

"Oh, I figured I'd see her at choir and tell her there," she said.

"So, you talked about Monday and Tuesday," Stumpo said. "We were curious, what were you doing on Wednesday?"

Mary Jane explained that on that day—the day Rhonda was shot—she had left her house at five minutes to 11 for an 11:30 appointment at Holiday Hair in Quakertown. Her brother was home and saw her leave, she said. After her hair appointment, she went shopping at Jo-Ann Fabrics in the same plaza and was home around three.

Stumpo and Egan looked at each other and, although they were careful not to visibly react, they both knew they were thinking the same thing. Five minutes to 11—that was the exact time the computer forensic expert had estimated

Rhonda was shot, based on when the Internet activity abruptly stopped in the church office.

That time of death had not been publicized. It struck both men as quite suspicious that Mary Jane would mention it precisely.

The troopers had something here, and they both knew it. But they continued asking their questions, determined not to let Mary Jane know their suspicions.

"We've been checking, and according to state records, you own a gun," Egan said. "Where's your gun?"

"Oh, I threw that away a long time ago," she answered quickly. "I got rid of it."

"What do you mean got rid of it?" Stumpo asked.

"I just threw it out somewhere," she said. "I threw it out of the car along the road or in the woods."

The troopers were dumbstruck. They had never heard of anyone just throwing away a gun. They didn't believe her.

"Well, Mary Jane, aren't you concerned that someone could find that gun?" Stumpo asked. "Like a child could find the gun on the side of the road?"

"Well I threw it in a lake, some lake somewhere," she said. "I threw it in Lake Nockamixon, somewhere in the deep end down by the boat docks."

Mary Jane claimed she got rid of the gun because she had been having problems with a woman at the Denny's where she used to work. During an unemployment hearing after losing her job there, she had been accused of threatening her former manager, Diane Anderson, with a gun, Mary Jane explained. She had the gun in her car during that hearing, she said, under the driver's seat. Mary Jane claimed she was so nervous that police would find the gun and believe she wanted to hurt Diane that she threw it away that very day.

She had fired the gun just once, she told the troopers. After her father disappeared, a newspaper article had come out in *The Philadelphia Inquirer* that had made her look like a suspect. The portrayal upset her greatly, and she was so depressed that she began contemplating suicide. To test the gun, she had fired it into her yard, but its loud sound had scared her.

The troopers still didn't believe Mary Jane's explanation about where her gun was—they thought she still had it—but they doubted she would admit the truth now. Plus, they were in a church—not the best location for a true interrogation.

Besides, Mary Jane was already off on another topic. She started to tell the troopers about how, on the Sunday before Rhonda died, she had stood up in front of the congregation to thank the group for the financial assistance they had provided to her.

"Nobody told me this was going on," she said, her voice somewhat strained. "No one asked me to help."

Stumpo looked at his watch and saw it was 7 o'clock. Choir was starting downstairs and they should return Mary Jane to the group.

But Mary Jane seemed to be in no rush to end the interview. She continued talking right up to the point that Stumpo and Egan walked her to the door.

"Well, I really enjoyed talking to you guys," she said. "I just have so much to talk about."

"Hey, well maybe at some point we'll call and we can get back together and talk some more," Stumpo said, setting the groundwork for another interview in the future. "I'd love to hear everything you have to say."

"Okay, that would be wonderful," she said, starting down the stairs. "Great."

Choir rehearsal was under way when the troopers got back downstairs. Mary Jane had talked for so long that it was too late to interview any of the other members. But Stumpo and Egan felt more than satisfied about what they had gotten from her.

There was the fact she had mentioned the time of five minutes to 11—the exact time they believed Rhonda was shot. And the fact Mary Jane confessed she knew Rhonda was working at the church that week. Only two other people had known that, Pastor Shreaves and Deb Keller, the church council president.

Then, there was her sudden mention of how the church assisted Rhonda. Mary Jane seemed angry, even jealous about it.

And the troopers simply could not believe Mary Jane's story about the gun. She had thrown it into a lake fourteen years ago? They didn't believe her for one minute.

It all added up to one thing: Mary Jane Fonder had killed Rhonda Smith. Now they just had to prove it.

While Stumpo and Egan were interviewing Mary Jane at the church, troopers Gregg Dietz and Pat McGuire went to her home to try to talk to her brother alone.

It was fortunate Dietz had been there before, because the Fonder home was hard to find. Winding Road proved to be a very fitting name for the curvy street in that especially rural part of Springfield Township. House numbers on mailboxes don't perfectly align with addresses across from them, and the Fonder home was not visible from the road.

Dietz and McGuire drove their car up the quarter-mile driveway to the small, blue ranch home. The grass was long, as if it had not been mowed for months or longer, and weeds covered the walkway that led them to the front door.

Ed Fonder, wearing a cardigan sweater and his usual bland expression, answered the door. Dietz recalled that Ed seemed uncomfortable having outsiders at his home and did not invite him in the last time he visited, so this time Dietz asked whether he could come inside. Ed obviously did not like the idea, but he sheepishly stepped aside and motioned for them to enter.

And, although both men had seen their fair share of filthy homes during their time in law enforcement, the Fonder residence still made their skin crawl.

The place was a mess. Actually, more like a pigsty. Dietz, McGuire, and Ed stood in a small foyer with doors that led to the kitchen and living room. Piles of papers stretched from the floor almost to the ceiling. Glancing into the living room, Dietz noticed jugs half filled with water in one corner of the room that were covered with cobwebs spreading all the way up to the ceiling, the kind that must have taken years to form.

There were boxes and boxes of assorted junk covering nearly every part of the floor. Where the carpet could be seen, it was so worn that the plywood underneath was clearly visible. Other parts of the floor were marred by birdfeed and animal feces. Dietz could feel his shoes starting to stick to the floor as he stepped, as if he were walking through a college fraternity house right after a big party.

"Don't tell anyone I invited you in here," Ed grumbled. "We don't like people in the house."

Ed said he told Mary Jane that the troopers had previously stopped by and that she was planning to call them. Mary Jane was again not home, Ed explained. She was at church and would not be back until around 9 o'clock. As he previously told the police, Ed explained he attended a different church in New Jersey, where he used to live while teaching physics in New York. He only moved to Springfield Township in 2001 so he could stay with his sister after their father went missing.

That brought the discussion to a topic the troopers had hoped to cover: the disappearance of their father. It was clear to Dietz that Ed didn't feel entirely comfortable discussing the matter, and wondered why the troopers wanted him to talk about it at all. Nevertheless, Ed started to explain some of the family dynamics: His mother had passed away in 1992, he explained, and he always felt his father could not cope with her death.

Mary Jane and their father frequently fought after that, he explained, but Ed didn't believe Mary Jane had anything to do with his disappearance. He truly believed his father simply walked away that day. Something akin to an Eskimo going onto an iceberg at the end of his life, he said.

Mary Jane was deeply upset by the way Springfield Township police handled the investigation into their father's disappearance, he added.

"Were you ever concerned for your safety?" Dietz asked. "I mean, did you ever buy a gun for protection or anything?"

They had a .22-caliber rifle, Ed explained, but the police had taken it and never returned it. Long ago, when their family lived in Philadelphia, he saw a handgun in the basement that his father claimed belonged to him. He did not know if his father brought the gun with him when the family moved to Springfield Township.

Ed said he also did not know whether Mary Jane owned a gun when she was living here alone, but he knew he had never seen one.

"Do you remember the day the woman was shot at Mary Jane's church?" McGuire asked. "Do you remember what you were doing that day?"

He did not, but Ed explained that he kept a detailed ledger of his comings and goings. After leaving the officers for a few moments, Ed returned carrying a composition notebook, one of several he owned. As Ed was a physics teacher, the notebooks contained not regular lined paper, but graph paper with rows and rows of tiny squares, which Ed filled with small, almost illegible script handwriting.

Rather than a diary or journal like any normal person might keep, Ed seemed to take note of every little detail of his life, complete with specific times and places minor events in his life occurred. The notebooks struck Dietz as extremely strange.

After flipping through the pages and reading a bit, Ed said he had been at his church the night before and didn't return home until 11 p.m. After such late nights, Ed said he usually slept late the next day. On January 23, he only had made note of a single late-afternoon phone call from a friend.

Ed said that must have meant he was home all day. He did not know his sister's whereabouts that day. The troopers asked Ed if he knew anything else about Rhonda's death, but he claimed he did not.

The troopers thought that was the end of the interview, but then Ed suddenly started talking again. Mary Jane had been upset lately, he explained, but they didn't talk about it much. She had been too upset to go to Rhonda's funeral, so Ed went in her place, he said.

At a luncheon after the funeral, Ed had picked up some pamphlets about feelings and dealing with grief, he said. Ed gave them to Mary Jane, who said the information in the pamphlets reflected exactly what she was going through. She said she was feeling a little depressed and stressed out, and had recently started having nightmares. Ed claimed Mary Jane was upset over Rhonda's death and recent developments in their father's case, although he didn't volunteer what those developments were.

With that, Ed ended the interview. He assured the troopers he would be willing to answer any questions they might have in the future, and also would let Mary Jane know they had stopped by.

CHAPTER 19

With only Stumpo, Dietz, and McGuire working in the criminal investigation unit of the Dublin barracks, the state police could no longer afford to dedicate all three of them to the Rhonda Smith case, let alone for the twelve- to sixteen-hour workdays they were putting in. Dietz, in particular, had a number of other cases stacking up, since he was in charge of the sexual crimes and child abuse cases in the barracks' coverage area. Dietz and McGuire were ultimately pulled off of active participation in the case, leaving Stumpo to work more frequently with Bob Egan.

The day after speaking to Mary Jane at the church, the state police's first stop was the Holiday Hair salon that Mary Jane said she had been to the day Rhonda died. Egan and Bucks County Detective Greg Langston drove out to the salon in Quakertown, where they were provided the customer sign-in sheet for January 23. Mary Jane Fonder's name was on the sheet, with a sign-in time of 11:22 a.m. The officers were unable to talk to the stylist who did Mary Jane's hair that day because she was not scheduled to work.

With Mary Jane's arrival time now in hand, Egan and Langston drove two different routes from Mary Jane's house to the salon. They wanted to determine whether Mary Jane would have had enough time to leave her house, stop at the church and drive to the salon within the timeframe they believe Rhonda was shot.

During their first trip, they traveled directly from her house to the salon, a 10.2-mile route that took about seventeen minutes to drive. On a second route, the officers first drove from Mary Jane's house to the church, which was 3.2 miles and took about five minutes. Driving from the church to the salon was another eight miles and took fourteen minutes. The officers were careful to abide by all speed limits and stop at all stop signs on the way.

If Rhonda was shot just after 10:54 a.m.—as police suspected because that's when her Internet activity abruptly stopped—Mary Jane would indeed have had enough time to get from the church to the salon by 11:22 a.m.

Stumpo and Egan followed up a few days later with Mary Jane's hair stylist at her home. Cindy Moser knew Mary Jane as a regular customer, though she had not come by for an appointment for a long time prior to her January 23 visit.

On that day, Cindy saw Mary Jane pull into the shopping center parking lot and park her car in the handicapped parking spot in front of the salon. Mary Jane had not made an appointment that day, which was usual for her, and she signed in on the walk-in sheet, Cindy said.

Cindy told the officers that when she took Mary Jane for her hair styling, Mary Jane followed her normal routine by taking off the wig she was wearing to have her own hair washed and styled. Mary Jane didn't appear to be acting particularly strange that day. She did mutter to herself a bit while her hair was drying, but that was normal for Mary Jane. She was talking a little louder than usual, Cindy said, but she didn't catch what Mary Jane was saying.

After Mary Jane left, Cindy realized she had left her wig behind. Cindy put the wig in a plastic bag and put it aside for Mary Jane to retrieve at a later date. But since Mary Jane had not returned, and hadn't called inquiring about the wig, Cindy told the troopers she believed it was still back at the salon.

The troopers thanked Cindy for her time, and immediately

drove back to the salon. That wig, Egan thought, could be the
break they needed to solve this case. It could have retained
gunpowder residue from the shooting, and both Stumpo and
Egan wanted to quickly get their hands on what could be a
major piece of evidence.

The wig was easily found under the front counter when
the troopers arrived, but they could not take it with them
without a search warrant. They reached out to Bucks County
First Assistant District Attorney David Zellis, who filed for
one as quickly as possible. Zellis, who had been made the
district attorney's point man on the investigation into Rhonda's death, was just as excited about the wig's potential evidentiary value as Egan and Stumpo. Zellis thought the wig
would give them enough cause to search Mary Jane's house
for her gun. Then, if they could find that, the case would be
closed.

The wig was picked up and entered into evidence the next
day. Stumpo also returned to the salon to interview another
stylist, Bridget Wolters, who had done Mary Jane's hair on
February 13. While she was there that day, Mary Jane had
asked Bridget if the salon keeps records of "who got a wash
and set." Bridget told her no.

Well, did the salon destroy the records? Mary Jane asked.
Bridget didn't answer her.

The state police didn't want to wait long to get the gunpowder residue test results back on Mary Jane's wig, so
Corporal Paul Romanic personally took the five-hour drive
on February 15 to bring the wig to RJ Lee Group, a private
laboratory outside of Pittsburgh.

Five days later, Stumpo received a call from the lab. Two
elements found in gunpowder residue were found on the wig,
but not a third element required for it to be a sure match.
The study would have to be marked inconclusive.

Egan, working on his seventy-sixth homicide case, knew
this was one of the many ups and downs that came with investigations, so he took the news in stride. But Stumpo, working on his first homicide case, was much more disheartened
by the lab results. His office had stacks and stacks of cold

cases, some going back fifty years, and he did not want the murder of Rhonda Smith to become one of them. He felt if he couldn't solve it now, how could another officer solve it years down the road?

In addition to checking out the Holiday Hair salon, Stumpo and Egan had a lot to follow up on from their interview with Mary Jane Fonder.

They also took a trip up to Hellertown, where Mary Jane said she had been the day before Rhonda's death looking at an apartment next to Rhonda's. The officers met with Rhonda's landlord, who did not remember meeting Mary Jane, even when shown a picture of her.

That struck Stumpo as a red flag. After all, Mary Jane was such a strange character, how could anybody *not* remember her if they had indeed met her?

As the officers stood outside Rhonda's apartment, they noticed how busy the road out front was. Not only was Route 412 the borough's Main Street, but it was also a well-traveled state highway.

This, along with the landlord's unfamiliarity with Mary Jane, led the troopers to form a theory: Mary Jane didn't go to Hellertown to look at the apartment, she went to scope out whether it would be a good place to kill Rhonda Smith. And, upon discovering the lack of privacy and abundance of cars driving by, she must have realized this wasn't the right place to do it.

Perhaps that was the moment, the troopers thought, when she decided to kill Rhonda inside their church.

Egan and Stumpo also paid a visit to Nockamixon Sports Shop, the Quakertown-area store where Mary Jane had bought her gun fourteen years earlier. Mary Jane had not been back any time recently to buy ammunition or anything like that, they were told, but the officers were able to pick up the receipt from when Mary Jane first purchased the gun.

The officers also organized a large search of Lake Nockamixon, where Mary Jane said she had thrown her gun many years back. The officers didn't believe that story, but they thought it was possible she might have discarded the gun while returning home from the hair salon.

Going past the lake from Quakertown, Mary Jane would have first passed the bridge on Route 563 closest to Route 313, so officers looked there first. In early February, there was still a lot of snow on the ground, so the officers used a metal detector to help in the search. It proved fruitless.

Also following the interview with Mary Jane, Egan called his colleagues at the Criminal Investigation Assessment Unit to ask them for their take on the case. They, like Stumpo and Egan, were convinced Mary Jane still had her gun.

For an outsider, the idea of a sixty-five-year-old church-goer like Mary Jane Fonder killing somebody might seem impossible. But Egan, who had seen a lot in his twenty-five years on the job, knew that it was perfectly likely. In fact, he had worked on a case in 2005 where a seventy-three-year-old woman viciously beat another woman to death with a hammer in Northampton County. The murderer, Kathy MacClellan, beat the eighty-four-year-old Marguerite Eyer to death after Marguerite confronted Kathy about stealing her belongings. Marguerite activated her medical alert device before she died and, when paramedics arrived to help, Kathy was sitting on Marguerite's porch and said to them, "It's too late. She's dead already."

The sad truth, Egan knew, was that anybody was capable of murder.

CHAPTER 20

Following church services on Sunday, February 17, several church members took part in a discussion about loss. Although the discussion was not specifically about the loss of Rhonda, she was nevertheless on many of their minds as the conversation went on.

Judy spoke about how her twenty-year-old son, Ricky, had died in the house fire back in 2001. She described how much she missed him, and how the passing of time had done little to blunt her grief. Then she turned to Mary Jane.

"And there's Mary Jane," she said to the group, "Her dad has never been found."

Judy had meant the statement as a way to include Mary Jane in the conversation and make her feel welcome. But Mary Jane was uncharacteristically silent for the rest of the conversation, and Judy feared she might have offended her.

Two days later it was Judy's birthday. That evening, she checked her answering machine to find she had a very long, rather disjointed message from Mary Jane.

"People are evil," Mary Jane said in the recording. "We should get a staff and wave it over everybody and ward off all the evil." The bizarre, cryptic message went on like that for about five minutes. Mary Jane kept constantly talking about evil and darkness, to the point that Judy didn't know whether to be confused or disturbed.

Then, abruptly, Mary Jane said with a perky voice, "Happy birthday Judy!" before ending the message.

Judy believed the church discussion about loss must have sparked something in Mary Jane. A few days later, Judy heard from her again. She opened up to Judy about her life, about how she hadn't had a good upbringing and that her father was mean to her and mean to her mother when she was sick.

"I'll never forgive him for that," Mary Jane told Judy. "Never."

Even after all this time had passed, Pastor Greg Shreaves was still having trouble feeling comfortable around Trinity Evangelical Lutheran Church. Aside from her parents and family members, Rhonda's death probably affected him more than anybody. Every day he had to work in the building where she had died, and every night he had to return home to a house only a few short steps away from where somebody shot her to death.

He didn't feel safe at either place. And as more time passed, his fears seemed to grow more and more irrational and intense. He feared that a crazy person was out to destroy the church, and that they would burn down his house or kill him, too. He was starting to think he couldn't stay on as pastor there.

For respite, the church council insisted Shreaves start taking a week off each month from his duties. He would visit his parents in Virginia and, on one occasion, he went to Ocean City, Maryland, for a short stay.

But it provided little relief. Whenever he was at the church, he would do his job but tried to avoid anything beyond that. Personal conversations were just too much for him. Whenever somebody tried to strike up a chat, he would push them away, claiming that he was still in mourning.

Pastor Shreaves did try to tackle his grief, as well as the grief his entire congregation felt, through his sermons. For several weeks after Rhonda's death, Shreaves centered his sermons on the issues of death and tragedy, anger and forgiveness. But after about a month, Shreaves could tell his congregation was growing uneasy with the topic. No one said anything to him about it, but as he stood in front of them, he could see all their eyes and body language. The whole topic made them feel uncomfortable, and rather than address the issue that loomed over everybody, they preferred to sweep it under the rug, stop talking about it, and pretend it never happened.

Shreaves felt he had to respect these wishes, and soon he stopped preaching about the subject. But their reaction troubled him. Shreaves felt like they had an opportunity to learn from this experience and pull at least one small positive thing from this tragedy, and he hated to let that opportunity slip away.

Isn't it tragic, he thought to himself. *We talk about sin and grace and evil and here it is right in our midst and we don't want to talk about it when it happens right here on our doorstep.*

Shreaves began to regret distributing copies of *Amish Grace,* the book about the Amish schoolhouse shooting, to members of the congregation right after Rhonda was killed. At the time, it seemed like there were a lot of parallels between the two crimes and the church leadership felt it could help the congregation learn how to cope with tragedy. But when those five children were killed at that schoolhouse in Nickel Mines, they demolished the school building altogether and erased all traces that it was ever there. That wasn't how Shreaves wanted to handle things at Trinity Evangelical. This was still their church.

The congregation's resistance to addressing the situation added weight to his struggle over whether to stay at the church. He was still carrying around all these feelings, but his parishioners didn't want to deal with them. *How do I deal with that as a pastor?* he wondered to himself.

Finding a therapist with whom he could discuss these issues and feelings helped him greatly.

It also comforted him to learn more about the investigation into the case. Stumpo and Egan had asked him several times about Mary Jane Fonder during their meetings together, but Shreaves never thought much of it. After all, they had asked him about so many different people, so many times. But then, during one meeting in early February, when the subject of Mary Jane came up yet again, Stumpo leaned in and said to Shreaves, "We know a *lot* about Mary Jane Fonder."

Shreaves would never forget those words from Stumpo. In that moment, the pastor put it all together: The police believed Mary Jane had killed Rhonda! Strangely, this brought Shreaves some peace. No longer was he afraid of the unknown; he only had to be concerned about one person.

Of course, the idea of going to church every week with a possible murderer did frighten Shreaves. But at least now he had some idea what to watch out for, and was not suspicious of the whole world, as he had been before. Prior to Stumpo saying that fateful sentence, the idea of Mary Jane as the killer had never even passed through Shreaves's mind. But all of a sudden it made sense: All the phone messages she left for him, the confession of her romantic feelings for him—they gave her a motive.

Feeling at least somewhat more comforted, Shreaves started having second thoughts about leaving Trinity Evangelical. Besides, what would it say about him if he went to a new church while his old church was in their hour of need? What if he went to a new church and there was a new tragedy there? They would probably fear he would leave at the first sign of trouble. No, Shreaves decided. He was staying here.

CHAPTER 21

After the wig testing and lake search proved fruitless, Stumpo and Egan's next step was to set up another interview with Mary Jane. After leaving a message on her answering machine on February 21, Stumpo got a return call the next day.

When he picked up his telephone, there was a woman on the other end rambling about how her brother had been chopping wood in the parlor.

"Is this Mary Jane?" Stumpo asked.

"Oh, yes, it's Mary Jane! My brother has been chopping wood in the parlor, and it's just a mess!"

Confused, Stumpo replied, "Mary Jane, you can't just chop wood in the parlor!"

"I know!" she responded enthusiastically.

Stumpo paused for a moment, still a bit stunned, then continued.

"So how are things going at church?" he asked.

"Things are the same at the church. There's something in the atmosphere—they're getting over it," she said in one breath.

"The new church secretary quit," she continued. "The girl was disturbed over it; it's a hard act to follow."

"Mary Jane," Stumpo asked. "So would you be willing to meet with me and Corporal Egan again?"

"How about Monday?" she volunteered. "I could come down to the station."

That was just what Stumpo wanted, and he did not even have to suggest it. It's easier to control an interview at a police station than it is in somebody's home. If someone is at home and starts to feel pressure, it's much easier for him or her to come up with an excuse to end the interview. Not to mention the fact that a police station is a far more intimidating setting than one's own house.

Stumpo and Egan had a very simple interview strategy: Let Mary Jane talk for as long as she wanted. Given her tendency to ramble, they weren't sure they would be able to keep her focused on a single topic anyway. So the plan was just to let her go on, and even if it took a few hours to get any useful information, eventually she would wear herself out. Besides, Stumpo felt he wasn't a good enough interviewer to keep her focused on one subject.

Egan, though more experienced, also favored the strategy of just letting Mary Jane go on and on. The most important thing in an interview is to let that person feel relaxed so they open up to you. The more people talk, especially when they are lying, the more authorities are ultimately going to be able to use their words against them, Egan thought. When you are telling the truth, the truth is always going to come out the same. But when you are lying, the lies change a little bit each time.

Mary Jane Fonder started talking the moment she walked through the door.

Egan and Stumpo met her in the lobby of the Dublin barracks, and she immediately started talking about her father. The two troopers were surprised. They were expecting Mary Jane to be talkative from their last experience with her, but not before they even made it to the interview room.

"Sorry if I seem nervous," Mary Jane said as Egan and Stumpo escorted her through the hallway. "I just couldn't get any sleep last night. I don't know why."

As they walked, Mary Jane continued talking right up until they reached the interview room. She was going to be an unusual challenge, Egan thought. Usually it was hard to get someone to talk. In this case, it would be difficult just to keep her on topic.

Mary Jane sat at the 4×3 foot table in the middle of the otherwise barren interview room. Stumpo took a seat at the corner of the table next to Mary Jane, while Egan sat directly across from her. Stumpo rushed to turn on the tape recorder, to avoid missing anything more Mary Jane had to say.

"Okay, Mary Jane," Stumpo said. "You were talking about your father, and . . ."

Mary Jane interrupted, "The only reason why I'm even mentioning it, about my dad, is these things came to my mind as a result of the incident that happened at the church. It was upsetting to me, I had so much on my mind at the time, and what bothered me so much was this terrible, heinous thing to happen to our friend."

Before Stumpo could speak, Mary Jane continued, "You gentlemen mentioned to me during the questioning session, had I owned a .38 revolver? I do know the handgun, and you might have known the caliber, but yes, it was a .38."

This was a good sign, Egan thought. The troopers weren't expecting a confession, but one of the things they hoped to learn in this interview was an explanation of where her gun was. It was promising to see her bring it up so early in the interview.

Mary Jane said she bought the gun in 1993, while working as a waitress at Denny's Restaurant in Center Valley. She said the cook there suggested she buy it for self-defense because she worked late nights and often drove alone.

"My mother and I used to go to the restaurant and eat a lot, and we traveled around at Roy Rogers and Burger King, and that's what I'm telling you she loved the best," Mary Jane said. "She said to me several times, 'Why don't you try a job as a waitress. You know, do what the Romans do, go along with the flow, anything that's practical.'"

Stumpo felt like he had to interrupt. "Ms. Fonder, let's take a break here. We just want to let you know you're not under arrest. If you want to leave, you can go any time you want to.

You can stop any time you want to. You understand that, right?"

"Yes," Mary Jane said. "So, this matter of this, uh . . ."

"This gun," Egan said, the first time he spoke during the interview.

"This gun," she said, appearing suddenly nervous. "Right. That's basically what we're trying to get around to getting. But the . . . uh . . . I'm sorry, guys, um, oh, let me get my bearings. . . ."

Egan asked, "You carried this gun when you worked at Denny's, for self-defense?"

"I carried it in my car, under the seat," Mary Jane said. "I know I did it during that period of time when I left Denny's. Then I was working at Burger King for quite some time, until July, when I needed out-patient surgery."

Mary Jane proceeded to explain some of the abdominal pains she was experiencing at the time, as well as her knee replacement surgery and pains she was experiencing in her left hand. Egan officially abandoned hope of getting a clear answer about the gun anytime soon.

"Let's talk about the hearings," Egan said, hoping to steer her back on track. "You had this unemployment hearing?"

Mary Jane frowned as she recalled her visit to the Bethlehem unemployment board office. "They didn't let me say anything," she said. "That's their prerogative. They said that I had threatened her with a handgun. That's the reason for not wanting to give me unemployment."

Mary Jane leaned forward, looked at Egan and smiled. "I said, 'My dear, you're not worth killing.' Can you imagine thinking you're that important?"

Stumpo steered back to the topic of the gun. "When we spoke the previous Wednesday, you had made reference that something caused you to get rid of the gun."

"Yeah, well, what happened was, I was absolutely petrified when I realized that's what she was accusing me of," Mary Jane said. "I just thought, 'Dear God, my car, it's in the car outside, under the seat right now.' "

Mary Jane closed her eyes and shook her head. "Oh God, I never bought the gun for that reason," she said. "You know, I was too chicken to use it. I shot the gun once, outside the house, in 1994, and it was terrifying. It was so loud, I was afraid of it."

Mary Jane kept looking down at the table as she spoke, and Stumpo realized she was constantly glancing at the tape recorder on the table, almost speaking into it rather than to the troopers. Obviously unnerved by the presence of the device, she picked up a pencil from the table and started tapping it next to the recorder. Fearful that the constant tapping would drown out the recording of their interview, Stumpo picked up the recorder and slid it further away from Mary Jane, hoping to take her focus off of it.

"I was suffering from a lot of embarrassment then," she continued on. "A lot of bad press from the articles that were written in *The Inquirer* about my father. He was going through all kinds of aging processes, developing Alzheimer's. Dad was upset over my mother passing away, he couldn't cope with it. It seemed that my father and I, it just seemed we had one problem after another."

Determined to return to the subject of the gun, Stumpo decided to feign ignorance. "So, when you left the hearing, honestly I can't remember what you told us, about when you got rid of the . . ."

"Oh, yes, well," she said. "I just didn't want anything to do with the thing. I put it away at the house, I did it at the house, and thought, 'You know, thank God it's not in the car.' You know, it was a very rare, rare situation happening at the house, with my father's living system. I was his main caretaker."

Soon, Mary Jane was on another tangent, talking about the stress from dealing with her father and the various surgeries she thought she needed.

"I somehow developed a terrible strep throat," she said. "My neighbors suggested I get Benadryl, and it helped with the cough. My face felt hot, my head got red, quite red. I felt pain at the top of my head—"

"Mary Jane," Stumpo interrupted, slightly more forcefully

now. "What did you do with the gun? When did you get rid of this gun?"

"Oh," she said. "Uh, '94. In the wintertime of '94."

But Mary Jane immediately changed topics again, this time talking about the day her father disappeared.

"I woke up on the 26th, I guess it was late morning, oh 10, 10:30, 11 o'clock in the morning. I heard my father come down the hall, and I thought, 'OK, good, dad's okay.' And then I heard the front door close and I said, 'Good, Pop went down to get the paper.' This is nothing new from my father, so I dozed off again."

She continued, "I woke up, I went down and looked. There's the dining room lights on over the table and all this filthy shaving stuff's on the table. And there's his cereal bowl and all his stuff, and I thought, 'What the heck's wrong here?' I mean, he's usually sitting there reading the paper at the table. There's no paper, and no Pop. I thought, 'God, what the hell's happened?'"

Mary Jane paused and looked at Egan, "Excuse me," referring to her use of the word "hell."

She continued, "I looked all over. I looked in his room, he wasn't there. I started calling and calling for him, 'Dad, where are ya?' And I thought, 'Geez.' I looked outside, and I was terrified. I ran down the driveway, but I wasn't finding him. The paper was there."

She added, "So I thought, 'My God, I lost my father.' You know, how do you lose your dad?"

Mary Jane continued to describe the days after her father's disappearance. She talked about her neighbors and cousins who came by to help search the area for her dad. She described the police, the dogs, the news coverage, and the four extremely thorough searches around the property, all of which yielded no results.

"Is it about this time you said you got rid of the gun?" Stumpo asked. "Or did you have the gun then? I would imagine you'd keep it now, because you were scared."

"And then what happened," Mary Jane continued, as if she hadn't heard the question, "they got a court order and all, because of course, I'm the chief suspect. He was with me. They were looking for wet cement in the cellar, thinking maybe I, ah . . ."

When Mary Jane failed to complete the thought, Stumpo added, "There's wet cement in the cellar?"

"They were looking for patches of wet cement, you know?" Mary Jane said, looking down at the table.

"Oh, they were looking for patches," Stumpo said.

After a long pause, Mary Jane suddenly looked up, "The helicopters, they chased me all over the property there."

"Chased you?" Egan asked.

Mary Jane started to describe an incident in May 1994 when, while walking along her property lines in the woods, she started to hear what sounded like propellers.

"I look over and, before I know it, my God, there's a helicopter!" she said. "I'm not bothering anybody! Not the trees! But it's zeroing in on me, so I started running. I was terrified they were going to pick me off from the air!"

"I said, 'What's going on here? I just had someone in a helicopter chase me from one end of my property to the next!'" she said. "They claimed he was doing an aerial search on the property. Aerial search? What the hell? Buzzing around me! What are they chasing me for? Can't they waste the taxpayer dollars with something else?"

At a loss for how to delicately transition back on track, Egan said, "But let's get back to . . . tell us why you got rid of the gun."

She laughed, "Yeah, yeah, we're off track. The reason I got rid of it was because I was so despairing over the major newspaper articles of my father and myself."

Mary Jane described someone whom she called a "very lovely lady" from *The Philadelphia Inquirer,* who interviewed her for a newspaper story while her father's disappearance was still an open investigation. The woman was very nice, Mary Jane said, and spoke to a lot of her neighbors and friends. When they parted, the reporter promised to portray her in the best light possible, Mary Jane said.

"She did a wonderful, big fancy interview with me," she

said. "But when the article came out, she very neatly eliminated things I said. She took certain things out of context, rearranged what I said. "

Mary Jane grew angrier and angrier as she talked about the story. She was particularly upset that the article claimed she only came up to visit her parents a few days before her mother died, rather than the six years she spent with her before her death.

"When the article came out in the paper, I had to run over to Martha's Store to pick up a copy of the thing," she said. "I couldn't wait to see the article. Then I looked it over and oh my God, it made me look so horrible. Like a mean, nasty, unpleasant girl taking advantage of her poor ailing parents. I said, 'This is not me, that's not what happened.' I got very depressed.

"All I could think of was doing away with myself," she said. "I didn't like myself, I didn't like myself, I just couldn't stand myself! I was thinking of taking my life with my handgun."

Mary Jane said she considered going out to the pier to shoot herself, but decided "that wouldn't work." She considered simply sitting outside in her comfortable Hawthorne chair and shooting herself in the heart, and "dying comfortable in the sun."

But while sitting outside in her lawn chair and contemplating suicide, Mary Jane said she decided against it after a visit from the Jehovah's Witnesses. She said during her worst moment, two members of the Restorationist church movement visited her and spoke with her for hours, and she decided she wanted to live after all.

Given Mary Jane's seemingly unlimited capacity for conversation, Stumpo couldn't help but think, *Mary Jane might be the one person who would be happy to see the Jehovah's Witnesses.*

"And that's when I got rid of the gun," Mary Jane said. "I just didn't want to . . . I really didn't want to do that."

"How did you get rid of the gun?" Stumpo asked.

"I don't really recall where I threw it," Fonder said. "I

threw it into Lake Nockamixon. Over the bridge, you know where the bridge crosses over 563? I'm pretty sure I threw it out as far as I could throw into the lake."

Three weeks had passed since Egan and Stumpo first talked to Mary Jane, and the absurdity of the claim still hadn't worn off. In all his years in law enforcement, Egan had never heard of somebody disposing of their gun in such a fashion, unless they had something very serious to hide.

"So, you had financial problems at this time," Egan said. "Did you think about selling the gun back? Because you could have gotten money for the gun."

"Naw, that didn't . . . that didn't seem like a feasible idea," Mary Jane said, quickly adding, "It's funny, even other items, if I purchase something, that's it. I'm just one of those people that when I buy something, I keep it. It's mine, I'm not taking it back. I never thought of selling it back. It didn't seem like a feasible idea."

Stumpo resisted the urge to shake his head in amazement. *It doesn't make any sense,* he thought to himself. *She knew the question about the gun was coming. She had that answer ready. But she didn't plan on this, she didn't have all the details, and now she's making it up as she goes along.*

After a few silent moments, Mary Jane added, "However, I should have turned it in to the police."

"You could have done that," Egan said.

"You know, over the last few years, you develop wisdom. You think, 'Gee, why didn't I do this?' Or, 'Why didn't I do that?'"

"Well, a concern is that someone else could get their hands on the gun," Stumpo said.

"Sometimes, you're involved in a controversy and you really, you're not thinking, your mind doesn't come up with the right answer at that time," Mary Jane said, rambling as if she had not heard Stumpo. "Why didn't I do this, and why didn't I do that? That's, ah, yeah, at this one period in time, one woman came over to the house, an officer was coming over to the house every week, checking up, Officer Triol was her name."

"From Springfield?" Stumpo said.

"Ah, from Springfield Police, yeah," Mary Jane said. "That was from the time Pop disappeared. They kept tabs on me, and she, all through the winter, she used to stop by, and I liked her. I developed a very comfortable relationship with her.

"But then one time she came over there," she said. "She tried to break me, to break me down and make me confess to killing my dad."

"Oh yeah?" Stumpo said.

"I was so heartbroken, so deceived," Mary Jane said. "Right in my, right in my living room. She's sitting there, having a coffee with me, and I thought, 'What in the hell, right in my own house!' And I said to her, why isn't this something you would do down at the township building? Why didn't you take me down and question me there? 'Oh Mary Jane,' she said. 'Don't you remember anything? Do you remember anything at all about this and that?' I broke down and I cried. . . ."

CHAPTER 22

"Let's talk about something a little less strenuous for you," Stumpo said, changing topics.

Mary Jane started to discuss the difficulties of living with her brother in such a filthy house, which quickly led the conversation back to Rhonda when she started talking about how Rhonda helped her look for apartments in Hellertown.

"It was a Mecca up there for apartments! I got so excited, Hallelujah!" Mary Jane said. "But it was too much. It was $850 for a small place, plus they told me they put $14,000 into fixing this apartment up. Plus you have to pay all the utilities, the phone utilities, the cable, the heat, hot whatever, everything."

"I wonder how Rhonda was affording it," Egan said.

The question seemed to catch Mary Jane by surprise. "Huh?"

"I wonder how Rhonda was affording that apartment," Egan repeated.

After a pause, Mary Jane said, "With the money I guess she had from people who were helping her. . . ."

"Was that right?" Egan said.

"Uh-huh," Mary Jane said. "Mrs. Bieber told me that the pastor had, um, made a request during a church service to help one of the parishioners who needed financial help and, ah, if, ah, they could possibly give him a hand in helping."

She continued, "She didn't tell me how much, but I thought, that's the first time Reta had mentioned that to me, that the pastor had made a request for financial help for that lady."

It struck Stumpo as cold the way Mary Jane referred to Rhonda as "that lady." *The woman's dead,* Stumpo thought. *She was murdered in a church. And a fourteen-year member of the church is calling her "that lady."*

"It sounds like Rhonda was very well liked," Egan said.

"Mm-hmm," Mary Jane nodded.

"Very well liked by the congregation," Egan said.

"Judy said she loved having Rhonda around. Rhonda loved Judy, she took to Judy like a duck in water. Which is good. They sure did become friends."

She continued, "I'm afraid that I personally never was . . . I was never involved deeply with that group of ladies until I joined the choir. I didn't join the choir right away like Rhonda did. I enjoyed being in the audience listening. You're either a performer or appreciator, and I was the appreciator. I enjoyed that thoroughly."

Mary Jane paused before continuing, "There's a certain group of that five or six women that click together. Like, sit together all the time and they go places. They're in their houses, or at each other's homes, or on the phone, you know? I mean, going to Tupperware parties. What's strange about it is, I never was involved with this group, going to parties, going to places, events outside the church. But Rhonda knew these ladies outside, and there were a great number of them in the choir that knew each other, that socialized and fraternized at each other's homes. I mean, no matter how many years I'm here, I never knew them in that capacity."

Stumpo could see this was making Mary Jane upset. It had never even occurred to her to join the choir until Rhonda Smith came along. The thought simply never crossed her mind. But even after she joined, she just couldn't seem to become part of the group like Rhonda had.

"Did the church ever help you out financially?" Stumpo asked.

"Ah, no, they did not," Mary Jane said. "Never financially,

no. I was encouraged by the pastor. He was very warm and a very friendly kind of guy, and he took right to me.

"He's a real man, Pastor Shreaves. He's a hell of a man, a real man," she continued, smiling. "If I ever needed a man, yup yup! He put me on my feet, he gave me courage. He's an affectionate, friendly man. If I misjudged this man before, I didn't really get to know him but I said, oh, that was some good guy. He was attractive. He was kind to me, asked me nice, said, 'Listen Mary Jane, I know you're having a terrible time right now.'"

Egan had grown somewhat more accustomed to Mary Jane's chattiness by now, but listening to her talk about Pastor Shreaves in this way made him think back to the long, rambling messages she would leave on his phone. Egan imagined there hadn't been too many men in her life.

"I just think it's odd that the church helped Rhonda but hasn't helped you in the past, don't you?" Egan asked.

"Nope," Mary Jane said. "Doesn't tick me off."

"No?" Egan asked.

"No one ever helped me," she said. "My parents raised me to take care of myself. I'm really trying to take care of myself and figuring a better way. I want to live in a nicer home, I like to have nice things around me, you know, I'm heartsick looking at the place I have."

"Yeah, I mean, that could get you depressed and . . ." Egan started.

"It's like living in a bombed-out place," Mary Jane said.

"Right," Egan said.

"It's like, it's like a bombed-up mess, and it does something. It works on your brain, it works on your mind, and it worked on my mind for so long."

Mary Jane seemed to hesitate before adding, "I'm sorry they never approached me for money. This hurts me, because . . . It hurts me. . . ."

"'Cause you're active in the church for fourteen years," Stumpo said.

"I'm active in the church and around these ladies, I know these people, why wouldn't they?" Mary Jane said. "If they had other issues, they could have come to me for money. You'd be surprised, the person that might not have much is willing to give more money than a person that does. I'll cut out something that I want and give, you know, that type thing. I'm very charitable and generous. I'm always like that, and I know the pastor always appreciated it."

Mary Jane continued speaking about some of her financial difficulties, and eventually steered into a discussion about taking care of her mother. Stumpo, feeling the conversation start to spin off into another tangent, tried to bring Mary Jane back into focus.

"So listen," he said. "Corporal Egan and I are investigating Rhonda's death."

"Yeah, yeah," Mary Jane said.

"We're looking for some answers and I personally don't know that there's going to be any closure at that church until we find some answers," Stumpo said. "We're talking to a lot of people and you seem like you're an active person in the church and so forth, so if you know anything, maybe you could tell us."

After pondering the question for a few seconds, Mary Jane started to discuss an adult Sunday School class she had participated in recently.

"We were discussing the forgiveness idea, and we were talking about what do we think grace is, forgiveness and everything, and John Catino, that's the name of our adult Sunday School teacher, he turned the subject to this business with Rhonda. And I thought, 'This is not what a Sunday School person is supposed to be talking about.'"

Mary Jane looked at Stumpo, "I believe John Catino expressed, what I gathered, he feels there is a possibility that one of us in this congregation could have done it."

"Really?" Stumpo said.

"He said he pooh-poohed the idea of the one-armed-man doing it. You know, Richard Kimble?"

Stumpo nodded, aware that Mary Jane was referencing the main character from the old television series, *The Fugitive*.

"No one believed Richard Kimble," Mary Jane said. "They were chasing him like he did it, but he knew it was the one-armed man. And Mr. Catino mentioned the fact that this stranger had supposedly stopped at the church."

"Right," Stumpo said. "Some mysterious, out-of-town man."

"Mr. Catino pooh-poohed the idea. The idea that some stranger did it," Mary Jane said. "He didn't say it with the same wording but he made insinuations. I found that to be irritating because with my heart and soul I love to be comfortable in church, I want to relax, we're trying to find closure on this whole thing."

"But that is a possibility," Egan said.

"It can't . . ." Mary Jane said.

"That is a possibility," Egan repeated.

"That is a possibility," Stumpo echoed.

"That somebody within the church did this," Egan said.

"It's possible it could have been a friend of hers, it could have been a neighbor," Mary Jane said. "It could have been anybody."

"That's what I mentioned earlier," Stumpo said.

"What?"

"About there being closure at the church," Stumpo said. "Because some people are like Mr. Catino, they don't . . ."

"They don't want to give up, they do not believe, they don't want to . . ." Mary Jane started.

"There's a lot of pressure on the church," Stumpo said.

"I know," Mary Jane said.

"There's a lot of pressure on us," Stumpo said.

"That's right," Mary Jane said.

"There's a lot of pressure on Pastor Shreaves," Stumpo said. "And Pastor Shreaves has been at that church for only a short period of time. I talked to him, and how he's been, I don't think he's doing well. We don't know. For him, we want to find the answer. We want to find answers for Rhonda's family, and for Pastor Shreaves 'cause he's under a lot of pressure. And the congregation itself. They're scared, they're nervous, they're worried."

Mary Jane nodded, "Of course. They were so close to her. Many people were very close to her. I can appreciate the position he is in because he's done counseling work. I know how he was like with me, how friendly and open and nice he was to me. I enjoyed his company. I liked sitting there singing and, you know, laughing. They were a lot of fun, he's a nice guy."

Stumpo said, "But we don't know how long he's going to be able to be like this."

"He was probably that way with Rhonda. He was probably that way with Ronnie," Mary Jane said. Egan felt throughout the whole interview, Mary Jane had been trying to create an impression that she and Rhonda were close friends, and that Rhonda's death had upset her deeply. But they had been talking for about an hour and forty-five minutes now, and this was the first time they had heard her refer to Rhonda as "Ronnie."

Mary Jane continued, "I realize what happened, it could change into where he might not want to be with the church and may want to move on."

"Absolutely," Stumpo said.

"The pastor, he's going to say, 'How can you face this thing?'" she said. "He would be in a better position, to start over somewhere else or ask the church for a transfer to a new location."

"The whole church might really think to do that themselves," Stumpo said.

"That's right, they might," Mary Jane said. "And I think it's a shame."

"That's why we need to find out what happened," Egan said. "Because it's affecting the pastor and it's affecting the church. This question has to be answered because this church will never be the same."

"It's not going to be the same," Mary Jane agreed.

"It will never be the same," Egan said.

Egan wanted to steer the topic to the murder itself. "What do you think happened, Mary Jane?" he asked.

"What I kept thinking was it was a freakish thing that

happened, just some freak accident, it would have to be," she replied. "Truthfully, I don't see how anyone in my church could do that. I couldn't do a thing like that."

"Well, what do you think happened?" Egan asked.

"Do you remember Charles Stockbrother?" Mary Jane started in. "The cases of Charles Stockbrother and his girl-friend, they went on a rampage all over the United States kill-ing people. These things are going on all the time around the country." Mary Jane was mistakenly referring to Charles Starkweather, who murdered eleven people in five states dur-ing the late 1950s.

"So you think that's a possibility?" Egan deadpanned. He had no idea who she was talking about.

"It could be a possibility," Mary Jane insisted. She paused and continued, "I'll tell you, I always liked the pastor. I had very sexual kind of feelings, warm feelings about the man, but that's not a reason to hurt, you know, do this lady in."

Stumpo interjected, "When Bob and I find out who did this, what do you think should happen to that person? Let's say they're a member of the church. Can you forgive them for that?"

Mary Jane thought it over.

"What if they decide that I did it?" she asked rhetorically. "It's like a double standard, one thing applies to me but something else applies to other people. Someone over here would have psychiatric exams, love, kindness, and forgive-ness on both sides of the fence. If it was me that did it, I'd get my head blown off, too."

"So you'd be treated differently?" Egan asked.

"I would be treated differently, that's correct," she an-swered with a twinge of hurt in her voice.

"Why is that?" Egan asked.

"Why is that?" Mary Jane shot back, the anger increasing in her tone. "Because that's the way my whole life is. My life's always like that."

"You get the lousy end of the stick," Egan offered.

"I would get the lousy end of the stick," Mary Jane said

in agreement before pausing. "And I'll tell you, I didn't do anything to Rhonda. I may have been upset, I had all kinds of things I was upset about, but it had nothing to do with her.

"She made me nervous," she continued. "I understand she had a nervous condition. She did make me nervous, I have admitted that."

The troopers were intrigued. "She made you nervous?" Egan asked. "Why did she make you nervous?"

"She did. Her personality, she had a nervous problem. Her nerves affected my nervous system," Mary Jane said.

"Really . . ." Egan prompted, wanting to hear more.

"And I felt this a lot of the time," she continued. "But it was a whole different atmosphere in the choir. In regular church, I wasn't part of this emotional group of people, but I was very intensely part of this group during the holidays. In the choir, I got into a social group."

"Were you involved in anything else like that?" Stumpo asked.

"I was involved with Stitches of Love," she said. "I like to crochet. I crocheted blankets in 2006 through the winter. I was a very happy girl. I did a wonderful job through the encouragement of the people of the church."

"And the Prime Timers, were you involved in the Prime Timers?" Stumpo continued.

"I've been with the Prime Timers for years, oh yes," she answered.

"None of these other groups are the same as the choir with the clique?" Stumpo asked.

"The Prime Timers is the only other one. The choir is one facet of it. That's the one where all the major people are involved and I'm getting along fine with everybody in there. The pastor's friendly, he flies in there . . ." she trailed off.

"Oh, geez, about the man. I still like him," she continued. "And I know it's hard for the pastor, having had this happen. I'm sure he was a good friend of Rhonda."

Suddenly, a new thought occurred to Egan. If Mary Jane was really as religious as she let on, he thought, then surely this murder must be weighing on her conscience at some level. Egan, pausing before broaching his next question, decided to try to draw on that faith and see how she reacted.

"Now the person who killed Rhonda, do you think they can be saved from going to hell?" he said in a strong, clear voice. The question struck Stumpo as downright eerie, and he was impressed with Egan for pulling it off. *It's like something out of a movie,* he thought.

"I mean, you go to church every week, you're very religious," Egan continued. "Could they be saved?"

Mary Jane got quiet and didn't say anything for a few moments. "Yes, they can be saved," she responded.

"How?" Egan continued.

"Because you believe in the Lord Jesus," she said matter-of-factly.

"Jesus will save you?" Egan asked, believing he was on to something.

"Jesus will save you," she said. "And I'll tell you something—"

Egan cut her off, "As long as you hold yourself accountable for what you did, He'll save you."

Mary Jane got quiet again, and her voice trembled a bit as she began talking again, "Pastor, I know, would love to get the person who did it. Sometimes people have these gut feelings, they think someone did this to her."

She was rambling again, Egan thought. Determined not to get off the subject this time, Egan started to speak, but then, in a flash, Mary Jane's eyes narrowed as she raised her head and stared directly at the troopers.

"I didn't do it to her, okay? I believe I'll be saved, I truly believe this because," Mary Jane hunched over the table and slowly emphasized each word, ". . . I . . . didn't . . . do . . . it."

CHAPTER 23

When Mary Jane professed her innocence, her voice had completely changed into a slower, low-pitched, angry voice that shocked both troopers. It was a voice they hadn't previously heard in all the hours they had spoken to Mary Jane. A voice that struck them as just plain evil. Egan felt as if Mary Jane's sweet old lady façade had been cracked, revealing something else altogether hidden underneath.

This was probably the Mary Jane that Rhonda saw right before she died, Egan thought.

After a few long moments, Mary Jane continued, back in her normal voice, "I feel sorry for anyone that has a terrible thing happen like that, anyone that murders somebody else, takes a life, anyone that commits a robbery, all these manner of things, I think they are in hell."

She stopped for a moment, before something came to mind that got her upset all over again.

"There's a chance that some people at the church think that I did this to Rhonda," she said. "First of all, they never cared for me. They may not like me and that could give them good cause to, you know, blame it on me."

Mary Jane stopped talking. The troopers desperately hoped she would continue, but when she didn't, Stumpo prompted her again.

"Has anyone accused you?" he asked.

"Not to my knowledge," Mary Jane said, starting again. "Mrs. Brunner and Mrs. Zellner, some of the ladies have been a tight knit group of friends for years and I have been on the perimeter. They would have a party, they would go out to dinner together, but they would not think of asking me along with them. It's that kind of thing. That hurts my feelings."

Stumpo started to offer up some sympathy, "Fourteen years in the church . . ."

"That's a long time," Mary Jane said, nodding her head in agreement. "You really do always hope that you are liked, but you can't expect everyone . . . the truth is you can't expect everyone to like you."

Egan changed the subject, "Have you spoken to the Smiths since Rhonda's death?"

"No, I haven't had the occasion," she responded. "I sent flowers and things to the funeral. I couldn't get close to anyone and they don't know. Ah, too much on my nerves. I was having such chest pains and stuff, I just couldn't stand it. I was getting medical attention, psychologically. I got depressed, okay, I was very, very depressed."

Egan was intrigued again. "Recently?" he asked.

"It was since this thing with Rhonda," Mary Jane said. "Over the years, I've had medical psychological problems. I get panic attacks. I always got something, panic attacks from fretting and frustration and just trying to make a living and live, you know."

Stumpo brought the conversation back to another topic the troopers had hoped to cover. "Let me ask you something, Mary Jane," he said. "How did you find out about Rhonda's death? How did you find out about that?"

"I'm trying to remember . . ." her voice trailing off a bit. "But I did find out. I think someone called me at the house."

"Do you remember when that was?" Egan asked.

"I don't know, I don't remember," she said, a bit flustered. This lapse in memory struck Stumpo as significant. How could anyone in the church community forget how they learned that one of their own was killed?

She doesn't remember because it wasn't important who

told her, Stumpo thought. *Because she already knew Rhonda was dead by then.*

"I know it had to be . . . It had to be the day it happened," Mary Jane continued. "But then, I had been to town that day. See, I had my hair done."

"That's right, you mentioned that," Egan responded and paused, wondering where to take the interview next. Maybe they could ask her to explain her timeline again of the day Rhonda died, to see what matched up and what didn't. It was the same as any other case, Egan thought. When somebody tells the truth, they always tell it the same way. Only when they lie do cracks start forming in their story.

"What else about Wednesday?" he asked. "You went to the hairdresser . . ."

Mary Jane picked up the conversation, "Yeah, so I went up, I wander, I go on into the Jo-Ann's Fabrics store. I'm looking around there after I get out of the hairdresser. I got home around 3:30."

"Did you talk to anyone when you got home?" Egan asked.

"My brother was there when I got home. I can't remember, but I'm pretty sure he was still there," she said, then insisting, "He was there, he had to be there."

"Did you call anybody on the telephone?" Egan asked, continuing the line of questioning.

"Ah, let's see," she said, thinking. "Not that I know of."

"You know, that reminds me," Stumpo interjected, hoping to cover some more critical terrain. "We got the phone records from the church. Remember you said you spoke to Rhonda on Monday?"

"Yes, I did," Mary Jane responded.

"And what we thought was interesting was there were actually three phone calls from your house to the church," Stumpo continued. "Do you remember making more than one phone call to the church?"

"At the time I talked to Rhonda, no," she responded.

"No?" Stumpo prodded.

Mary Jane thought for a moment. "I thought maybe,

maybe I called twice, I might have called twice," she spat out. "I asked her if they had a new directory in yet. I needed a couple addresses and she said, 'Well let me look around the office.' So that's when I called back. I called back and she said she wasn't able to find any. We chatted about a couple other things, but I don't recall calling her three times."

"There's three phone calls," Stumpo insisted. "The first one was just for a couple seconds. . . ."

Mary Jane shrugged. "It's possible, it's possible I called for a couple seconds," she said.

"The first call was a couple seconds, so you might have called to see if she was there," Stumpo continued.

"And poor Judy, I bothered her, jeez, 'cause I don't know, it must have been after Rhonda had been, after this happened to Rhonda," Mary Jane started in. "I called to get something from Judy from the directory. I needed her mother's address, I didn't have the current one at home."

The troopers were confused. "Whose mother?" Egan asked.

"Rhonda's mother," Mary Jane replied. "I wanted her address and my directory didn't have it, so I asked if she would be kind enough, and she was very annoyed. I called her at a decent time, 8:30 or 9 in the morning. I'm sorry I aggravated her, but I wanted to send her mother a . . ." Mary Jane trailed off.

"Right, she sounded annoyed that you were calling her," Stumpo prompted, trying to get her to continue.

"Yeah, she was a little annoyed and I felt bad about it," she said. "I said, 'Touchy, touchy.' Of course, she's upset."

"But she found Rhonda," Stumpo said.

"What's that?" Mary Jane asked. "She was crazy about Rhonda."

"Well, she *found* Rhonda," Stumpo said, emphasizing his point again.

"She did, she found Rhonda," Mary Jane said in agreement.

"Well it's got to be pretty traumatic for her," Egan contributed.

"Oh, yeah," Mary Jane said.

"Terrible," Stumpo chimed in.

"You know it, it was terrible," Mary Jane said. "At the time, I was afraid to tell anybody that I had talked to Rhonda."

"Yeah, you said you hadn't told anyone," Stumpo said.

"That's correct, I was afraid to," Mary Jane said with a nod. "I was afraid, really look at all these people, so many other people had called her on the phone. I said, I'll just wait to tell you guys. . . ."

"The pastor," Egan said, changing the subject a bit. "I mean, he's realizing he could lose this whole congregation."

"I know," Mary Jane said glumly.

"Because of what happened," Egan continued.

"I know it," she offered. "You know, I've had feelings of not going in. I've had feelings of backing out, feelings of only going to one service in the morning."

"How many are you going to now?" Stumpo asked.

"I go twice," Mary Jane answered. "Since he saved me—that man saved me a lot. He was a wonderful guy and he really inspired me. He's a damn nice fellow."

It seemed there was nothing Mary Jane could do to hide her infatuation with the pastor, Egan thought. *She just keeps bringing it up,* he thought. *She's playing into our hand here.*

Jumping at the opening, Egan said, "But someone has to save him right now. Somebody has to save him because this is never going to leave the church."

"What can I do for the pastor? What can I do for him?" Mary Jane wanted to know. "I'm a grown woman, you know. A wonderful guy . . .

"I have no information I could give him other than what I'm telling you fellows," she continued. "I mean, I can help him if I could do something. I've offered to help him at the church. I will say this, I at many times as a friend offered, in a friendship way, 'Please, let me help you out.' I at many times approached the pastor and he never needs any help."

"Well he needs help now," Egan prompted.

"I would gladly go over there," Mary Jane offered.

It wasn't registering with her. Egan tried again, "And the help comes through us."

Mary Jane continued, but not where Egan was hoping. "I, truthfully, you know, between you guys and myself, the pastor is a wonderful guy and I'm crazy about this pastor," she said. "He's a swell man, and he's a real man, a real man."

"But we need to find out who killed Rhonda," Egan said, trying one more time.

"I can't help him by saying anything or telling him who did it, I can't give him any ideas," she responded. "I didn't do it. It's not the help he's going to get because I didn't do a thing to that lady, okay? And I'm sorry, I did not do it, I'm not touching, didn't do a thing. . . ."

Mary Jane trailed off and the three sat in silence for a few moments.

"Do you have any ideas who did?" Stumpo asked.

"Of course not, I don't know," Mary Jane answered. "If I did, I'd tell ya. If I had an idea, I'd tell ya. I certainly would."

"So you had nothing to do with her death?" Egan asked, steering the conversation back to Mary Jane.

"No, and I'd do anything, like I said, to help the pastor," Mary Jane said. "Over all the last couple years, how many times have I offered to help that man and he doesn't need any help. I've offered to help him many times, I could sit here, say he needs a secretary and he needs someone to sit in the church or stay in the church, I was willing to volunteer my time.

"He is supposed to have two people in the church at all times now because of this thing happening and I'd be willing to go over," she continued. "I'm not working and it's no excuse unless this pastor doesn't care for me, or is suspicious of me. You cannot say I did not offer my help to this man many times."

Egan tried to pick up on Mary Jane's reference to the pastor's possible suspicions. "Do you think some people in the church think that you killed Rhonda?" he asked. "Do you think that that's the case?"

"No," she answered, refusing to take the bait.

"You don't? Because you had mentioned a Mr. Catino kind of inferred it was somebody in the congregation. Do you think . . . ?" Egan prompted.

"He's not saying it about me," she answered.

"Well, what I'm thinking is if people are thinking that, are they going to push you out of the church or away from the congregation?" Egan inquired. "Do you think that's possible?"

"It certainly is possible, and I certainly hope if they feel that uncomfortable in me they can certainly call me, talk to me, or discuss that with me," Mary Jane said. "They ought to be big enough and honest enough to talk it over with me. I say confront your accuser, and confront me. I don't like dealing with phonies, people that don't like me, that kind of crap."

She was getting more and more worked up, her voice getting higher and higher. "How would the pastor like it if I thought he did it? How would the pastor like it if I thought to myself, 'Pastor Shreaves, did you have any personal thing with that lady?' How would I know? I don't know what he does personally outside the church. I don't know his activities outside the church."

She thought for a moment before continuing, "It's a possibility that my pastor's reputation is at stake. I thought this, too, lots of people think maybe my pastor was involved with that lady. I thought she was friendly, she's pretty, she's attractive, she's warm, and she's very approachable and people liked her. And I thought, 'My God, how do I know?' Even today, this thought came to me when I was up at the doctor's office, 'Oh God, I wonder if the poor pastor was in love with that lady.' "

"Maybe he was just being a pastor and helping her," Stumpo suggested. "There's no indication there was any love connection there."

"That's right," Mary Jane said.

"So there's a lot of rumors flying around and you know—" Stumpo started in.

"Since I've never been asked, I never touched a hair on his head, he never touched a hair of mine," Mary Jane interjected. "I always liked him."

"Right," Egan said, looking for more.

"There's a lot of other ladies that have affection to that man," Mary Jane insisted. "He's a popular man with the ladies."

"Sounds that way," Egan said.

"And I'll tell you something, just because I'm one of those ladies that liked that guy doesn't mean anything," she said. "It could have been anybody, because they're so ingrained with this clique at church."

Egan continued the back-and-forth. "It sounds like there's quite a clique at church," he said.

"There is quite a group of them at the church, and maybe I'm not as intimately involved outside as they are together. Still, Sue was my neighbor, I liked her," Mary Jane said. "We have this inner group of people who were intimately friendly with Rhonda, sponsoring Rhonda. I wasn't sponsoring Rhonda, I was never told a thing about her. The whole world's going around this lady and I don't know it."

Mary Jane started in on a story, "But one thing I didn't tell you about, Wednesday, the week before this happened, Wednesday night was choir practice. Rhonda was a little late coming, but she came and Mrs. Catino came and we had a very nice time and a wonderfully happy time.

"The group disbanded and I was getting my things," she continued. "Not a soul in the choir room, not a soul in the kitchen, the lights were out. I went to get my car and I looked in the parking lot and there were all these cars, everybody's car was in the parking lot.

"I thought, 'Where did they go?' It was all really funny. If I'm not mistaken, I was checking around and found out I believe Rhonda's birthday was on the 17th. It would have been that night, that maybe they had a birthday party for her. It was nice of them to have a birthday party for her," she concluded.

Egan and Stumpo looked at each other. "If they had, we don't know if they had. . . ." Egan said.

"I'm making a statement and I just say it's possible they did," Mary Jane insisted. "Those cars were parked, six, seven cars parked there. Maybe they went somewhere. It was a mystery to me."

"So, Wednesday," Egan said, changing the subject. "The day Rhonda was killed, were you at the church at all? Did you stop by the church at all?"

"No, I didn't," Mary Jane said.

"Okay. So you went from your house to the salon?" Stumpo said, returning to the timeline.

"To the hairdressers, yeah. I had been there the other week, and I saw, usually you write up on the sheets . . ." she trailed off, trying to remember.

"The sign-in sheet," Stumpo offered.

She nodded. "There is a time when they used to take sign-in sheets and they would save the information. I found out they don't do it anymore. There's no way of indicating I was there."

"Well, what about the person that worked on your hair?" Stumpo asked. "They would remember you, wouldn't they? You've been going there for a while, right?"

"Yeah, there's about eight or nine girls in that place and I don't know what the girl's name was," Mary Jane said, thinking. "Cindy. Her name was Cindy."

"And what do you get worked on at the salon? 'Cause you told me the last time we spoke to you that you—" Stumpo started.

"I get a wash and set," she interrupted.

"But you wear a wig," Stumpo said.

"Yeah, I like a wig," she responded.

"So that's your own hair?" Egan asked.

"This is a wig," she answered.

"That's a wig?" Egan clarified.

"But my own hair is under here, yeah," she said.

"It looks different than when we spoke that one Wednesday," Stumpo interjected.

"Yes, it does look a little different," she said. "Well, I brushed it better and I have two or three wigs."

"Do you have all your wigs?" Stumpo asked.

"Yeah, as far as I know, I have them all," Mary Jane said.

"We have one of your wigs," Stumpo said, hoping to rattle Mary Jane.

It worked. "You do?" she said, clearly surprised. "You're joking."

"No," Egan said in a completely serious tone. He was impressed with the way Stumpo had brought up the wig, and was pleased with the impact it seemed to have on Mary Jane.

"You're kidding me, really?" she asked, still shocked. "How come you have my wig?"

"'Cause you left it at the salon," Egan offered.

"Did I really?" she asked.

"They said you forgot it and you left it there," Egan continued.

"It's a joke—you're kidding me!" she said with a half-hearted laugh. "Isn't that a scream that after that I would lose my . . . Ah, thank you, I'm glad you have it."

"Yeah, we have it," Egan said, not breaking his serious tone.

"So you know, we have your wig, but we're not going to be able to give it back to you just yet," Stumpo said, serving her up another surprise.

"Okay, so you want to hold it," Mary Jane said, becoming more serious.

"Well, we sent it out to a lab looking for some information," Stumpo said.

"In the hair—you're getting information out of the hair?" she asked. "That's good. Interesting."

They had her where they wanted her. Both men noted that Mary Jane appeared to be digesting the information in her mind even as she spoke, trying to figure out the best thing to say.

She's freaked out, Stumpo thought.

Egan continued, "'Cause there's a lot of things they can do with a wig these days, for instance, looking for molecules and different things."

"So I'd be happy to talk to you about the wig, if you'd like," Stumpo interjected. "Are you curious to know anything about the wig?"

Mary Jane nodded. "I'd like to know what you're going to tell me about the wig."

Rhonda Smith, 42, who was shot to death inside her Pennsylvania church on January 23, 2008.

(Courtesy: the Smith family)

Rhonda Smith during a Christmas celebration at her parents' house in Lower Saucon Township, Northampton County, Pennsylvania.

(Courtesy: the Smith family)

Trinity Evangelical Lutheran Church in Springfield Township, a rural area of Bucks County, Pennsylvania.

The Trinity Evangelical Lutheran Church office where Rhonda Smith was working when she was shot.

Pastor Gregory Shreaves had only been with Trinity Evangelical for three years before Rhonda Smith was murdered.
(Courtesy: WFMZ-TV)

Dorothy and Jim Smith mourning the death of their daughter, Rhonda.
(Courtesy: WFMZ-TV)

Jim Smith speaking to reporters about the death of his daughter, Rhonda. (Courtesy: WFMZ-TV)

Trooper Gregory Stumpo was the main investigator on the Rhonda Smith murder, his first homicide investigation. (Courtesy: Pennsylvania State Police)

Corporal Bob Egan, a 24-year police veteran, was called in to assist Trooper Gregory Stumpo with the case.

Mary Jane Fonder, 65, a long-time church congregant, was eventually arrested for Rhonda Smith's murder.

(Courtesy: WFMZ-TV)

Mary Jane Fonder as a young woman.

(Courtesy: Rosalie Schnell)

Mary Jane Fonder playing with her dog at her childhood summer home in Springfield Township.

(Courtesy: Rosalie Schnell)

Eight-year-old Garrett Sylsberry found the gun at this spot along Lake Nockamixon while fishing with his father, Doug.

Bucks County First Assistant District Attorney David Zellis personally handled the Fonder case.

Mary Jane Fonder hired defense attorney Michael Applebaum to handle her case.

Mary Jane Fonder's murder trial was held in courtroom #1 of the Bucks County Courthouse.

Mary Jane Fonder being escorted to her murder trial at the Bucks County Courthouse. (Courtesy: WFMZ-TV)

"Well, I can tell you about the wig, but I'm going to have to read you your Miranda rights beforehand, and you don't have to talk to us," Stumpo said.

He was under no obligation to read Mary Jane her rights, as she was not in custody, but Stumpo decided he'd rather be on the safe side. On the off chance that Mary Jane was about to confess, he didn't want some slick lawyer to have her statements thrown out because she wasn't aware of her legal rights.

Mary Jane nodded and said "um-mm" as Stumpo continued to explain she could leave whenever she wanted. The entire time she read Mary Jane her rights, she simply continued to say "um-mm" over and over.

"That was a surprise that you have my wig," Mary Jane said when Stumpo had finished the legal procedure. "I'm shocked that I left it at the salon that day."

The troopers were glad she was back to the wig. "Yes, and it's amazing what they can do these days with science and with gunpowder residue," Stumpo said.

Mary Jane thought for a moment. "I'm sure that nothing has appeared in my wig because I don't have a gun and I didn't do anything," she said.

Stumpo decided it was time for a more direct route. "You were at the church on Wednesday," he said.

"No, I wasn't," she responded.

"You didn't see Rhonda on Wednesday, January 23?" Stumpo asked.

"No, I did not," she said, continuing to assert her innocence.

"You left your house . . ." Stumpo said, starting in.

"I left the house at five of 11, I got to the hair salon at 25 after, had my hair done," she offered.

"You stopped by the church before you went to the hair salon," Egan interjected.

"No, I did not. I did not," she said, getting upset. "Are you trying to tell me that you found gunpowder residue in my wig? Which is ridiculous because there is none. There couldn't possibly because I don't have a gun, it's impossible."

"Then who did this to Rhonda?" Egan asked.

"I have no idea," she responded.

"You didn't do this to Rhonda?" he tried again.

"No, I didn't," Mary Jane said.

"Did you like Rhonda?" Egan asked.

"I liked her. I found her friendly and thought she was nice, yes," Mary Jane responded.

"Do you think Rhonda was having a relationship with the pastor?" Egan continued.

"I have no idea. Just as I spoke to you earlier, it's a conjecture," she said. "I feel sorry for him, I feel sorry for all her friends, but like I said, there is always a question of his reputation.

"Since you read me my Miranda rights, it has to do with my reputation, too. Heaven help me," she said, with a little laugh. "Heaven help anybody."

"How's your reputation going to be tarnished?" Stumpo asked. "What happens here today stays in this room."

"It doesn't," Mary Jane insisted. "It stays on the tape recorder, which can be removed from the room. We could keep going back and forth, back and forth, back and forth, as you, like Officer Triol tried to get me to do in 1993."

"What's that?" Egan asked. "Get to the truth?"

"No, try to make me confess to killing somebody, which I did not," Mary Jane said. "I did not do a thing to Rhonda. And we could go on and on forever. You seem to feel you have some information of some kind on my wig and I don't see how there could be gunpowder on it because it's impossible, I don't have a gun."

"When was the last time you fired a gun?" Stumpo asked.

"The last time I fired a gun was in 1994 into my yard," she answered.

"Have you been around anyone firing a gun lately?" Stumpo asked.

"No," she answered.

"So if there's gunpowder residue on your wig, you wouldn't be able to explain that?" he continued.

"Of course not, of course not," she said.

"But there shouldn't be any on there," Stumpo offered.

"I don't believe that there is any gunpowder on it, I really don't, because there couldn't be," she said.

Egan leaned in, his voice deeper than before, and he bluffed. "Why else would we be talking to you for four hours if there wasn't anything in your wig?" he asked.

"Yeah, that's interesting," Mary Jane said, a bit wistfully. "It's getting more interesting the whole time."

After a pause, she said, "I think I shall pursue an attorney. I'm sorry it's taken a turn like this, but you know, too bad. I didn't hurt the lady."

CHAPTER 24

Though exhausted by the nearly four-hour, ramble-filled interview, Stumpo and Egan were pleased with the results they had achieved. They did not get a confession, but neither man really expected to, although Stumpo thought Mary Jane was on the verge of cracking when she became so frazzled about the wig testing. But confession or not, they learned a whole lot more about Mary Jane and her feelings toward Rhonda and the church.

And then there was that moment when Mary Jane hunched over, her voice taking on a new, evil tone, she vehemently insisted, ". . . I . . . didn't . . . do . . . it." It was a new side of Mary Jane, one that, in the troopers' opinions, showed she was capable of murder.

A few days later, Stumpo and Egan made plans to meet with First Assistant District Attorney David Zellis. They thought they had obtained some valuable information, but wanted his take on it as well. As he rose in the ranks throughout his nearly twenty-five years with the Bucks County District Attorney's office, Zellis had handled many of their most important cases. A bit shorter than average, with wide eyes and a big smile on his round face, outside of the courtroom he didn't necessarily look like a hard-bitten trial lawyer.

But he knew his way around a courtroom: He was always

well researched, seldom caught off guard, and knew how to take the gloves off when he had to.

While conducting the interview was not easy for Stumpo and Egan, listening back to it was downright agonizing. Zellis, who had never met Mary Jane, was floored by her complete inability to stay on one topic. She would go off on tangents to such an unbelievable degree that Zellis wondered if she had some kind of mental defect that affected her ability to keep her thoughts straight.

However, by trudging through the tapes, the trio began to realize what valuable material they had on their hands. Throughout the course of nearly four hours of chatter, Mary Jane had inadvertently laid out her motive for killing Rhonda.

She admitted she had romantic feelings for Pastor Shreaves, and that she suspected he might be involved with Rhonda. She also discussed how she was upset she was never invited to social outings with the other church ladies, but that Rhonda seemed to fit in well with them.

Also, Rhonda made her "nervous," she told the troopers. Then there was the jealousy Mary Jane had voiced over Rhonda being given financial assistance from the church and her working as the substitute secretary, two privileges never afforded to Mary Jane.

"The whole world's going around this lady and I don't know it," she had said.

Zellis, Stumpo, and Egan also took notice of Mary Jane's mention of a birthday party for Rhonda the week before she was killed. The notable events were starting to add up in that week: the birthday party the Wednesday prior, Rhonda thanking the congregation for their financial assistance on Sunday, Mary Jane finding out Rhonda was serving as the substitute secretary on Monday.

The jealously must have grown in Mary Jane throughout the week, Zellis thought. Her misinterpretation about the birthday party must have lit a fuse in her, which grew stronger and stronger until it ultimately detonated in an explosion when she killed Rhonda, he thought.

The law enforcement officials didn't need a motive to arrest Mary Jane, but it helps in a trial. People—including jurors—are always curious why one person kills another.

If their theory was correct, however, much of what drove Mary Jane to murder was in her head. The birthday party, Rhonda's supposed affair with Shreaves, these were little more than figments of her imagination. On the surface, it could seem hard to believe that Mary Jane could bring herself to the point of murder based on such delusions. But to Egan, it made perfect sense. In his experience, he knew that even the tiniest disrespectful comments or smallest gestures were sometimes enough to drive people to kill.

In fact, Egan had seen even stranger motives for murder in his day. He recalled Patricia Rorrer, a woman from a murder case he worked in 1994. Living in North Carolina, she called her ex-boyfriend of ten years one day only to have his wife, Joann Katrinak, answer the phone. Joann told her never to call again and hung up on her. The next day, the furious Rorrer drove all the way to Catasauqua, Pennsylvania, abducted Joann and her three-and-a-half-month-old son Alex, drove them into the woods and killed them.

For Mary Jane, her resentment had been building even before Rhonda joined the church, even before Mary Jane joined the church herself. She had been left out her whole life, Egan thought, and she probably had built up a whole lifetime's worth of resentment as a result.

On February 27, two days after interviewing Mary Jane Fonder, the police launched yet another search of Lake Nockamixon, this time expanding the area to another bridge near Route 412 as well as the one at Route 313. Nobody really expected it to be any more fruitful this time than the last, and sure enough, no gun was recovered, although they planned to conduct another search weeks later when some of the snow-covered areas around the lake had melted.

By now, Stumpo and the other investigators were paying close attention to any bit of information that came along about Mary Jane Fonder. The day of the Lake Nockamixon search, Stumpo spoke with church choir director Steve Wysocki, who said he had received an unusually short message from a distressed-sounding Mary Jane, where she told him, "I won't be at church and choir for a few weeks. I am taking a break from choir and church to get some things in my life straightened out."

Upon reviewing Mary Jane's phone records, Stumpo and Egan found that she had called her neighbor, Rosalie Schnell, the day of Rhonda's murder on January 23, at around 2:45 p.m. On March 3, Stumpo and Egan visited Rosalie, who described herself as one of Mary Jane's longest and closest friends. Rosalie said she could not remember the phone conversation from that day, but recalled that she and Mary Jane had discussed Rhonda's death during a day of shopping in Quakertown a few days after the murder.

Schnell seemed to recall that Mary Jane had said she didn't know Rhonda all that well but thought she was a nice young woman, and that there was talk it could have been a suicide, not a murder. She also thought she vaguely remembered Mary Jane saying something about buying a gun for protection—something that certainly caught the attention of Stumpo and Egan—but she did not remember ever seeing a gun or hearing Mary Jane bring it up again.

Besides, Rosalie insisted, she couldn't imagine Mary Jane ever even holding a gun, much less using one. Yes, she'd heard all the rumors and all the talk about Ed Fonder's disappearance, but to this day she just didn't believe it. Mary Jane was a sweet lady and a good friend, and Rosalie didn't believe she could possibly be a killer.

As they were leaving Rosalie's home, the troopers saw that Mary Jane and Ed didn't appear to be home, but had left their garbage cans out for pickup. They knew it was a long shot, but with nothing to lose, Stumpo and Egan pulled the trash bags out of the cans and brought them back to the station with them. But after a thorough search, nothing of value was found, and they were discarded in a Dumpster outside the station.

The next few days were relatively uneventful in the investigation, but Stumpo and Egan continued speaking to various people from the church community. On March 11, they visited Judy Zellner's husband, Les, in Allentown, where he worked. He had very little to share aside from the typical church rumors Stumpo and Egan had encountered numerous times before.

But Les did offer one interesting tidbit, even if it wasn't particularly useful. Back before Shreaves arrived at Trinity Evangelical, when Donald Hagey was still the pastor, Mary Jane had approached him at the church, wearing an overcoat. Her cat had recently died, and Mary Jane asked if the church would be willing to bless her deceased pet. Hagey smiled warmly and nodded yes, of course he would. That smile quickly melted away, however, when Mary Jane opened her coat and showed she was holding the cat's corpse underneath it.

Suffice it to say, Zellner explained, Hagey did not bless the cat that day.

CHAPTER 25

It was around noon on March 12, a Wednesday afternoon, when the phone rang at Jim and Dorothy Smith's Lower Saucon Township house. Dorothy picked it up and Jim, seated comfortably in his favorite living room chair, could hear a woman's voice on the other line.

"Oh, hello Mary Jane," Dorothy said.

Jim grimaced. Neither he nor his wife knew Mary Jane Fonder very well. To them, she was just another member of the church, and one they had never gotten to know particularly well. The last thing he wanted today was to hear from anybody from the church. Six weeks had passed since Rhonda was killed, but time had done nothing to blunt the heartache he felt for his lost little girl. And, likewise, time had done nothing to dampen the distrust he had developed for just about everybody at Trinity Evangelical.

I don't want anything to do with any of them, he thought. *I don't want anything to do with anybody.*

"I was wondering if you wanted an apple pie that I baked?" Mary Jane asked. "I made too many."

Dorothy put her hand over the receiver and asked her husband, who immediately and vehemently shook his head no. Dorothy felt the same way and, speaking back into the phone, she politely declined the offer. Seemingly unoffended, Mary Jane simply responded, "Okay."

Dorothy was relieved. She barely knew Mary Jane, and the last thing she wanted today was a visitor. Besides, Dorothy had already encountered Mary Jane earlier in the week. After a church service that past Sunday, Mary Jane had gone up to Dorothy and, out of nowhere, started talking about how much she missed Rhonda. She also mentioned that she had spoken with Rhonda the Monday before she died, something Dorothy had never heard before.

"I don't know how this happened," Dorothy remembered Mary Jane saying, before the woman inexplicably started to cry. The tears seemed a little forced to Dorothy, and she was a bit annoyed with the idea of having to comfort someone else about her daughter.

Three hours later, the phone at the Smith residence rang again. This time, Jim picked it up, and he was more than a little annoyed with what he heard.

"Hi Mr. Smith, this is Mary Jane Fonder," she said, her voice sounding a little distant, as if she was distracted. "I'm up here on the highway. How do I get to your place?"

Jim frowned. *I thought we said we didn't want you here,* he thought, but didn't say aloud. It didn't matter, she was already here, driving up and down Route 412 looking for their house. Everybody had trouble finding the Smiths when they visited for the first time. Not only was their home heavily concealed by a row of thick bushes, but the driveway ran along a rear alley that started several houses away, and visitors had to loop around and take a hidden path before they could reach the Smiths' home.

"Now look, it's a dangerous highway, I don't want you to get hurt," Jim said, nervous about her talking on her cell phone while driving on Route 412. There had been plenty of accidents on that road in his time, and the last thing his conscience needed right now was for a sixty-five-year-old woman to crash her car looking for his house.

"I'm going to come up with an apple pie," Mary Jane said, her enthusiasm apparently unaffected by Dorothy's rejection a few hours earlier. "How do I get to your place?"

Reluctantly, Jim decided to direct Mary Jane to their

driveway before she hurt herself. A few minutes later, Dorothy was greeting Mary Jane at the backdoor. With a pie in her hands and a big smile on her chubby face, Mary Jane looked around at the small kitchen as she stepped inside. Dorothy politely accepted the pie and, after placing it on the kitchen table, led Mary Jane to the living room, where she sat on the couch next to framed photos of Rhonda.

As usual, Mary Jane did most of the talking. In her typical manner, she rambled on and on, discussing one subject for a few moments before abruptly going off on another tangent altogether. Dorothy barely said a word, mostly listening and nodding every few minutes. Jim sat in his chair, watching television and doing his best to pretend he wasn't paying attention at all. But he was listening to every word Mary Jane was saying, and growing inside him was that blistering feeling of distrust he had been harboring for everyone at the church over the last two months.

The conversation soon turned to Mary Jane's brother, Ed, and the deplorable conditions of the home they shared together. "He don't clean up," Mary Jane said. "He has everything a mess." In fact, Mary Jane said, her brother was so hard to live with, she had visited an apartment near Rhonda's apartment in Hellertown just the day before Rhonda was killed.

"You know, it seems a little odd that I would be looking for an apartment when I own property, but I don't get along with my brother sometimes," Mary Jane said.

The line of conversation made Jim and Dorothy uncomfortable. They didn't even want Mary Jane here, and they certainly didn't want to hear her talk about their daughter. But, fortunately, it wasn't long before Mary Jane was off the topic altogether and rambling about something else.

Dorothy was distracted by Mary Jane's shoes, a worn, odd-looking pair of black rubber shoes that almost resembled a pair of galoshes. Jim, too, had noticed them right away when Mary Jane came in the house. Motioning toward her feet, Dorothy asked, "Can you use a pair of sneakers there?"

Yes, Mary Jane nodded, her shoes were a bit worn out.

"We've got some of Rhonda's old shoes," Dorothy said, standing up from the couch. "I'll see if they fit." She went through the kitchen and into the cluttered first floor bedroom, where they were keeping a number of Rhonda's old things, including several pairs of her old shoes and sneakers. She grabbed one pair of each and brought them back to Mary Jane, who had already slipped off her rubber shoes and happily fitted Rhonda's sneakers onto her feet.

Mary Jane stood and walked back and forth between the living room and the kitchen a few times, the floor creaking a bit under the pressure of the shoes that Rhonda had worn in that house so many times in the past. Suddenly, Mary Jane stopped, and a big smile crept across her face.

"Yes ma'am," she said. "They sure do fit, ma'am."

By 5 o'clock, after two hours of politely enduring Mary Jane's visit, Dorothy led her back out the door and wished her good-bye. As she closed the door in front of her, she looked at the pie sitting on the table. Jim came into the room and waved his hand dismissively.

"I wouldn't eat that," he said.

Dorothy agreed. She had absolutely no appetite anyway, she thought, as she picked up the pie and brought it to the downstairs freezer.

Later that day, Mary Jane showed up for choir rehearsal about forty minutes early. Choir director Steve Wysocki was the only one there when she arrived, getting everything ready before the practice began. Steve thought it strange that Mary Jane had shown up so early.

In fact, he was struck by her overall pattern of attendance at church functions over the last few weeks. Before, she would miss the occasional service or two, and sometimes would go a few weeks at a time before she attended any of the church's special events. But ever since Rhonda died, it seemed, Mary Jane hadn't missed a single church function. In fact, she was not only attending church every Sunday, but going to both Sunday morning services every week.

As Mary Jane entered, she extended her arms and gave Steve a big smile.

"I feel so good tonight," Mary Jane told him. "Tonight, everything feels peaceful."

Mary Jane continued on about how positive a mood she was in today, and explained that she had just visited Rhonda's parents, Jim and Dorothy. The visit went great, Mary Jane explained. They had a lovely talk, Mary Jane brought them a pie, and they even gave her a pair of Rhonda's old sneakers, she said.

"Everything feels back to normal and fine," Mary Jane said, almost like a declaration. "I think Rhonda's spirit is finally at rest."

She continued on and on like that, repeating over and over especially that last phrase, about Rhonda's spirit being at rest. Steve frowned. Personally, he was not sharing those sentiments.

"Mary Jane, I really need to finish getting ready for rehearsal," he said in as polite a voice as he could muster, then resumed his duties getting ready for the rehearsal.

Pastor Shreaves had started getting phone messages from Mary Jane again.

They weren't coming as often as they were before, but between the calls she made to his house and to the church, he was still getting four or five messages a week. And they certainly hadn't gotten any shorter, or any less unfocused or rambling.

"Peace be with you, Pastor Greg," one of the messages started. "Hoping sunshine will be blooming in your office! A big pot of sunshine or something, 'cause you'll need a nice happy day!"

If the messages were a nuisance to Shreaves before, they were nearly unbearable now. Ever since the police had hinted they were looking into Mary Jane, Shreaves had been doing his best to avoid her, which was no easy task in a small church like Trinity Evangelical. While Shreaves used to linger after services to talk to people, now he was leaving so Mary Jane wouldn't get the chance to chat with him.

This hadn't gone unnoticed by Mary Jane, as she pointed out in one of her messages.

"I wanted to stop and talk with you at choir practice, but you were in a hurry to leave and, ah, well anyway, I wasn't able to stop you," she said. "I think we, I could come over to sit and talk with you, but I can't, I know . . . It's up to you if you wanted to talk to me. I got so much I wanted to discuss with you, but that's the way it goes."

Nowadays, it became very difficult for Shreaves to even conduct a service while Mary Jane was in the pews. If she would so much as squirm during a sermon, Shreaves would get nervous, irrationally wondering to himself if she was reaching for a gun.

Once, when Mary Jane asked if she could help with communion, as she often did, Shreaves said yes, thinking to himself, *If I say no, she'll shoot me.*

Just like before, Mary Jane's messages bordered on incomprehensible at times, and varied widely in tone. In some, Mary Jane was chipper and pleasant, while in others she sounded bleak and depressed, as if the weight of the world was on her shoulders.

"Dreary, dismal, terrible day," Mary Jane said in one.

"Right now, it seems like everyone you bump into has some tragedy in their life or some sad problem," she said. "Some of the terrible things that happened to our Lord are actually happening to us, and it's just we're in terrible times. Lord knows it's always something. Some devil somewhere, or some terrible person or some terrible thing or maybe a friend doesn't love you anymore or doesn't like you and that is very hard to take, but you know, it's like you roll with the waves of the sea. It comes in and it comes, it comes back and forth sometimes, the sad part washes away and sometimes it goes to its end and another beginning starts again."

And, while most of the messages were long, some were more casual or uplifting. At times, Mary Jane simply called the church to see if they needed any supplies, or to see whether they had any luck finding a new church secretary. When Shreaves would take a few days away from the church, he would usually return to a message from Mary Jane, telling him she hoped the rest had done him good.

"The offer's always open if you need anything," she said. "Give me a call and I can always dash over to town and get things for you if you need any errands run, okay? So keep it in mind, and you're always on my mind."

As uncomfortable and stressed as the messages made Shreaves feel, everything he was going through was made harder by the fact that he couldn't tell anybody that the police suspected her. With the way gossip traveled around the church, what if word got around to Mary Jane and she tried to run away or—worse yet—hurt somebody? Or, on the other hand, if she were innocent, it would permanently and irreparably harm her reputation.

Shreaves decided he would call the new church council president, Paul Rose, and insist that he call Mary Jane and demand she stop the phone calls, stop talking to Shreaves in church, stop everything. The pastor had made that request to church council months ago, but they didn't want to deal with it, but now they'd just have to. There wasn't much Shreaves could do to make himself feel safer or more comfortable, but this much, at least, he could do.

By mid-March a core group of church members was routinely calling the police, with several providing information about Mary Jane. On March 13, Don Ludlow called Trooper Stumpo to tell him he had remembered that Mary Jane gave Pastor Shreaves $100 for a Christmas gift in 2006.

The next day, Stumpo and Egan verified the gift with Shreaves, who also said Mary Jane had given him checks and restaurant gift certificates worth $25 and $35. He gave the gifts to other church members in need of some financial assistance.

On March 16, Stumpo spoke to Steve Wysocki, who had grown so concerned about Mary Jane's behavior that he started jotting down notes on scraps of paper after speaking with her, then saving them in his wallet to share with police later. Steve told Stumpo about the choir rehearsal Mary Jane had shown up early for, and told him all about how she had just visited the Smiths and kept declaring that Rhonda's spirit was finally at rest.

On March 18, Don Ludlow called Stumpo with a similar story. He had been at Bible study the previous Sunday with Mary Jane, and he heard her mumble Rhonda's name. Curious, Don asked her what she was talking about, and Mary Jane burst out, "I'm feeling much better about Rhonda now." Don asked her why, and Mary Jane said it was because she had visited with Rhonda's parents for a few hours.

The next day, Les Zellner called with another tip about Mary Jane. She had been helping around the church more than usual, he told Stumpo, and had a new dress.

With now two reports of Mary Jane visiting Rhonda's parents, the police wanted to hear about it for themselves. Stumpo followed up with a call to Jim Smith, who retold the story for him. Mary Jane had been the only person from the church to visit them since Rhonda died besides Pastor Shreaves and the Zellners, Jim Smith said.

Mary Jane also sat with the Smiths at the breakfast held at the church for Easter, where she gave Dorothy Smith a hook rug as a present, Jim Smith told the trooper.

As Jim hung up the phone, he turned to his wife.

"They're after that woman," he said. "They haven't been asking us about any other church people."

But Dorothy Smith still found it hard to believe that Mary Jane Fonder could have killed her daughter.

CHAPTER 26

The circumstantial evidence against Mary Jane was mounting, but police still lacked the physical evidence needed to shore up the case.

It had now been two months since Rhonda's death, and a month after their big interview with Mary Jane, but they hadn't gotten very far since then. With all the searches for the gun coming up empty, they were starting to get frustrated.

One day, while Egan and Stumpo were brainstorming about what to do next, Egan came up with what Stumpo thought was a wild suggestion.

"Let's go get her car," he said.

"Bob," Stumpo responded, confounded. "We can't get a search warrant for the house, how are we supposed to get one for the car?"

Egan was not discouraged. "I don't know, I just thought maybe we'd talk about it."

Stumpo shook his head. "It's not going to happen," he said. "We just don't have enough now."

But Egan did not let it drop, and a couple days later, he brought it up again.

"You know, I think I'm going to work on that search warrant for the car," he announced.

Still not convinced, but not looking to argue any more, Stumpo begrudgingly gave in.

"Go ahead," he said. "Go work on it."

Egan was not sure a judge would grant a search warrant for Mary Jane's car with the evidence they had, but he felt they had to try something. The case was getting into its third month, and if it went on too much longer, Mary Jane was going to get away with murder, possibly for a second time.

Egan had worked a previous case where he was able to find gunshot residue in a car several months into an investigation, and he hoped that would be the case with Mary Jane's car. Steering wheels and turn signals are stickier than average surfaces and retain gunpowder for a much longer time.

Egan included that argument in his search warrant application, and also details of Mary Jane's timeline on January 23 that showed she would have been in her car immediately following the shooting. He also included the transcript of her long interview to police, which showed she had a possible motive in the homicide.

On March 25, Zellis signed off on the search warrant and submitted it to Common Pleas Judge Albert Cepparulo, who approved it that same day.

On the morning of March 25, Mary Jane Fonder left a message on Sue Brunner's answering machine while Sue was out of town in Florida.

"I see a lot of cars around your house. It looks like there's so many; I didn't know what the situation was. Is everything okay up there?

"I'm trying to get a hold of my housework," she continued. "I sure hope I can get working on it. Everything's going okay down here, I'm trying to do the best I can with my housework.

"So many disturbing things are bothering and upsetting me. Like unhappy moments. They're stealing my spirit. Nothing seems to be right. So sad these days. Too many losses, too many disappointments, too many sad things this year. Some we don't understand."

She concluded with an eerie warning that stuck with Sue Brunner for a very long time.

"Endings come and you just never know," Mary Jane said before hanging up. "You never know when your ending is going to come."

At 8:45 the next morning, Stumpo and Egan went to Mary Jane's house to serve her with the search warrant for her car. They brought Troopers Anthony Rhodunda and Joseph Miller, parking multiple cars outside her property. They wanted to make the visit look like a big deal because they wanted to rattle Mary Jane. They wanted her convinced that they were going to keep coming back to her over and over again until they got the gun. Until she was behind bars.

Mary Jane greeted them at the door with an enthusiastic hello, as if the troopers were just friends paying her visit.

"Oh, hi Bob!" she said. Then, inexplicably, she removed her wig from her head. It was not the reaction the troopers were expecting and, under different circumstances, Stumpo would have laughed.

But when they handed her the search warrant, she instantly became quiet and went inside to talk to her brother.

"I want a lawyer," she said, when she stepped back to the door.

"You can call a lawyer," Stumpo responded. "But we're still taking your car."

The tow truck was running a little behind, so the troopers waited outside until it arrived. Stumpo went back to his police cruiser while Egan waited next to Mary Jane's car. As he waited, Mary Jane came out of the house and approached him, asking to get something out of the car.

"I want my laundry," she said.

"You can't have it," Egan responded. "You can't get anything out of your car."

Mary Jane looked at Egan with an angry glare and stormed off into her house. But after a few minutes, she reemerged from the house, stormed back toward Egan and started screaming at him. The trooper let her talk, and for a few minutes Mary Jane went on a tirade, angrily ranting on and on.

Later, Egan would barely be able to remember what specifically she said, but he would never forget her tone. It reminded him of that eerie moment during their long interview when Mary Jane's voice dropped to an evil-sounding pitch and she insisted she was innocent. Like then, Mary Jane had dropped any pretext of being a sweet old lady, and a hidden side of her had emerged. The side of her that was probably the last thing Rhonda Smith ever saw, Egan suspected.

Ed Fonder rushed out of the house and, while Mary Jane was still on her tirade, grabbed her and started pulling her back toward their home. "Shut up," he said. "We're calling a lawyer."

The police towed Mary Jane's car to the Dublin barracks, where it was searched by Trooper Louis Gober, who was the main crime scene investigator the day Rhonda's body was found.

He first photographed the car before taking samples to be tested for gunpowder residue from the gear shift, steering wheel, seat belt strap, door handle armrest, turn signal knob, and the driver seat. He also took several items for evidence, including the brake pedal cover, gas pedal cover, the driver's side floor mat, and several blankets Mary Jane had on her passenger seat.

Gober also vacuumed the floor mat and other carpeted areas of the car to capture any evidence they might contain. The samples were all sent to the same Pittsburgh-area laboratory that checked for gunpowder residue on Mary Jane's wig. It would be several weeks before they would get results.

Meanwhile, Mary Jane, in a panic, tried to contact Pastor Shreaves. She put in a call to the church, and Judy Zellner, there on one of her regular cleaning visits, answered.

Pastor Shreaves wasn't there, so Mary Jane confided in Judy.

"I'm in trouble," she told her.

"You're in trouble?" Judy repeated back. "Well, what did you do?"

"Well, the police just came and took my car," Mary Jane

answered. "They're looking for something under my seat. Something I got rid of back in 1996 or '97."

"Do you need any help?" Judy offered, hoping Mary Jane would say more. "Do you need to go anywhere? I'll take you."

"No, no," Mary Jane responded. "I can use my brother's car."

As they said their good-byes, Mary Jane made another startling statement.

"What happened ten years ago with my father is coming back to haunt me," she told Judy. "Rhonda and I are in this together."

CHAPTER 27

Doug Sylsberry and his eight-year-old son, Garrett, had been fishing for about an hour, with absolutely no luck.

It was a cold and windy afternoon on March 29, and the smell of mist was in the air as a light drizzle fell down on the tranquil waters of Lake Nockamixon. Although far from the perfect conditions for a day outdoors, Doug was determined not to let the weather ruin a day with his son. It was the first day of trout season, and the two so rarely got to go fishing together.

Doug lived in Quakertown, a Bucks County borough just a dozen miles west of Nockamixon State Park. A forty-year-old contractor, he was a slim man with a goatee and short haircut that contrasted with the brown mop of hair atop Garrett's head. A second-grade student at the Neidig Elementary School in Quakertown, Garrett was Doug's eldest son by four years and, although unusually short for his age, what he lacked in size he made up for in energy.

Being the first day of trout season, Doug assumed everybody would be fishing in the nearby creeks, so he decided to take his son to the lake instead. As a result, there were few boats on the water, and absolutely no other fisherman milling around the edge. Seeking a little shelter from the elements, Doug and Garrett had made their way under the Haycock Run Bridge, which provided some overhead cover but still

opened up to an excellent view of the wide-open lake and
beautiful green trees.

As they stood fishing on the rocky surface underneath
the bridge, Doug noticed the water was unusually low, with
at least three or four feet more surface than usual exposed.
What he did not know was that the state police had drained
part of the lake a few days earlier, searching in vain for
Mary Jane Fonder's gun.

Before long, Garrett started to get a little restless and lost
his focus on the fishing, setting his rod aside and exploring
around the lake's edge. Off in the distance, he noticed a
great blue heron wading in the water, and he told his father
he was going to head out for a closer look at the bird. While
Doug continued fishing under the bridge, Garrett followed
the rocky path along the shoreline of the lake.

A wooded ledge ran alongside the surface where Garrett
was walking. Route 563 was clearly visible just fifteen feet
away atop the hill, and the sound of passing cars was so loud
it resembled a roar. Down at the water, the surface was
coated by layers of foam left over from the rain dropping
down on the recently exposed rocks.

And in that foam, Garrett saw something.

A glare from the sun gave the object half emerged in the
water a bright shine, but as Garrett approached it, the water
made it look blue. As Garrett got closer, his eyes widened as
he realized what it was . . . a toy gun! He wrapped his fist
around the barrel and lifted it from the water, pointing it out
toward Lake Nockamixon like a Wild West gunslinger.

But the weight was heavier than Garrett expected, and he
quickly realized it could not be made of plastic. He looked
down at it and noticed it was black, not blue. There was
some minor rust where the revolver had been exposed, and
some wear and tear along the cylinder and interior of the
barrel.

It's real, he thought.

Garrett quickly pointed the gun down at the ground.
Rather than continue grasping it, he loosened his grip, extended his arm forward and held it by a few fingers on the

barrel, as if it might contaminate him somehow. Garrett doubled back toward the bridge, where he found his father still fishing underneath.

"Dad, I found a gun!" Garrett said excitedly, holding the newly found item in the air.

Doug would never forget the image of his son coming around the bend with that gun in his hand. A lump caught in his throat, and his feeling of shock was overwhelmed by an instinctive pang of terror for his son's safety. He quickly rushed toward Garrett and carefully snatched the weapon out of his hand.

"Garrett, you know better than to pick that up!" Doug said. He owned a handful of guns himself, and had always gone out of his way to teach Garrett how to act properly around them. Doug believed strongly in his Second Amendment rights, but always stressed to his children never to touch the weapons at his home.

Doug opened the wheel and his fears were confirmed: In addition to three empty casings, two live hollow-point shells were inside the gun. Doug asked Garrett to take him back to where he found the weapon and, as they walked, he shook the empty casings loose from the barrel and tossed them into the lake. By the time they had walked back to where the gun was recovered, he had removed the live rounds and tossed them into the lake, too. He knew how unstable wet ammunition can be, and didn't want it anywhere near his son.

Everything around the lake was state game land, so Doug's first thought was that the gun had been dropped by some hunter, or by a fisherman who brought his pistol along with him. After looking around a bit and finding nothing else of interest, Garrett and Doug went back down the path to the bridge. Doug placed the now-unloaded gun in his pocket, and the two once again picked up their fishing rods.

"Garrett," Doug said. "Don't you dare tell your mom that you touched the gun. Don't say you touched it."

They continued fishing for another three hours until the sun went down, almost completely forgetting about the gun altogether. Once they left Haycock Run Bridge, Doug called his brother, a friend, and his wife to let them know about the gun. None were particularly surprised or disturbed by the news, except for Doug's wife, Karen, who immediately suspected something was wrong and insisted Doug call the police when he arrived home.

"Doug, there's dirty dealing here," Karen said. "There's dirty dealing."

Trooper Andrew Mincer was working at the communications desk at the Dublin state police barracks, and it was around quarter after eight when the phone rang. It was Doug Sylsberry, a Quakertown man who claimed to have found a Rossi .38 caliber while fishing at Lake Nockamixon near the Haycock Run Bridge.

Mincer, of course, knew that Mary Jane Fonder's gun was a Rossi .38 caliber, and he felt a twinge of excitement as he asked Doug for the serial number: AA362102. He plugged it into the National Crime Information Center, a computerized index of criminal justice information, and sure enough, the gun belonged to Mary Jane.

"Stay right there. We'll send someone over right away," Mincer said to Doug, who knew from the trooper's urgent tone of voice that something major was going on. His wife was right. Dirty dealing.

The first person Mincer called was Greg Stumpo. He was off that Saturday, but had already been called in to work earlier that morning as part of the Special Emergency Response Team, a program in which state police respond to emergency or high-risk incidents. Earlier that morning, a man with a gun had barricaded himself into his car, and Stumpo was among the team that responded to the potentially dangerous situation. He was still wearing his SERT gear when he got Mincer's call.

"You won't believe this," Mincer said, before giving him the news.

"You're kidding me," Stumpo said, a mixture of disbelief, amazement, and relief striking him all at once. He had been convinced Mary Jane still had the gun, and that they would have to build enough evidence for a warrant to seek it. The idea of a random citizen stumbling upon the gun alongside a lake just seemed too good to be true.

Stumpo's first instinct was to rush over to Doug Sylsberry's house himself, day off or not. But he had promised his five-year-old son he would spend the day with him, and he had already been called away for most of the morning. His son was visibly upset when Stumpo had to leave for the SERT assignment, and was just as obviously happy when he came back. As much as Stumpo wanted to get out to that gun, he knew he couldn't let his son down. Besides, Patrick McGuire was on call. Pat was a perfectly competent investigator, and there was nothing he would do differently than Stumpo.

Mincer also put out calls to Bob Egan and Dave Zellis, both of whom were home for the evening, and were just as shocked as Stumpo to receive the news.

"What are you talking about?" Zellis first responded. The more Mincer told him about the recovery of the gun, the more stunned he got. "Wow. That's amazing."

Egan felt great, as if everything was now finally coming together. He had hoped Mary Jane would make some sort of mistake in response to losing her car, but this was better than he could have hoped. At first glance, it appeared she had hurriedly tried to get rid of the gun, and had botched the disposal so poorly that an eight-year-old boy found the weapon by accident.

Sometimes, you just need luck to solve these things, Egan thought. *You need good strategies, you need good investigators, but sometimes, you just need plain old good luck.*

Trooper Gregg Dietz had a similar reaction. He knew firsthand how much work Stumpo and Egan put into the investigation, but also knew from experience that sometimes, you need a bit of luck to close a case. He could recall several of his own cases where the police work was solid and everything was done right, but ended up going unsolved because he needed that little bit of luck and never got it.

But even as they thought it, the two men knew they were not giving the police work enough credit. The finding of the gun might have appeared serendipitous, but if Mary Jane had indeed only recently disposed of her gun, it was only because the police had taken her car in the first place and made her nervous.

McGuire and Trooper Joseph Longmore Jr. were called and dispatched to the Sylsberry household in Quakertown, along with additional patrol units. Mincer also ran a background check on Doug, but found no criminal history. It was a little after nine thirty when they arrived, and both Doug and the Rossi .38 were waiting for them. It wouldn't be until later that Doug would learn who had owned the gun. At that point, it didn't even occur to him that it was connected to a local crime, and he believed it had been discarded by a criminal from Allentown or Philadelphia just passing through the area.

The gun was placed into an evidence envelope and secured in McGuire's police car while Doug ran through everything with the troopers. He told them about the discovery of the gun, as well as the rounds he removed and discarded into the lake. McGuire asked whether Doug would be willing to go back to the Haycock Run Bridge to look around and try to recover the casings, and Doug agreed without hesitation.

It was quarter after ten and dark by the time they arrived at the bridge, but Doug led McGuire and Longmore down to the area where the gun was found. Troopers Nicholas Desantis, William McDermott, and Justin Oliverio were all brought in to help with the search, scanning the beams of their flashlights along the shore and water as Doug pointed out areas he believed the casings might be.

After only a few moments, Oliverio and McDermott spotted something shiny sitting in the water, just along the bank. One of the officers reached down and picked up one of the three empty casings, lying just where Doug said they would be.

"I found 'em!" one of the officers called out.

"Don't touch them!" McGuire ordered.

Doug watched as the trooper froze, the casing still in his fingers, a slightly panicked look over his face. "I already touched one," he said, slowly and guiltily. Doug found it amusing, but it appeared McGuire did not. It was clear that they had caught a lucky break in finding the gun, and they didn't want to make a stupid mistake now that could eventually help Mary Jane Fonder's defense attorney.

After they had secured the empty casings, the two discarded live rounds were found only a few moments later. They had what they came for, but the troopers planned to do a thorough search of the area to see if anything else came up. After sending Doug back home, the police spent about forty-five minutes searching before McGuire and Longmore spotted a silver and blue cardboard box, submerged in about eight inches of water just a yard or so off the shore.

It was a box of .38 special high velocity hollow-point rounds, still about two-thirds full with thirty-two unexpended bullets. The exact same type of ammunition from Mary Jane's gun, presumably discarded into Lake Nockamixon along with the gun.

The items were taken back to the Dublin barracks and entered into evidence, along with the gun. The next day, they were submitted for analysis to ballistics expert Corporal Mark Garrett. Fortunately, he was available that Sunday due to another case he was working on in the crime lab, but after this case was explained to him, Garrett agreed the situation was sufficiently important enough for him to drop what he was doing and focus on the Fonder case.

Garrett tested the gun that very day and confirmed what Stumpo, Egan, and everybody involved in the case had already suspected for some time: Mary Jane Fonder's gun was used to kill Rhonda Smith. Now all that was left was to make the arrest.

Meanwhile, on the evening of March 31, church council President Paul Rose prepared for what he expected to be a very long and awkward phone call: He had to ask Mary Jane Fonder to leave Pastor Shreaves alone.

It was a call that was long overdue, but one that Paul knew had to be made. It had been months since the pastor—

rattled by the long phone messages and Mary Jane's strange admission of her romantic feelings toward him—asked the church council to speak with her. Paul wasn't president of the church council at that time, and he knew the council leadership was uncomfortable with the idea of getting involved, and consequently nobody ever reached out to her.

Now that task fell to Paul, who had started his term as council president in February, about a month later than usual due to the circumstances of Rhonda Smith's death. In the chaos of everything that had happened since then, Paul hadn't had a chance to call Mary Jane until now, but Shreaves seemed to have only grown more and more uncomfortable around her, so he decided it was time to speak with her.

Paul had been a member of Trinity Evangelical for about twelve years. He always liked Mary Jane and would always give her a big hug whenever they saw each other after service. Sure, she could be a bit flighty at times, but he never knew her to be anything other than a friendly, happy-go-lucky woman, one that Paul felt others in the congregation didn't really know as well as they thought they did.

That night, Paul told Mary Jane that she couldn't talk to Pastor Shreaves anymore: no more phone calls, no more conversations after services, nothing. To his relief, she didn't seem angry at the news, but rather a bit puzzled.

"You've got to do me a favor," Paul said. "You've got to leave the guy alone."

"I don't understand," she replied. "I haven't done anything wrong. I was just being sociable."

"I understand, Mary Jane. I just need you to do me this favor."

Although obviously displeased, Mary Jane seemed to begrudgingly accept this and did not press the matter. Instead, she launched into a tirade about how horribly the police were treating her. They wouldn't leave her alone, she said, and now they had taken her car. Mary Jane was convinced they believed her to be a suspect in Rhonda's murder.

"They're out to get me," she said.

Paul could tell Mary Jane was a nervous wreck over the matter. She kept rambling on and on about how she had nothing to do with Rhonda's death, how she had nothing against the woman, how she was getting her hair done that day and couldn't have possibly hurt her. Mary Jane went on for nearly an hour, and Paul felt like he hadn't spoken for more than two minutes the entire time.

"They're putting me under all sorts of pressure," she said.

Paul tried his best to comfort her, adding, "If you didn't do it, Mary Jane, you've got nothing to worry about."

After a few more minutes of conversation, Mary Jane and Paul concluded their conversation. As he hung up the phone, Paul got the impression that his comment had done little to put her mind at rest.

CHAPTER 28

The morning of April 1, Stumpo and Egan spent about an hour with Zellis discussing the criminal complaint in the Smith case before seeking Mary Jane Fonder's arrest warrant. By now, they were sure they had more than enough information to seek a warrant, but the two troopers—especially Stumpo—didn't want to leave any room for error. They had no idea what kind of a defense Mary Jane's lawyer would one day present, and with her incarceration just around the corner, they didn't want to make any stupid mistakes now.

After meticulously combing through every detail of the complaint, Zellis assured them everything was in order, and Bucks County District Attorney Michelle Henry approved the warrant. The troopers took it to the office of Magistrate District Judge Charles Baum in Perkasie, a Bucks County borough about a half hour south of Trinity Evangelical. The judge signed off, and everything was in order for the arrest.

Meanwhile, Mary Jane and Judy were together in the church kitchen that morning, getting the food ready for the noon Prime Timers meeting. It was still a few hours away but Mary Jane had arrived early, much to the discomfort of Judy, who did her best not to show any outward signs of her uneasiness. By now, between her husband's prediction after Rhonda's death and the fact that the police had taken her car, Judy had little doubt that Mary Jane had killed Rhonda.

Pastor Shreaves came into the kitchen and, upon seeing Mary Jane, also tried to conceal his anxiety. She had been looking terrible lately, and today was no exception. Her skin was red and clammy, her forehead sweaty, the hair on her wig somehow more disheveled than usual. *She knows something's up,* Shreaves thought. *She knows her days are numbered.*

Immediately upon noticing the pastor, Mary Jane frowned and, in a confrontational tone, asked him about the phone call she had received the previous day from Paul Rose.

"What does he mean, I can't ever call you?" she asked.

Shreaves was finding it increasingly difficult with each passing day to keep his frustration with Mary Jane at bay. How many times did Mary Jane have to have this explained to her? How much clearer could it be? Although he had tried not to do anything that might excite or upset Mary Jane ever since learning she was a suspect in Rhonda's murder, Shreaves just couldn't take it anymore. Judy watched as Shreaves motioned for Mary Jane to step out of the kitchen.

Although the two moved into the large multipurpose room outside the kitchen, Judy could still hear their conversation through the large window connecting the two rooms.

According to Judy's recollection, the following conversation took place:

"Mary Jane," Shreaves said. "What part of Paul's phone call don't you understand? Do you understand that you cannot call me anymore?"

Obviously upset, Mary Jane asked, "Does that mean I can't be counseled by you or talk to you about the church?"

"You cannot try to get a hold of me in any way, shape, or form," Shreaves said. "You have to stay away from me and the phone."

Mary Jane paused a moment to take this in, then asked, "How about if it's not, like, a pastoral concern? If I just wanted to say hi or something?"

"No," Shreaves asserted. "You can't talk to me at all. Not until this is resolved. You just can't."

With that, Shreaves walked away and left Mary Jane standing in silence. After a few moments, Mary Jane slowly walked back into the kitchen, where Judy tried her best to pretend she hadn't heard a word.

"I . . . I don't feel good," Mary Jane said. "I'm going home."

"Okay," Judy said, masking her relief.

A few hours later, around noon, other members of the Prime Timers started arriving at the church. Shreaves returned and asked Judy where Mary Jane had gone. After Judy explained, Shreaves frowned, and it was obvious to Judy that he felt guilty for talking to Mary Jane the way he had.

"You'd better call her," Shreaves told Judy. "See if she's all right, and ask her to come back."

Judy called as instructed, and was secretly disappointed to hear that Mary Jane sounded much more cheery than she had a few hours ago. "You know, I'm feeling better," Mary Jane's voice came over the receiver. "I think I'm coming back."

By the time Mary Jane had arrived, everybody was already gathered and assembled for the Prime Timers meeting. Normally, the meetings included some sort of a guest speaker, but today they were just watching a video about the church and parsonage of Pastor Shreaves's parents. Judy watched Mary Jane as she joined the others and, when Mary Jane took her seat, Judy could barely contain her horror.

Mary Jane sat down in the vacant seat right next to Dorothy Smith.

Stumpo and Egan wanted to take Mary Jane as quietly as possible and avoid any excitement, which meant making the arrest without her brother around. They drove by the Fonder residence and saw that Ed's car was not in the driveway. With Mary Jane's car still impounded, she would have had to take her brother's car if she went out. The troopers drove to the church and, sure enough, Ed Fonder's green 1997 Honda was among the other vehicles in the parking lot.

They didn't want to barge into the church to arrest Mary

Jane, especially since they were unsure whether her brother was with her. So instead, Stumpo arranged for Trooper David Turnbow to wait in a marked police car in the parking lot of the Springfield municipal building, on Township Road just a half mile south of the church. Mary Jane had to pass the building on her way home and Stumpo wanted to make sure she was picked up by a marked car with sirens driven by somebody other than Stumpo or Egan. If she thought it was just a routine traffic stop, perhaps she'd act more calmly and not try anything unexpected.

Stumpo also arranged for Greg Langston to wait in an unmarked car across from the church parking lot and keep watch for Mary Jane. Stumpo and Egan waited elsewhere in a separate car for Langston's call. It was Stumpo's hope to pull Mary Jane over with as little drama as possible. He couldn't help but recall the famous televised images of the slow-speed O. J. Simpson chase, with dozens of police cars following his white Ford Bronco down the California highway. Such an incident was the last thing Stumpo wanted.

However, for all of Stumpo's efforts, the police cars didn't exactly go unnoticed. As Pastor Shreaves left the church that early afternoon to attend a pastoral visit at St. Luke's Hospital, he noticed Langston sitting in the unmarked car across the street. Although he recognized the detective, Shreaves didn't think much of it.

Other church parishioners, however, took greater notice of the police. Despite Stumpo's wish that Turnbow wait alone at the municipal building, several other marked state police cars had parked there as well. Under the guise of providing additional backup, the troopers really just wanted to be part of the excitement of the biggest arrest the area had seen in years.

All the cars, however, attracted the attention of Reta Bieber after she left the Prime Timers meeting early. Bieber, who also played organ for the nearby St. John's United Church of Christ, was on her way there to practice when she saw the police cars gathered together. Much to the surprise of the troopers, she pulled over right next to them and casually asked, "Are there any problems, officers?" The troopers shook their heads no, that they were just parking there that afternoon, and Bieber went on her way.

After some time had passed and the Prime Timers meeting ended, members started leaving the church and pulling out of the parking lot. Langston watched carefully, waiting for Mary Jane to step outside, but even after most of the cars were gone, she was nowhere to be seen and the green Honda sat undisturbed. Minutes passed, then a half hour, then an hour, and still she did not emerge. Stumpo and Egan began to feel restless.

Where is she? Stumpo thought.

Judy watched as Dorothy Smith left the church after the Prime Timers meeting, her sympathy for the woman matched by her shock that Mary Jane would have the audacity to sit next to her after all she had done to the Smiths. *She talked to her like it was nothing,* Judy thought. *I don't see how you can do that. I think she has two personalities or something.*

As Dorothy and the others left, Mary Jane stayed behind with Judy, Sue Brunner, and Carol Gregory. She casually mentioned to Sue that she had baked a pie for the Smiths and brought it to them a few weeks ago.

"Oh, Mary Jane, that's so nice," Sue said.

"I know that John really likes blueberry pie," Mary Jane said with a nod, referring to Sue's husband, John Brunner. "I saved some blueberries, so when I get home today, I'm going to make him a blueberry pie and bring it to him."

Over the next several minutes, Mary Jane lingered in the church long after almost everybody else had gone. At first she busied herself with idle work in the kitchen but, after a while, she dropped all pretext of doing anything productive, and was simply standing around. Judy, Sue, and Carol were waiting politely for her to leave so they could lock up, but when time passed and Mary Jane hadn't budged, Carol said, "Well, I'm just going to go outside because I notice some of those plants outside have to be trimmed."

They exited the side door to the parking lot expecting

Mary Jane to follow, but instead she simply nodded and stayed behind, as if she were hesitant to leave the building. The three women didn't understand, but stepped outside and waited, expecting Mary Jane to eventually follow. Several long minutes passed as Judy, Sue and Carol pretended to tend to the flowers, but Mary Jane still hadn't come out. Finally, Sue walked back inside and called, "Mary Jane, we're all leaving."

Finally, with what appeared to be a great effort, Mary Jane sighed and followed Sue outside to the parking lot. As Carol and Sue dispersed to their cars, Judy stayed behind to lock the door behind her. As Judy turned toward the parking lot, Mary Jane suddenly wrapped her arms around Judy in an unexpected, awkward hug. Internally, Judy cringed, but she voiced no objection as Mary Jane embraced her.

Less than a half mile away, Stumpo's radio squeaked to life as Langston called to report that Mary Jane was coming out to the car, and her brother was nowhere to be seen. *Finally,* Stumpo thought as he radioed Turnbow to make the arrest.

Unfortunately, it was reported back to him, another trooper car had just been arriving to relieve Turnbow, so Stumpo's hope for having just one marked police car waiting for Mary Jane was already shot.

Oh well, too late to worry about that now, he thought as he pulled out and headed toward Township Road.

As Stumpo and Egan approached, they could see their attempt at discretion had failed more miserably than they expected. All the police vehicles in the municipal lot made it look like some sort of massive police sting, Stumpo thought. Fortunately, it appeared Turnbow had pulled over Mary Jane without incident just a few hundred yards away.

Stumpo brought his car to a halt just behind Turnbow's vehicle, then he and Egan stepped outside and slowly walked toward Mary Jane's front window. They found her sitting there silently with both hands in the purse on her lap, although it became immediately clear that she was not reaching for any kind of weapon.

"Oh, hi," Mary Jane said, as if she had simply run into Stumpo and Egan at the supermarket.

"Hi, Mary Jane, how are you?" Stumpo asked.

"Oh, I'm okay," she casually responded.

Stumpo politely asked if Mary Jane would come down to the station with them to discuss the investigation, but she replied that she would rather just go home and speak to her brother and an attorney. Stumpo, more sternly this time, told her they could not let her leave, and a look of understanding crept across Mary Jane's face. Stumpo asked her to step out of the car.

"I had a feeling you guys would be coming today," Mary Jane said. Motioning toward her purse, she added, "I was going to go home and put some underwear in a bag. I thought you would have come over to the house."

When Stumpo asked why Mary Jane thought that, she shrugged and replied, "You took my car. You could take my house."

Stumpo informed Mary Jane that she was under arrest for the murder of Rhonda Smith, and read her the Miranda rights as he clamped his handcuffs onto her wrists. As he led her toward their unmarked police car, Stumpo felt a sense of relief, but only the slightest bit. There was still so much preparation, so much work to do, and he knew he would not feel at ease until a favorable result was rendered at her trial.

As Stumpo guided Mary Jane into the backseat of their unmarked car, she mumbled something that the trooper couldn't make out. He and Egan took their seats in the front and, after they had started the car, Mary Jane said, "I didn't do nothing to that sweet girl. I didn't hurt that girl." It was the only sound she made for the rest of the trip back to the Dublin barracks. For the first time since they had first spoken to her before her choir practice about two months earlier, there was an uncharacteristic silence among the three.

CHAPTER 29

It was around quarter after three when Stumpo and Egan led Mary Jane through the Dublin station into the holding room. For liability reasons, there was no cell at the barracks, so they asked her to sit on a metal bench against one side of the stark room. After taking off her handcuffs, Stumpo asked her to remove her shoes, jacket, and jewelry. Mary Jane did so with a polite smile, showing no outward signs of fear or hostility. It seemed to Egan that she was still putting on an act that, despite where she was and what she was accused of, she was still a kind, normal lady.

Stumpo placed a handcuff back onto Mary Jane's left wrist and secured the other to a post next to the bench. Egan asked Trooper Gregg Dietz to stay behind to monitor Mary Jane while they finished the necessary paperwork. Dietz had been with the state police for over fourteen years, spending most of his career in the Gettysburg area before he was moved to Dublin in October, only three months before Rhonda was shot. Slim but fit, the good-looking trooper had close-cropped brown hair and looked younger than his forty years.

Normally, the task of babysitting a suspect would fall to someone with less experience than Dietz, but the troopers wanted someone they could trust there in case Mary Jane started to talk.

They couldn't question her without her attorney, of course,

but if Mary Jane were to say anything unsolicited, the police
wanted to be sure they got every word of it down on paper.
Mary Jane had been advised of her rights and knew anything she said could be used against her in court. Under
normal circumstances, it would be highly unlikely that a
suspect in this situation would have much at all to say, but
they were well aware of Mary Jane's tendency to ramble and
wanted to be prepared.

Dietz took a seat across the room from Mary Jane, holding
in his lap a police report for an unrelated case. Pen in hand,
Dietz started working on the report, waiting to see if Mary Jane
would say anything. For the next ten minutes, however, they sat
in complete silence, with Mary Jane showing no visible emotion whatsoever. At one point, Mary Jane started fiddling with
the handcuff on her left wrist, and Dietz asked whether it was
too tight, but she politely replied that it was fine.

After another five minutes of complete silence, Mary
Jane bent down to adjust her socks, which Dietz noticed had
numerous holes in them.

"These socks need mending," Mary Jane said simply.
Dietz responded with an affirmative nod of the head.

Mary Jane looked Dietz directly in his eyes and mumbled something about her brother. When the trooper apolo-
gized and said he hadn't heard her, she said, "My brother, he
is at home and he needs the car to go to Greek class at the
church. You know, he goes to New Jersey an awful lot."

Dietz nodded and said, "I know your brother goes to
church in New Jersey. I've spoken with him before."

For the next few, long minutes, Mary Jane was silent once
again. Then, all at once, it was as if a light switch had been
flipped on. She was chatting with Dietz as if she had known
him for years, her words coming quickly and crammed together, as if she didn't have nearly enough time to say everything she hoped to say.

"It is amazing what they are doing to me today," she said.
"They think I did something to this girl. I didn't do anything
to her."

Dietz moved aside the police report he was working on

and began to take notes about what Mary Jane was saying. He responded to her by nodding his head up and down, and Mary Jane continued.

"I don't know what they found in my car," she said. "You know, they took my car."

It quickly became clear to Dietz that everything he had heard about Mary Jane, from her extreme chattiness to her bizarre demeanor, was absolutely true. Mary Jane changed topics no less than three times over the next sixty seconds, describing the house she shared with her brother, her love for Trinity Evangelical and the topic of the Prime Timers meeting she had just attended.

She looked down at her shabby socks and said, a bit of annoyance in her voice, "Those guys took my car and it has my laundry in it. We are Laundromat people. We go to the Laundromat with lunch. It is a fun day. I was ready for a real nice day last Wednesday."

Dietz wrote down every word Mary Jane said. Just when he thought it couldn't get any more unusual, she added, "Oh well, I have enough underwear at home. . . ."

As Egan continued working on Mary Jane's paperwork, Stumpo stepped away to search Mary Jane's purse for contraband. There would clearly be no bail in this case, so her belongings would have to be secured at the prison after Mary Jane was incarcerated. He found nothing unusual or dangerous: just her wallet, a few odds and ends, and what appeared to be a small black checkbook.

Stumpo flipped the book open, and immediately, he spotted Rhonda Smith's name.

It was not a checkbook at all, but rather an eighteen-month pocket calendar. Stumpo had coincidentally opened the page to January 2008, the very month of Rhonda's death. At the top of the page was an innocuous photo of a Springer Spaniel, his rear facing upward as he rested his head and front legs on the ground.

Several of the calendar's date blocks were filled with the sloppy scribbling Stumpo recognized to be Mary Jane's handwriting. Under January 17 were the words "Rhonda's BDAY," and sprawled from January 23 to the 26th were the words, "Someone called from church to tell me of incident." Under February 25, the day of Stumpo and Egan's four-hour interview with Mary Jane, were the words, "Dublin S.P., They Say They HV Wig, TRiED To MK ME CONFES." The writing there appeared particularly sloppy, as if they had been written with a sense of urgency and anger, especially the item about the wig, which was circled.

But Stumpo's eyes were immediately drawn to January 23, the day of Rhonda's murder. In big letters, above a circled notation about Mary Jane's hairdresser appointment, Mary Jane had written the words "Rhonda MURDered."

The notation alone struck Stumpo as unusual. He was positive that he could go through the day planners of every other church member and not find any such note written on that date. *I don't see an innocent person taking those notes,* he thought.

Stumpo immediately closed the planner, put it back in the purse and took the purse to be secured for the prison. He didn't want to read a single word more until he had obtained a search warrant. The last thing he needed was for Mary Jane's lawyer to have the evidence thrown out on allegations of an improper search and seizure.

Mary Jane had been silent for the last five minutes, but soon she was at it again.

"I know Rhonda's car is here," she said, looking up directly at Dietz. "I was looking for it when I was coming in."

Dietz looked back at her and said nothing.

"You know, for the investigation," she continued.

"I don't know what you mean," Dietz said.

Mary Jane said she expected Rhonda's car had been impounded to the police station, which led her into a long tangent about a time in 1976 when she visited Philadelphia and her car was impounded. Dietz took it all in, writing down every jumbled, seemingly irrelevant word.

One of his fellow officers passed by in the hallway and

glanced into the room. He smirked at Dietz, silently and jokingly mocking the trooper for having to sit there and babysit this seemingly crazy old woman. Although Dietz was inwardly a bit annoyed with the trooper and concerned that the interruption might silence Mary Jane, Dietz simply smiled in response as the trooper in the hall walked away.

The smile seemed to stir something in Mary Jane, who said to Dietz in a joking tone, "You are bright eyed and bushy tailed!"

Hiding his confusion, Dietz responded simply, "I will take that as a compliment."

"Please do," Mary Jane replied. Then, with a laugh, she added, "I guess I'm doing all right. I haven't fallen over yet."

Dietz had no idea what to make of the comment, but asked that if Mary Jane felt she was about to fall down, she warn him. Another few minutes of silence followed, but soon Mary Jane was talking again, indiscriminately switching from topic to topic at a jarring pace. She spoke again about her brother, how often he drove back and forth from New Jersey, how messy their house was. She described her arthritis and back pain, how much she hated to live alone, how she and her brother took care of each other.

Throughout the one-sided conversation, Mary Jane remained completely calm and unemotional, as if she were simply speaking with a friend she had known for years. Dietz had known in advance of Mary Jane's chattiness, but still couldn't help but be surprised by the tone.

She knows why she's here, she knows she's under arrest, Dietz thought. *Yet she's chatting like I'm just the guy sitting next to her on the bus.*

Soon, her conversation turned to the church itself and, in particular, Pastor Shreaves.

"You know, he encouraged me to join the choir," she said. "So sad. I regret joining the choir, with Rhonda being murdered, me in having a good time. I was so optimistic, cruising all over the place, getting a kick out of singing, looking at the clouds, talking to people. You know, Wednesday was choir rehearsal. I spent a lot of time at church over the holidays."

Mary Jane abruptly stopped talking and just started staring at Dietz. Dietz said nothing, simply waiting for Mary Jane to act, even as an awkward ten, twenty, thirty seconds passed and she continued her staring. And then, just as suddenly, she said, "You know, I like talking to you, always smiling and laughing," and she entered into a short, uncontrolled laughing spell.

It was unlike anything Dietz had ever seen in a suspect before. Again, he decided to say nothing and simply wait for Mary Jane to stop laughing. Eventually, she did, and continued speaking.

"Today, I was at least glad to see people at the church. The last fourteen years . . ." she sighed, then continued. "That is my family. Fourteen years. All the problems I had with my pop. You know, he left and is missing."

Dietz shook his head no.

"I was home to have an operation, but we were doing fine," she said. "We got along pretty well, until a couple of cousins stopped by on a hit-and-run visit."

Mary Jane's tone remained neutral and unemotional just as it had been since she began talking, but Dietz could tell by the way she described the visit that the matter was a sore subject for her. He nodded in an affirmative manner, and she once again started to simply stare at Dietz. It was no less awkward than a moment ago, only this time, there was no laughing, no smile from Mary Jane.

"They just showed up from Hatboro," she said. "They were old women, and they brought my pop a cake, and they just started getting him worked up. They came with this big surprise, it was late afternoon, and they pushed this cake at him and began lambasting me about how I don't treat him right and I never do anything for him and we never go anywhere."

Mary Jane was talking a bit faster now. "My father liked to stay at home, he liked to work around the house. They criticized me and stayed for about twenty minutes. I only wanted to do nice for him. They set my father off. I remember seeing his eyes, they got as big as saucers and he changed after that. They made him that way."

Hoping to keep Mary Jane talking, Dietz said, "Is that right? I'm sorry to hear that."

"My cousins, they are old and dead now," Mary Jane said, matter-of-factly. "His personality changed. He was angry and Pop slammed the door and it went dead quiet like you could hear a pin drop. He went from happy to a solemn, quiet guy. This went on for about two or three weeks. I couldn't reach that damn brother. His sleeping patterns changed. He used to stay up all night and sleep in late."

Mary Jane touched her fingers to her throat, then said, "I am getting dry." She took a sip from a water bottle Egan had brought her earlier, then started speaking again.

"I just accepted it. He wasn't angry at me, just because . . ." she mumbled a few things, then continued. "A couple of weeks later, I heard him walking down the hallway to get the morning paper as usual. I got up and didn't see him. Went outside, and the dog was there. Because he was a missing person, I called Chief Bell and the state police. I checked all around and I was heartbroken. Never, never found my dad. Talked to the neighbors. Where would an eighty-year-old go?"

Mary Jane's thought process seemed to be growing more fractured, less focused. She spoke in spurts of sentence fragments, and her voice trailed off until she stopped speaking altogether. Then, suddenly, she lifted her eyes to meet those of Dietz.

"I was a suspect," she said. "They feel . . ."

Dietz stared back at Mary Jane, returning her gaze and waiting desperately to hear what she would say next. It was unbelievable to him that Mary Jane had brought up her father in the first place, without any prodding. And now, although Dietz had absolutely no expectation that Mary Jane might make a confession, it seemed she might be on the verge of one.

"Feel . . . feel sorry for her. She was popular, attractive, well liked." Dietz realized that suddenly, somehow, Mary Jane had switched topics altogether. She was no longer speaking about her father at all, but rather of Rhonda Smith.

"Never got to know her," she said. "I am older than everyone in the choir. Rhonda, the girl that was murdered, her mother is not much older than me. You know, I visited her mom and dad?"

Dietz shook his head no.

"I am depressed about this, what a terrible thing," Mary Jane said. "At Easter breakfast, I sat down at their table at church. I was not chowing down. They had amazing food, anything you could want."

Just like that, it was over. That growing agitation Dietz had detected since Mary Jane brought up her cousins had subsided, and she was talking about her visit to the church as if she was talking with a friend or fellow parishioner. Any hope for a confession had completely dissipated.

"I probably would have chowed down," Dietz said, if only to keep the conversation moving.

"I don't chow down like I used to, not much of an appetite," she said. After a short period of silence, she added, "It was a beautiful, sunny day. I got my tray and started to eat, and got dizzy. You know, my diabetes. I went home and took some medicine and back. Struck me as funny. I . . ."

Mary Jane stopped mid-thought, and suddenly, inexplicably, she was talking about her father again. ". . . never found him. I had lots of problems with the investigation. There wasn't any evidence."

Mary Jane's voice became very low, lower than at any point since she was brought into the room, and she appeared to be on the verge of crying, but no tears came. She stared at Dietz and started rubbing the handcuff on her left wrist.

"Now, it looks like I am a suspect," she said.

Before Dietz could reply, Mary Jane returned to the subject of her father, and described the investigation. She described Officer Triol's attempts to get her to confess, a topic that seemed to anger her.

"Office Triol tried to break me down, questioned me. She would check on me weekly. She read me my Miranda act in my HOUSE," she said, loudly pronouncing the final word. "I broke down and threw her out. I would have liked not to be questioned in my house. If it was at her station, I would have gone."

After some quiet, mostly incoherent mumbling, Mary Jane added, "I had a lousy life. Nothing to live for."

Suddenly, she looked back into Dietz's eyes. Throughout the entire conversation, Mary Jane had shown no outward sign of emotion. But now, there was a clear expression of anger on her face, and it was directed straight at Dietz.

"You have a lot to talk to me about, oh YEAH," she said, drawing out and particularly emphasizing the final phrase.

It was as if Mary Jane had realized for the first time that she was talking to a police officer, and what the ramifications of that could mean for her. Before Dietz could respond, Trooper Patrick McGuire entered the room and announced it was time for Mary Jane to be processed. As McGuire removed the handcuff from the post, Mary Jane looked angrily at Dietz and motioned toward his notebook, "You done taking notes?"

Dietz didn't know what to say, so he said nothing as McGuire led Mary Jane out of the room.

After Stumpo snapped a photo of Mary Jane for her criminal file, he realized she was still wearing her wig. He thought perhaps it would be best to get a photo without the wig, and asked Mary Jane to remove it.

She politely obliged, removing it from her head to reveal a messy, unwashed mass of hair that, to Stumpo, looked exactly the same as if she was still wearing the wig.

Stumpo took another photo and suppressed an urge to shake his head at the oddity that was Mary Jane Fonder. When he was finished, he led her to a seat in the processing room, where she was fingerprinted. It was around quarter to five when they were finished, and Mary Jane's left wrist was once again handcuffed to the wall while she remained seated. Dietz, who was once again asked to monitor Mary Jane, stood watching as Egan brought a copy of the criminal complaint and affidavit for her to read.

After leafing through the first few pages of the documents, Mary Jane started shaking her head and mumbling things like, "No, not me." After reading a few more pages, she threw them down on the table next to her and simply sat there, staring at Egan and Dietz. Gone were any traces of the sweet, kind old lady Egan had seen when they arrested her a few hours earlier, or the laughing, almost flirty attitude she had initially exhibited to Dietz in the holding room. They were replaced with an angry scowl, the look of a woman who no longer had to hide her irritation.

After about sixty seconds of staring at the two men, Mary Jane picked up the documents again. "I'll read through this and see what you have to say," she said.

As she continued to read through the papers, her demeanor grew angrier and angrier.

"That's pathetic, I am so disgusted with what he said to you," Mary Jane said. "If you could see his face. What a phony! Why in the name of God would he encourage me?"

At first, the two troopers didn't know whom she was referring to, but it became all too clear in just a moment.

"I cared for him, my dear friend *Greg*," she said, drawing out his name in a very sarcastic tone. "He is not at all what I thought. I did not make that phone call to him, untrue, absolutely untrue! I am telling you it is not true."

Mary Jane's voice was growing louder and louder with every word. "I am very disappointed at the pastor. He is so, why, disgraceful! How could he? Went to the church unannounced. That . . . that . . . cad!"

Mary Jane continued reading, her anger softening a bit, but she occasionally muttered things like, "absolutely revolting," "he is a liar," "impossible," and "I am heartbroken." At one point, Mary Jane angrily pointed at the information about Stumpo calling her former coworkers at Denny's. "I TOLD YOU THAT, about the restaurant!" Mary Jane almost shouted.

Egan had heard about Mary Jane's earlier statements to Dietz, of course, but he was still surprised. Suspects simply did not talk this way immediately after their arrest, at least not during their processing. Eventually, her anger returned to the pastor. *This is helpful,* Egan noted to himself. Anything she had to say now would only strengthen their case about the strong feelings she had for Shreaves. The motive that led her to commit murder.

"This is revolting. Just today . . ." she said, but failed to finish the thought. "Make me think he likes me. He is a chameleon, two faced."

She looked up at Dietz and said, "Sorry for the bad word." Dietz didn't know what word she was referring to, but shook his head in an affirmative anyway. Egan suppressed the urge to roll his eyes, recognizing the tactic of Mary Jane's from his interview with her.

"I will be happy to speak with the attorney about the pastor," Mary Jane continued. "He offered to have me come in for Sunday School classes. He loves to talk to me. This is revolting!

"That phony, fake, bullshitter. How dare he? Encourage *me* to come to service," she said, sarcastically emphasizing her words again. "I loved having him at service. He liked me. Encouraging me to come. That phony!"

Next, she turned to the page about the discovery of her gun in Lake Nockamixon, and her demeanor changed altogether. Egan was reminded of the bombshell about the wig Stumpo dropped on her during their four-hour interview. It was clearly something she hadn't expected at the time, and she had appeared to be processing the information even as she continued speaking. She was doing the same now.

"Oh my God, they found my gun," she said. "It . . . is . . . threw away years ago. How amazing. Hmmm. I didn't think you would locate it, I didn't think you would ever find it . . ."

She was still keeping up the act, Egan thought, still pretending she had thrown the gun away fourteen years ago, even though it was in near-perfect condition when it was discovered by the lake.

"My God," Mary Jane said, acting surprised. "Somebody used that gun! Oh my gosh!"

Egan couldn't help but feel a bit surprised. Confronted with proof that her gun killed Rhonda, Mary Jane had already started spinning a new story altogether: that fourteen years after she disposed of the gun, somebody had somehow found it and committed the murder with it.

"Well, I can see why you called me in," Mary Jane said.

"That it was from my gun, that is terrible. Thought it hit the water. 1994. I feel horrible. Someone else used my gun. I wouldn't hit that girl. Oh that pastor. Sorry it was my gun. I didn't use . . .

"Bob," she said, looking into Egan's eyes. "Bob, I am in terrible shape."

Egan nodded.

"There are two dead people at the church," Mary Jane said.

Egan and Dietz looked at each other, puzzled at first, but soon Egan understood. Mary Jane was referring to herself. She was the second victim: an innocent woman accused of a crime she didn't commit, who was facing the prospect of life in prison because her gun had been used by somebody else. Egan felt disgusted that Mary Jane would compare herself to Rhonda in such a way.

For the next several minutes, Mary Jane continued to speak in short, disconnected bursts of thought, as she had earlier with Dietz after the memory of her cousins caused her such distress.

"I am not a murderer." "Killed poor Rhonda Smith." "Just horrible, doesn't look good for me." "I wish I would have stayed away from the church, terrible thing." "I am hurting like crazy." "Hook, line and sinker." "I had no reason to attack that girl." "He is a liar." "Can't deny it was used on Rhonda. Unbelievable." "God, I am glad you found my gun, just not under the circumstances." "Okay, oh my God, how the hell am I going to get out of this?"

"It is a bitch!" Mary Jane blurted out suddenly, then laughed out loud. "Something from Neverland coming to get me. I got the Devil crawling on me. Most unfortunate."

Egan and Dietz said nothing. It was like nothing they had ever heard from a suspect before.

After a brief pause, Mary Jane said, "Okay, well guys, all right. I guess go see a judge?"

Egan explained that she was about to be arraigned before Magistrate District Judge Robert Schnell Jr. in Doylestown, but that given the nature of her alleged crime, she would not be entitled to bail. Mary Jane nodded that she understood.

"I know where I will be living," she said. "How long I don't know. I will have to try and convince a jury. Somebody had my gun. That pastor . . . what a cad."

She continued to mutter things about Shreaves, although Dietz was finding her harder and harder to follow.

"The man was all over me," she said. "Was a fan of women as women go. A ladies' man. Didn't take to him very much. Didn't push myself to see him. He didn't impress me. Very tall, unusually tall. Not that tall matters."

She put up a hand and added, "I can't call him a friend. He was interested in me. Because Rhonda got shot. He was friendly with both of us. Me and her were having a good time with him. Maybe he thought I did something. Just today . . ."

Mary Jane stopped. When she didn't continue, Egan asked her if she had any questions regarding the affidavit. She shook her head no. And, to the troopers' amazement, she still wasn't finished talking.

"I am sorry whoever found it used it on Rhonda," she said. "I couldn't figure out what direction my life was going the last couple of weeks. Hmmm. Always friendly with him. He always had a good time. We all want to come to a conclusion on who killed that woman."

Stumpo entered the processing room and announced that Judge Schnell was ready for Mary Jane. She finally stopped talking as Stumpo and Egan brought her out to a patrol car and left the Dublin barracks. Mary Jane, once again, sat uncharacteristically silent in the backseat. As they arrived in Doylestown, Stumpo pulled the car over into the Moravian Pottery & Tile Works parking lot, where they met another patrol car that was going to accompany them to the arraignment.

Mary Jane looked out the car window and said, "Look at the green grass. I guess I should get a good look at it. I may never see green grass again."

After a brief arraignment devoid of any press attention, Mary Jane Fonder was ordered to be held without bail and remanded to the Bucks County Correctional Facility.

CHAPTER 30

That afternoon, Rosalie Schnell got a phone call from Kathy, her friend from the nearby borough of Coopersburg. Kathy often liked to call for idle gossip or chit-chat, but Rosalie was caught completely off guard by what her friend had to share today.

"Did you hear the news?" Kathy asked. "You had a real experience in your area!"

"No," Rosalie replied. "I didn't watch the news."

"Isn't your neighbor's last name Fonder?" Kathy asked.

"Yeah . . ." Rosalie responded, startled.

"Mary Jane Fonder murdered somebody!"

Rosalie didn't respond. She just stood there, her hand shaking as she grasped the receiver, in such a state of shock that Kathy had to call out her name repeatedly before she could snap out of it.

Similar waves of shock would soon resonate throughout the whole Bucks County region. The arrest of Mary Jane Fonder would be met with feelings of horror, fascination, and incredulity from almost the entire population. Judy Zellner, like Rosalie, first learned of the arrest from a phone call, when her daughter called and instructed her to turn the news on right away.

"The defendant in this case had very strong feelings for the pastor in the church," Bucks County District Attorney

Michelle Henry was saying at a press conference. "She was jealous of the fact that the victim was getting attention from the pastor."

As Judy watched, her body began to shake uncontrollably. She had known for weeks, of course, that Mary Jane was under suspicion, but after hearing the words from the district attorney's mouth, Judy found herself overcome with fear and disgust, thinking back to the hug Mary Jane had given her earlier in the day in the church parking lot.

Oh my God, Judy thought. *I was with her all morning.*

Soon, Judy was on the phone with Sue Brunner, whose feelings were much the same as Judy's, although her first reaction to the arrest was one of humor: Sue laughed and said to her husband, "I'm sorry you didn't get your pie," a reference to the blueberries Mary Jane had mentioned having saved some earlier in the day.

But John Brunner found little humor in the situation. Despite everything, despite Mary Jane's eccentricities and all the rumors that had been flying about her father, the Brunners couldn't believe that Mary Jane could resort to such ghastly violence. John couldn't help but remember all the times Mary Jane would come over to their house, often uninvited, and leave cards, notes, food, and other gifts for him. Sometimes, she'd just let herself into their home without even knocking, including one instance when John was in bed asleep.

All the gifts and visits had caused the Brunners to believe Mary Jane harbored a little crush on John, something they had viewed as harmless and even a bit comical in the past. Now, the thought of it was nothing short of terrifying, especially considering the apparent jealousy toward Rhonda that authorities claimed drove Mary Jane to murder.

It could have been Sue, John thought to himself. *Sue could be the dead one.*

Later, Sue also recalled that she had spoken with Mary Jane just the day before her arrest, and Mary Jane had claimed she was feeling "bad vibes." Mary Jane quickly ended the brief conversation after that, and at the time it had seemed mostly insignificant to Sue. Now, it seemed downright eerie.

Within minutes of the announcement of Mary Jane's arrest, scores of news vans and reporters started swarming Springfield Township and its neighboring towns, both from the local media outlets and the larger Philadelphia market. The sudden explosion of attention was completely foreign to the quiet rural neighborhood, and not entirely welcome. The story of Rhonda Smith's murder—an innocent woman slain in the rural parish of Anytown, USA—had already been fascinating to the press. Now, the addition of an oddball elderly murderess and a twisted love triangle—however one-sided—made the story downright irresistible to them.

Although the affidavit Stumpo and Egan painstakingly prepared laid out the case in great detail, Dave Zellis still found himself fielding call after call from reporters anxious to learn more about Mary Jane's frame of mind. (His response: "How about if we leave that to a courtroom?") In the meantime, reporters were out in droves, knocking on doors, and visiting local businesses. Nobody answered at the Fonder residence, but there was no shortage of people willing to discuss the case and the unusual defendant.

"She had a horrible personality," Vera Lalli, owner of the favorite local spot Vera's Country Cafe, told a reporter. Both Mary Jane and Rhonda were frequent visitors and, although she described Rhonda as bubbly and cheerful, she painted a portrait of Mary Jane as a grumpy old lady. "I guess she was a sad individual," Lalli said. "She seemed to be kind of a loner."

Some said the arrest came as absolutely no surprise at all. Michael MacHukas, the Berks County man who Mary Jane had taken to court back in 1994, told his wife about the arrest, and she immediately broke down crying. They remembered how fanatical Mary Jane had appeared when she talked about the "very sacred area" of trees and they had the distinct feeling that she was perfectly capable of murder.

"She was a real nutcase, man," MacHukas later told a reporter from *The Morning Call*, the Allentown-based newspaper.

Others were more surprised that the seemingly kind old lady from their neighborhood would be capable of such a crime. Vera Deacon, the Trinity Evangelical parish nurse, could barely contain her shock when approached by *The Morning Call* for a comment: "I never saw any indication of any problem. It's amazing. It's amazing that it occurred in our church, and it's amazing that one of our members is now charged with it."

Todd Slotter, who lived not far down the street from Mary Jane on Winding Road, told the press she was always quick to say hello, and attended funeral services for his relatives, even when she didn't know them particularly well. Slotter admitted he didn't know much about Mary Jane, but told reporters, "It's not fair to me to pass on my own judgments because a lot of people have their own ideas."

Jim and Dorothy Smith had received a call from police early that morning, letting them know an arrest was pending, but they had no idea who the suspect was until they watched it on the news later, along with everybody else. And, like everybody else, they were in shock. This was the same woman who brought them a pie in their time of grieving. The same woman who they had given two pairs of Rhonda's shoes to as a gift, a thought that now filled them both with disgust. Dorothy reflected on the fact that, just a few short hours ago, she was sitting next to Mary Jane at the Prime Timers club.

"I was hoping they'd find somebody," Dorothy said. "I never expected she'd be sitting right next to me."

The whole idea of it was especially hard to accept because they barely knew Mary Jane, and to their knowledge, Rhonda had only ever talked to her a handful of times in passing. They listened to the news of Mary Jane's alleged motive for the shooting, but it made no sense to them. Jealousy? Feelings for the pastor? How could Mary Jane have believed their daughter had anything to do with any of this?

"I just wish she had said something to Rhonda," Jim said that day. "Instead of doing this, if she'd just said something to her. Rhonda would have helped her. That's how she was."

Nevertheless, the Smiths were relieved that somebody

had finally been arrested, and knew they were lucky that the gun had been stumbled upon the way it was; Jim made a mental note to give $100 to Garrett Sylsberry if he ever got to meet the boy. Gary Smith called his parents the day of the arrest and expressed shock at one particular detail he gleamed from the news reports: that the gun was found in Lake Nockamixon. The very same lake where Jim would often take his children for fishing trips.

"Can you believe it?" Gary said. "After all this time, can you believe the lake came back to reward us?"

Throngs of reporters knocked on the Smiths' door that afternoon, and Jim and Dorothy politely took each one into their house and spoke to them, one after the other. Jim sat in his favorite living room chair, next to a table with framed photos of Rhonda, and proudly shared with each reporter the four-page letter Rhonda had written to him the Easter before she died, thanking him for helping her get through her bipolar disorder.

When asked how he felt about Mary Jane, Jim refused to discuss it, insisting he would wait for the courts to handle that matter. "We can never have Rhonda back anyway, so I don't want to judge anybody." When one reporter expressed that this must be a difficult day for the family, Jim shook his head no. For months, he had been enduring speculation and gossip that Rhonda had committed suicide, something he knew was impossible. After everything she had overcome in her life, he knew his daughter hadn't killed herself, and now at last everybody else knew it as well.

"You can see how good I feel on my face," he said to the reporter. "You know why? Because she's free. She lost her life, but she didn't lose her name."

As reporters spoke to the Smiths, others were calling practically everybody involved in the Mary Jane Fonder case. Doug Sylsberry fielded several calls at his Quakertown home, but was careful to protect Garrett from the limelight and did not let anyone speak to his son. The press seemed to particularly love the detail of the eight-year-old boy finding the gun, and he had already heard his name mentioned several times on the television broadcasts.

"You're a real celebrity now!" his mother said to him, to which Garrett simply shrugged in response.

Doug similarly downplayed their role in Mary Jane's arrest. "We just wanted to do the right thing as any citizen should," he said during one telephone interview. As he explained where and how the gun had been found, Doug took a few moments to point out that this crime should not be reflective of all gun owners.

"I'm proud of my Second Amendment rights," he told *The Express-Times,* the Easton-based newspaper. "It's important everyone does what they can to keep gun crime down so people who enjoy their rights can enjoy them for a long time to come."

Meanwhile, Paul Rose served as the press spokesman for Trinity Evangelical Lutheran Church with the help of Robert Fisher, an assistant to the bishop in the Southeastern Pennsylvania Synod. Paul and Robert stood in the church parking lot while a seemingly endless stream of reporters and news vans pulled in to speak with him, or snap photos and record video of the two men or the church itself.

It was not a pleasant experience for Paul, who quickly grew tired of answering the same questions over and over, and of the barely veiled attempts by reporters to elicit some sort of shocked quote or sound bite from him.

It's either this, or paying my taxes back home, he thought. *I think I'd rather be paying my taxes.*

Paul was distrustful of how the press might spin the story. *They'll find three words to fit together to say whatever they want to say,* he thought. Particularly due to Mary Jane's feelings for Shreaves, Paul feared they would portray the murder as some sort of a love triangle, and that people might wrongly conclude that Shreaves was involved with Rhonda, or Mary Jane, or both.

Paul tried to convey to the reporters that this was not only a tragedy, but also a test for the entire church congregation, an opportunity for them to respond like Christians in the face of a terrible tragedy.

"We are going to rise above this," Paul told several reporters. "We will gather together in Christian fellowship and remind ourselves that our faith will get us through this."

Robert pledged to *The Morning Call* that the synod would do whatever it could to get the community through this period. "This is going to be a difficult time," he said. "We are saddened and perplexed that this kind of violence occurs within the church family."

But Paul didn't want to portray Mary Jane as a complete monster in all of this. After all, she had been with the church for nearly fifteen years, and had always seemed like a happy and friendly person, despite her obvious peculiarities. At the very least, she was entitled to her rights of due process just like anybody else, Paul felt. She deserved to be considered innocent until proven guilty.

Paul made sure to point out some of the good things Mary Jane had done for the church over the years, like the time she made paintings of the church on old stone slates when the steeple was replaced a few years earlier. After all, he had known Mary Jane for twelve years, and barely ever got to know Rhonda, who participated in activities at the church that Paul was less involved with.

"You'd never think she'd do something like this," Paul said of Mary Jane. "She seemed so harmless." Stressing that he meant no disrespect toward Rhonda, he added about Mary Jane, "The woman's been caught, but she hadn't been convicted. So for all we know, she's innocent."

CHAPTER 31

For the most part, Pastor Gregory Shreaves himself avoided the many press inquiries directed at him, although he did speak briefly to *The Philadelphia Inquirer,* to whom he expressed his disbelief at Mary Jane's arrest.

"Not in my wildest dreams, no one in the congregation could imagine that it could have led to this," he told the paper. When asked how he would lead the congregation through this time, he responded, "I'm going to have to just pray that I'll be given the right words to say."

But, of course, Shreaves had known for weeks that the police were focusing their efforts on Mary Jane, and he had long since grown convinced she was the one who killed Rhonda. Although the despair he voiced to the *Inquirer* was genuine, the single strongest emotion Shreaves felt following the arrest was relief. He no longer had to live in fear that Mary Jane would lash out and hurt him or someone else, no longer had to feel that sense of dread during his church sermons or when he went to bed at night in his own house.

But the media reports following the arrest were particularly painful for Shreaves to read. Mary Jane had retained an attorney named Michael Applebaum, a defense lawyer with a strong reputation in the area. In his younger years he worked as a longshoreman on the docks of Philadelphia, and traces of that working-class background could still be detected in Applebaum's rough voice and his slightly rugged face.

Nevertheless, Applebaum was known for his gregarious and conversational approach, which allowed him to engage his juries and make them laugh. He had worked four murder cases before taking Mary Jane as a client. One of his best-known cases involved the 1994 murder of Philadelphia teenager Eddie Polec, a sixteen-year-old who was beaten to death with bats by high school kids on the front steps of a church. Applebaum defended the eighteen-year-old Bou Khathavong. In a controversial split ruling, three of the boys were found guilty of murder, one was found guilty of manslaughter and conspiracy to murder, and two others, including Applebaum's client, were convicted only of conspiracy to commit murder. His client served five years in prison.

Mary Jane had contacted Applebaum shortly after her lengthy February 25 interview at the Dublin state police barracks. She and her brother, Ed, met in Applebaum's Allentown office with his associate attorney, Thomas Joachim, who would become second chair alongside Applebaum for her defense.

Joachim was a bit overwhelmed upon first meeting Mary Jane, who spoke incessantly and appeared to be in a panic. It was very difficult to keep her focused, and Joachim at first did not understand why she had even wanted to meet with them.

"I think I'm a suspect in a homicide case," Mary Jane had conveyed at the time.

She explained how two state troopers had interviewed her on multiple occasions, and how she felt they had become accusatory toward her during the conclusion of their most recent interview, which lasted nearly four hours.

"I can't understand why the police are focusing on me," Mary Jane told Joachim. "I just want the interviews to stop."

Following her arrest, Applebaum spoke to the press on behalf of his client: "From what we've determined, she's a good Christian, very active in her church, and hardly knew this woman except from the church. She bore her no ill will."

Many reporters were asking whether Mary Jane suffered

from some form of mental illness and, although Applebaum said he did not have enough information to answer, he was quick to identify her many physical health problems, including diabetes, arthritis, and high blood pressure.

"It all happened very suddenly," he said of her arrest. "She is very distraught. She's never had any run-ins with the police or been arrested. She's been uprooted from her home of twenty-one years."

Applebaum began to paint a portrait of his client as a kindly old woman who loved her church and its congregants, but was not loved in return. He even went so far as to compare their treatment of Mary Jane to the Salem witch trials. Applebaum believed that Mary Jane did not match the type of member the other congregants wanted at their church, so they shunned her.

It was uncanny how fast they threw her to the wolves because she was the odd one, Applebaum thought privately about his client. *They speak the words of the Christian philosophy, but they don't act it. It's directly contrary to what they preach.*

Although his public statements about the church weren't quite as extreme, Applebaum made clear to reporters there were cliques at the church from which Mary Jane was completely excluded, and hinted that the pastor was not there for Mary Jane when he should have been.

It was difficult for Shreaves to see his church portrayed as insensitive or uncompassionate toward Mary Jane. He felt as if a mirror was being held up to the congregation, and they were being forced to face a hard truth about themselves.

Some, like Paul Rose, believed the idea of cliques at Trinity Evangelical was nonsense, nothing more than a smokescreen presented by Mary Jane's lawyer that the press was eating up because it made for a better story. But Shreaves had a more pragmatic view. He knew there were cliques at the church, but he felt all churches had their cliques. There are cliques everywhere. But Applebaum's statements only added weight to a guilt Shreaves had been carrying since the murder.

What did I do wrong? he would often think. *What could*

*I have done better? There must have been something I did to
cause this, or something I could have done to prevent it.*

What bothered Shreaves even more than those accusations, however, were Mary Jane's own words. He hated to
read about the feelings Mary Jane apparently harbored for
him, and worried about the many different ways people could
misinterpret his own role in her imaginary love triangle. He
couldn't imagine anybody from the church believing that he'd
had a relationship with Mary Jane, but outsiders were free to
form whatever opinion they wanted. The idea that somebody
could suspect him of having some romantic involvement with
his congregants—whether Rhonda, Mary Jane or otherwise—
left Shreaves feeling truly uncomfortable.

But nothing bothered him more than the reports of what
Mary Jane told police during her various interviews about
her fears that Shreaves had fallen in love with Rhonda and
gotten involved in something he shouldn't have. As if she
was some sort of motherly figure trying to protect the naïve
pastor who was in over his head.

It burns me up, he thought as he read those reports. *What
the hell does she know about that stuff? Let me deal with
that stuff.*

The day after the arrest, Mary Jane Fonder was not far
from the thoughts of anybody at Trinity Evangelical. In a
way, it was as if she was still at the church, her presence
looming over every congregant no matter how much they
might like to avoid her. Choir practice proceeded as scheduled that day, but few were able to concentrate on the
music. Most of the ladies were still reeling from the shock,
the idea never having crossed their mind that it was one of
their own congregants, let alone the sixty-five-year-old Mary
Jane.

"Do you know anything?" Many of them asked Judy Zellner. "What's going on? What do you know?"

But although Judy had known more than most about the
case, she really had nothing satisfactory to tell them, short
of what was already being reported in the news. Most of the
choir members said nothing, keeping their thoughts silent,

but tension bubbled to the surface after Sue Brunner made a remark to Judy about her surprise over what Mary Jane did.

"Well, how do you know she did it?" snapped one of the congregants. "I don't think they proved she did it! How do you know she did it? I don't think she did it!"

A few others voiced support for Mary Jane, but they were few and far between. Some congregants wrote letters to Mary Jane in prison. Others supported Mary Jane in silence. One day, Judy noticed one of Mary Jane's old paintings was hanging in the choir room. *I don't want to look at it and be reminded of her,* Judy thought, and she took it down. The next day, however, Judy was surprised to see that somebody had hung it back up just where it had been. It has remained there ever since.

Reta Bieber maintained a regular correspondence with Mary Jane after her arrest. In the face of the evidence against her, Reta believed Mary Jane probably did kill Rhonda. But Mary Jane had always been sweet and kind to Reta in the past, and to her the woman who could have committed this crime was not the Mary Jane she knew.

That was just another side of her I had never seen and never expected to see, Reta thought. *She was always pleasant to me. I have no reason not to write to her.*

Although Paul Rose did not write to her, his own thoughts mirrored those of Reta. Despite his pleas that the media not rush to judge Mary Jane too quickly, he believed she had committed the murder, especially after David Zellis met with congregation members to explain the case they had against her. Zellis hadn't gone into too much detail, but just enough to set the church members' minds at ease, as neither the prosecutors nor the church council wanted them to learn all the sordid details from the press first.

"We've got a terrific case," Zellis assured them. "It's one of the most solid cases we've ever had."

But even though Paul was convinced of Mary Jane's guilt, he also felt there was still a lot of good left inside her.

There is a good Mary Jane and a bad Mary Jane, and the good Mary Jane had no idea what happened, Paul believed. *In her right mind, she's a very nice person. She just lost her way.*

That, however, was not the prevailing attitude around Trinity Evangelical. Few openly discussed Mary Jane, and those that did often spoke of her with scorn or disgust. It was not uncommon for Shreaves to hear the words, "She got what she deserved," "She's guilty," or "She's where she belongs," whispered from the corners of his church, and it disturbed him.

Although a large part of him was angry with Mary Jane, he didn't feel it was right for the congregation to feel any sense of victory or superiority over her. *Mary Jane's arrest should be a sad thing,* he thought. A tragedy, not a triumph. He did not want people to simply dismiss what Mary Jane did as the work of a two-dimensional monster, and preached about the fact that anybody was, in a way, capable of murder. Just because we don't murder with a gun, he said, doesn't mean we don't murder with a pen, or with a vote, or by spending money on products from a company that uses child labor. He didn't want people to feel they were superior to Mary Jane because she did something they would never do.

But Shreaves soon found that forgiveness toward someone close to the congregation, someone known to them, was far more difficult than forgiveness toward someone anonymous to them. To forgive a nameless and faceless person was easy, but when it was someone in their midst, they couldn't just speak it. They had to live it out. It reminded Shreaves of the ease at which his congregants discussed evil when spoken in abstract terms, but that when it was visited upon their doorstep, it became another matter entirely.

Shreaves found himself in a situation that reminded him of *Dead Man Walking,* the story of Sister Helen Prejean, which was adapted into a film starring Susan Sarandon and Sean Penn. Sister Prejean established a bond with Matthew Poncelot, a prisoner on death row for the murder of a teenage couple. Shreaves often thought of Sister Prejean and the difficult role she played, attempting to serve as a pastor for the convict and maintain respect for the victims and their families, all while attempting to reconcile her own conflicted feelings and deal with the criticism from those who felt the killer deserved no counsel or comfort whatsoever.

Mary Jane Fonder was still on the Trinity Evangelical prayer list, and Shreaves decided he would leave her name there despite the arrest. The decision did not come without conflict for him, but ultimately he felt it was the right thing to do. To take her off the prayer list, Shreaves thought, does that mean we've stopped thinking about her or praying for her?

In the end, she was still technically a member of the church, he thought. *People didn't have to pray for her if they didn't want to.*

But the decision proved to be particularly controversial among the congregation. Just the presence of the name alone was enough to discomfort some, and anger others. Tempers flared even further after one of the congregants posted Mary Jane's prison address at the church, in case anyone wanted to send her letters of support. When Shreaves declined to take the listing down, one man even went so far as to call him at home and threaten him.

"You'd better watch your back!" the man shouted, insisting he was leaving the church and would not return as long as Mary Jane's address was posted and her name was on the prayer list.

But he was the only one to leave the church after Mary Jane was arrested. In fact, attendance was as strong as ever, just as it had been immediately after Rhonda's death. This time, however, things felt different. Rather than the strong sense of unity the church felt at that time, the atmosphere was now constantly tense. Once the shock of Mary Jane's arrest had worn off, the feelings of many parishioners turned to anger, much of it directed at Shreaves. During all of those church services, they were sitting with a murderer among them, and Shreaves never said a word. Why, they wanted to know, hadn't he warned them? Judy and Sue tried to explain there was no way he could have said anything without jeopardizing the investigation, but that did little to comfort some.

CHAPTER 32

The ink was barely dry on the newspaper stories about Mary Jane Fonder's arrest before the press started digging into her past and was reminded of the disappearance of her father. That unsolved case added another layer of intrigue and drama to a story that wasn't short of either in the first place. The excitement in the press was palpable, and it was doubled when Bucks County authorities announced the Edward Fonder case had been reopened due to a renewed interest following Mary Jane's arrest.

"The disappearance of the father is being looked at in conjunction with the investigation of the current homicide," Springfield Township Police Chief Mark Laudenslager announced. "We're looking at it with State Police. Obviously, we're interested in any information on Mr. Fonder's disappearance that anyone would have to offer."

Neither Laudenslager nor any other authorities would confirm whether Mary Jane was considered a suspect in the disappearance, but the stories that followed the announcement did little to improve her public image.

Meanwhile, Stumpo and Egan continued to focus their efforts on strengthening their case. Egan sought and received a search warrant for Ed Fonder's composition notebooks. The trooper recalled how Ed regularly, almost obsessively, seemed to document every detail of his life into those books, and he was sure there was something on those pages that would be useful in the case against Mary Jane.

On April 8, Egan, Stumpo, Greg Langston, and Trooper Joshua Miller went to the Fonder home to serve the warrant. They found Ed outside the home, clutching one of the composition notebooks in his arms. He made no protest about surrendering the books.

Dietz and McGuire had explained that Ed wrote his thoughts and daily occurrences in these books, but as Stumpo and Egan sat down to comb through the pages, they realized this was a great understatement.

Page after page of the tiny, almost illegible script handwriting documented Ed's day-to-day activities in bizarre, excruciating detail. It included everything from routine activities and phone calls to references to people he spoke with and neighbors he watched outside his window. Each item included a notation of the exact time and place. Several pages were filled with which Evangelical Christian Radio speakers he listened to, what time they came on the radio, and what they said. Much like the filthy and disorganized state of Ed's house, the notebooks to Egan were a strong confirmation of Ed Fonder's eccentricity. The books were filled with such minutia, and the handwriting was so hard to read, that the troopers found it difficult to focus while searching for anything relevant. Stumpo in particular had to force himself to read the pages over and over after he found himself skimming over them.

Although Ed seemed to write down just about everything, his notes were focused entirely on himself, and he wrote very little about what Mary Jane Fonder said or did. But Stumpo and Egan soon found something they believed would be helpful. Not only did Ed write down where he was going when he drove his car, he noted the mileage before he left and after he arrived. According to the notebooks, Mary Jane Fonder had only ever borrowed Ed's car on two occasions: on April 1, the day she was arrested, and on March 28.

The day before Doug and Garrett Sylsberry found her gun. Stumpo and Egan showed this information to Dave Zellis and they developed a theory, which would later be used in court. On March 26, Stumpo and Egan had taken Mary Jane's car. She became nervous, knowing it was only a matter of time before they served a warrant for her house, where they would find the Rossi .38 revolver. Two days later, Mary Jane borrowed her brother's car, drove over to Lake Nockamixon and hurled the gun over the Haycock Run Bridge.

From Ed's notes in the books, it was clear Mary Jane had put more than enough mileage on the car to have driven to the lake and back. In fact, Zellis believed Mary Jane probably drove back and forth on the bridge several times, waiting for the right opportunity to throw the gun. He imagined Mary Jane was nervous, which is why she probably threw it from the moving car rather than get out of the vehicle and risk being spotted with it.

If you think about it, Zellis thought to himself, *it's not that easy to just throw a gun out of a window.*

And if that was how it went down, the police were extremely fortunate that Mary Jane was so nervous. Lake Nockamixon is a huge body of water, and searching for a gun there would have been like trying to find a needle in a haystack. Not only that, but Zellis later learned that only a few hundred feet from where Mary Jane discarded the gun, the water underneath the bridge was very deep. If she had dropped the weapon there instead, it would have gone straight to the bottom.

We never would have found it, Zellis thought.

On April 9, Egan received a call from Corporal Paul Romanic, who had some incredible news to share with him. Ed Fonder was sitting in the corporal's office in the Bethlehem barracks right now, and he claimed to have found something in his car that might be considered evidence against his sister.

Egan met the two at the Bethlehem barracks, where Ed explained he had gotten into this car that morning to go for an oil change, and saw sunlight reflecting off a metal object on the floor of the driver's seat. Ed thought it was an earring at first, but after he picked it up and took a closer look, it appeared to be some sort of discharged bullet. Ed placed the object back where he found it and immediately called his attorney, who suggested he turn it over to the police.

Egan asked for permission to search Ed's car and he agreed, signing a written consent form. The search confirmed Ed's original suspicions: A large bullet fragment was indeed discovered on the driver's side floor, as well as another smaller fragment elsewhere in the car.

When this later became public knowledge, many were stunned that Ed Fonder so willingly cooperated with police in handing over potentially damning evidence against his sister. But to conclude he was siding against his sister would be to deeply misunderstand Ed Fonder. He was not at all pleased about the investigation into his sister, and although he generally acted cordially toward the troopers, he made his displeasure clear to them on several instances.

On one occasion, Fonder and his attorney were speaking with Zellis about trial preparations, while Stumpo and Egan observed and listened. When one of the troopers briefly interjected or tried to clarify something, Ed looked at them with an icy stare, then turned to Zellis and asked, "Who's answering the questions here? Me or them?"

Nevertheless, Ed cooperated with police at every turn, and shocked many in the public when he eventually agreed to testify against his sister in court. Zellis, however, believed this had nothing to do with taking sides against his sister, but rather spoke to Ed's strong sense of morals and devout religious spirituality. He didn't believe he was siding against her, Zellis thought. He simply believed he was telling the truth, simple as that.

But among those who believed Ed had taken sides against Mary Jane was Mary Jane herself.

From the day she was arrested, Ed Fonder was one of his sister's few regular visitors. Police monitored their visits and calls, and it was clear to them that Mary Jane was not pleased with her brother. Zellis and the troopers believed her anger stemmed not only from Ed's cooperation over the bullet fragments, but also the fact that Ed was the last person to see Mary Jane before she left the house on January 23, the day Rhonda was killed. If Ed would just claim she was home up until a few minutes before her haircut appointment, it would help her defense a great deal. But Ed couldn't remember the exact time she left that day. That's what he told police, and it angered Mary Jane so much it caused her darker side to emerge again.

Zellis grew convinced that if Mary Jane were acquitted and set free, there was a risk that both Gregory Shreaves and Ed Fonder could become her next victims.

Also that day, Stumpo received a call from Elana Foster, an employee at the RJ Lee Group laboratory where the police had sent specimens from Mary Jane's car to be tested for gunpowder residue. A specimen from the turn signal handle and the driver's door handle both had tested positive for the presence of gunpowder residue, Foster told Stumpo. When Foster completed her tests a few weeks later, she would uncover another positive specimen from Mary Jane's driver's seat.

CHAPTER 33

It was the third week of April when Sue Brunner stepped through the visitor's entrance of the Bucks County Correctional Facility. She had never so much as written a letter to Mary Jane Fonder in prison, let alone visited her. Sue still felt too hurt, too confused, and the idea of having a nice little "Oh, how are you?" conversation struck her as impossible.

But she felt that this was something she had to do. She had to try to understand why Mary Jane had done what she did. She had to look her right in the eye and see if she was going to continue with the charade, or tell her the truth.

That she was somehow so angry with Rhonda, with this woman she really didn't even know that well, that she had to take her life, Sue thought. *It just doesn't make any sense to me.*

Upon Sue's entering the prison, a guard took her purse and locked it up, then asked her to step through a metal detector. A man standing behind a counter opened a door and motioned Sue into a bare-walled, uninviting room, one that struck her as downright ugly. Across from the entrance was a glass wall, a chair, and a telephone, just like what you'd expect to see in a television police drama.

A few minutes after Sue took her seat, she saw a door open on the other side of the glass and in walked Mary Jane, wearing a red jumpsuit, handcuffs on her wrists, and chain shackles around her ankles. She was smiling as she took her seat across from Sue, the same kind of smile she might have worn at a church service. Sue nevertheless felt a great sadness well up inside her. It felt horrible to see one of her fellow parishioners in a place like this.

The two made small talk at first. Sue talked about her pets and filled Mary Jane in on the latest talk around their neighborhood. Mary Jane spoke about life at the prison. The food was good, she said, and she was losing weight because she had plenty of opportunities to exercise outside. Mary Jane asked about improvements Sue was making for the house, mentioning that before she was arrested, she walked by Sue's home and noticed a painting truck outside. As she often did, Mary Jane quickly and abruptly changed subjects, discussing some nice women who had visited her home a few weeks earlier with religious pamphlets about the Bible. All in all, it was not unlike any given conversation Sue and Mary Jane might have had after bumping into each other during a walk on Winding Road.

It was Mary Jane who steered the conversation in the direction of the crime when, out of nowhere, she began to talk about Pastor Shreaves.

"Pastor didn't do anything wrong," she said. "He's just being nice to everybody. It's terrible the things they're saying about him. It's going to ruin his reputation."

Once the subject was broached, Sue found it slightly easier to ask, "Mary Jane, how did this happen? What happened with Rhonda?"

"I have no idea what happened!" Mary Jane said, her facial expression remaining unchanged. "Who would kill that innocent girl?"

Sue paused before replying, "But Mary Jane . . . it was your gun."

"Well, I can't figure out how anybody found that gun because I threw it away a long time ago," Mary Jane said.

And that was that. Mary Jane moved on to another topic, switching back to the more casual small talk of their earlier conversation, but Sue could barely pay any more attention.

She was struck by the matter-of-fact tone with which Mary Jane had spoken about Rhonda, how she had so casually brushed the topic aside despite the overwhelming evidence that she had killed the woman.

She kept up the charade, Sue thought. *Either she's a really good actress, or she really doesn't think this happened. Like she just kind of blocked it out.*

Soon, the conversation was over. Mary Jane was led back to her cell, and Sue left the prison with the uneasy feeling that Mary Jane was just as casual in killing Rhonda as she was in discussing her death.

It was just, "You have to die," Sue thought. *"This is a job I have to do, so I'm going to do it."*

Sue had come looking for some sort of closure, but instead just felt sad. Sad that all this had to happen, sad that Rhonda had to die, and sad that Mary Jane Fonder, a great artist, a woman who loved her church and her house, who loved animals and nature and plants, was now stuck in prison, probably for the rest of her life, while Rhonda Smith was six feet underground.

And for what reason? Sue thought as she walked back to her car. *Nothing. Nothing that makes sense to me.*

Around this time, Applebaum started seeking members of the church who would speak positively on Mary Jane's behalf as a character witness. It wasn't an easy task, and he had even assigned a private detective to try to find someone, but so far was having no luck.

He decided to contact the church directly himself and, upon speaking with Pastor Shreaves via phone, arranged to visit the church on a specific date to speak with congregants about the possibility of testifying. Applebaum explained to the pastor that he would be polite and discreet. He did not want to accost or embarrass anyone, the attorney said, but he believed there surely must be some people at Trinity Evangelical willing to speak for Mary Jane.

A few days later, however, Applebaum received a call from church council President Paul Rose explaining that

Pastor Shreaves had changed his mind, and did not want Applebaum to come to the church. Applebaum was furious, particularly with the fact that Shreaves had asked someone else to call him back rather than confronting him directly.

He doesn't even have the balls to talk to me himself? Applebaum thought. But he did not want to cause a scene with Paul or anyone else at the church, and there was little he could do but accept the cancellation in stride. The decision severely hampered his efforts to find character witnesses for Mary Jane and, to Applebaum, it was just another sign of the church turning its back on his client.

Applebaum had an expert conduct a psychological evaluation on Mary Jane. The results, which were never publicly released, found that his client was not mentally ill or legally insane. Although there was some indication of paranoia, and a few schizophrenic tendencies, the exam found she was not suffering from any major delusions.

Had Applebaum planned to pursue an insanity defense, he might have had another test conducted. But Mary Jane adamantly insisted she was innocent, and that left the possibility of an insanity defense out altogether. As Applebaum put it, "You can't say, 'She didn't do it, but if she did, she's insane.'"

Both privately and publicly, Applebaum believed his client was innocent. He found her to be a loving, caring individual who gave so much to the church, but got very little in return. Still, the attorney knew it would be difficult to convince a jury, particularly after the discovery of the gun and the fact that the bullets matched those that shot Rhonda. By far, Applebaum believed, that was the most damaging evidence.

Although Applebaum believed Mary Jane was innocent, Thomas Joachim was not so sure. While Applebaum had been a defense attorney for decades, Joachim had more of a prosecutor's background: In fact, straight after graduating from law school, Joachim spent three years working in the Bucks County District Attorney's office before joining Applebaum's firm. That background left Joachim less inclined to believe Mary Jane's claims of innocence, although he did have difficulty picturing the elderly woman walking into that church and pulling the trigger.

In any event, at no point during their time together did Mary Jane Fonder ever admit to either Applebaum or Joachim that she had killed Rhonda Smith.

CHAPTER 34

Rays of sunlight crept through the row of windows along the wall opposite the entrance to Magistrate District Judge Kay DuBree's Ottsville courtroom on May 2. A handcuffed Mary Jane Fonder, donning a red prison jumpsuit and fuchsia lipstick, sat beside Michael Applebaum at the defense table. She sat in complete silence, without a trace of her usual chattiness, but behind her the room was positively bustling.

Normally empty for something as simple as a preliminary hearing, the rows of tightly packed together chairs were full of spectators, including members of the media, state troopers, Trinity Evangelical members, and others who just came to enjoy the show. Also among the crowd were Jim and Dorothy Smith, along with their granddaughter Amber, who sat in silence directly behind David Zellis at the prosecutor's table.

It had already been decided earlier that the district attorney's office would not pursue a capital case against Mary Jane. Zellis had determined the murder did not meet any of the aggravating circumstances required for the death penalty, such as the killing of a witness or police officer, or the use of torture or ransom, or a victim under twelve years old.

Naturally, some in the public were disappointed with that decision, but to Bob Egan it made no difference whatsoever. As far as the veteran trooper was concerned, there was no death penalty in the state of Pennsylvania. Although it had been on the books in the state since 1976, only three executions have ever been carried out since, and even those were only after more than a decade of appeals. For the most part, pursuing a capital punishment case only means better legal representation for the defendant and a swell of support from anti-death penalty advocates, which only make the prosecution more difficult.

Four troopers testified for the prosecution during the preliminary hearing, including Greg Stumpo, who rehashed everything from Mary Jane's past history with the church to the discovery of her gun in Lake Nockamixon. Zellis took considerable time describing Mary Jane's long and often confusing police interviews, as well as her conflicting statements about how and why she allegedly threw out her gun fourteen years ago. Zellis described the day Rhonda thanked the congregation for providing her with financial assistance during her hour of need, and described it as the moment that sparked Mary Jane's jealousy so strongly that it moved her to commit murder.

Applebaum argued much of the evidence was circumstantial at best. But at a preliminary hearing, the prosecutors do not yet have to prove guilt beyond a reasonable doubt. They simply have to establish sufficient evidence exists that the case should be moved to trial. After ninety minutes of testimony, Judge DuBree found enough evidence indeed existed, and ordered that Mary Jane be held for trial. But not before Applebaum argued vigorously in her defense, offering Zellis a window into what he might expect from the defense at trial.

Applebaum argued that even though the gun was indisputably registered to Mary Jane Fonder, the police had no evidence that she was in possession of it on January 23, much less that she used it to kill Rhonda. Mary Jane had already claimed she threw the gun into the lake back in 1994. Applebaum indicated it was possible somebody else had found the weapon and killed Rhonda with it.

He even hinted that he might have another plausible suspect in mind, although he declined to elaborate before the trial began. Nevertheless, just the hint of it was enough to cause a considerable stir among the media in the room.

Neither Zellis nor Stumpo were particularly impressed with Applebaum's argument. For one thing, the gun was in nearly pristine condition. It had barely any rust on it whatsoever, and had obviously not been sitting in Lake Nockamixon for the last fourteen years. In order for a jury to find Mary Jane Fonder not guilty, Stumpo surmised, they would have to believe somebody else who had a motive to kill Rhonda Smith had fished the gun out of the lake in 1994, kept it for fourteen years, shot Rhonda to death, then put it back in the lake just in time for police to find it.

That's bizarre, Stumpo thought. *To believe that is ridiculous.*

Somewhat more troubling than that argument, however, was the way Applebaum seemed to target the police investigation itself. While cross-examining Patrick McGuire, Applebaum forced the trooper to admit police took no fingerprints from the gun or ammunition after it was found. The attorney claimed to be "appalled" by this revelation, as well as the fact that the crime scene where Rhonda was murdered was not preserved for the defense to eventually inspect.

"They did a poor job of preserving the evidence," Applebaum claimed.

Zellis countered that the church was still in regular use, and that the office could not very well have been preserved for months until an arrest was made. But Applebaum had made his point, and it was clear to Zellis that the police investigation would fall victim to further attacks at the trial—that Applebaum would argue they couldn't prove her guilt beyond a reasonable doubt because of their mistakes.

But at the end of the day, it was Stumpo's testimony about Mary Jane's day planner that ended up making the most headlines. When he described that Mary Jane had actually written "Rhonda MURDered" under the date of Rhonda's death, it was the first time that irresistible detail had been publicly released, and it sent the reporters—and later the public—into a tizzy.

For a fleeting moment, some in the courtroom believed Mary Jane had made the notation *before* Rhonda was killed, as a sort of "to do" reminder. But Stumpo's testimony made clear that was not the case, and that it was more likely it was written in later, perhaps with the intention of keeping her story straight while dealing with the police.

Zellis placed great emphasis on the notation, claiming the mere fact that it was written at all was important evidence. Applebaum did his best to downplay it, saying Mary Jane had written it later on, after somebody had notified her of the murder. Zellis tried to argue against this theory, claiming the police had never publicly disclosed whether Rhonda had been killed or committed suicide. Applebaum simply scoffed the argument away, and insisted that everyone in the community knew it was a murder.

"She went back and made notes after the church had called her," he said.

Although Stumpo was forced to admit upon cross-examination that he had no way of knowing exactly when the notation was written, he privately thought very little of Applebaum's theory. In his mind, it came down to the simple fact that the notation about Rhonda's murder was written *above* the note about the hairdresser, not below it. If Mary Jane had simply been taking note of the day that Rhonda died, she would have written it after the hairdresser appointment had already taken place, so it would have been written below the appointment.

Another set of notes in the planner appeared slightly more innocuous than the note about the murder, but was later looked upon by police and Zellis with great importance. Under January 16, Mary Jane had written, "Choir Practice 8:15–8:30 Everyone Disappeared Party?" Next to it, on the 17th, she wrote, "Rhonda's B'DAY?" It was only after reading this note that Stumpo and Egan remembered that during one point in their four-hour interview, Mary Jane had gone off topic and briefly mentioned that she'd seen several cars in the church parking lot a few days before Rhonda was killed, and she believed they were holding a birthday party for her.

Zellis had looked into the claim, but after speaking with several church members, he learned there had never been any such party. Much like Shreaves's apparent infatuation with Rhonda, it appeared to be simply a concoction of Mary Jane Fonder's imagination. But if she had believed the church had held a party for Rhonda, and that they had not invited Mary Jane and kept it a secret from her, it would play right into Zellis's theory about her jealousy toward Rhonda Smith.

Upon the conclusion of the preliminary hearing, Mary Jane remained silent as she was escorted from the courthouse, saying nothing to the swarms of reporters surrounding her except the word, "No," when asked whether she had committed the crime. The Smiths and their granddaughter also declined to speak to the media as they left.

As the reporters asked their questions and the excitement in the courtroom began to wind down, Bob Egan was approached by Judy Zellner, who had been watching from the audience. She told Egan the church had recently been notified that Mary Jane had purchased something for the church sometime before she was arrested, and that it had just arrived at her home. Apparently, it was some sort of an angel statue.

A statue dedicated to the memory of Rhonda Smith.

Later, Egan arranged for the statue to be obtained, and sure enough, it was a two-foot-tall stone statue with a winged angel draping its arms over a tombstone and weeping. Mary Jane had purchased the sculpture, which was apparently inspired by an original work from nineteenth-century sculptor William Wetmore Story, for $60 from an online home décor company. Upon the gravestone was an inscription, "The bud was spread/to show the rose/our Saviour smiled/the bud was closed. Anon."

Mary Jane made the purchase on March 14, which Egan noted was exactly two days after she had knocked on the front door of Jim and Dorothy Smith to offer them a pie.

To Egan and the other investigators, the statue was not just another confirmation of Mary Jane's eccentricity, but another sign of a pattern of cunningness that was becoming all too clear to them.

Police had already interviewed Mary Jane twice by the time she ordered this statue, and it must have been obvious to her that she was under suspicion. The statue, the pie, the sympathy cards she had sent to members of the church: Egan believed these were all part of a strategy Mary Jane employed to portray herself as a kind, sweet old lady who adored Rhonda Smith, and couldn't possibly have had anything to do with her death.

This theory was further supported, in Egan's mind, by Mary Jane's behavior immediately after the long police interview back in February. She went out of her way to visit Dorothy Smith in church, making a big show out of how much she missed Rhonda and making sure to mention that she spoke to Rhonda the Monday before she died. Mary Jane knew that now that the police were aware of that Monday phone call, they'd start asking questions about it, and she wanted to lay the groundwork so she could later claim she had nothing to hide.

Likewise, Mary Jane had gone out of her way to let several people know about the pie she had so graciously given Rhonda's parents. In investigating the gift, Egan learned Mary Jane had stopped by her friend Rosalie Schnell's home with a pie for her, and was sure to mention to Rosalie that she was bringing one to the Smiths. And then, a few days later, Mary Jane had called Steve Wysocki and Donald Ludlow to let them know about bringing the Smiths a pie.

To Egan, Stumpo, and Zellis, this showed that behind Mary Jane's apparently odd and senseless behavior was an intelligent, calculating woman who knew exactly what she was doing, and was taking measures to cover her steps.

CHAPTER 35

After the district attorney reopened the investigation into Ed Fonder's disappearance, county detectives began looking into his bank records. They were surprised to find he was still receiving monthly pension payments now, even fifteen years after his disappearance, and that Mary Jane Fonder controlled the account where they were being deposited.

The district attorney's office forwarded this information in May to the federal government's Pension Benefit Guaranty Corp. In July, the organization filed suit against Mary Jane, seeking back payment of the pension money she had collected since August 25, 2000, the date under Pennsylvania law her father would have been presumed dead with seven years passing since his disappearance. Ed Fonder's pension payments since that date totaled $32,913.63.

Mary Jane's attorney, Michael Applebaum, told *The Philadelphia Inquirer,* who broke the story, that he felt Mary Jane didn't do anything wrong, considering she had power of attorney over both her parents' finances.

"As far as I know, the police still consider [Fonder's father] to be a missing person," he told the newspaper.

Ed Fonder retired from his job as a machinist in 1976 and started receiving $353.91 in monthly pension payments in April 1979.

In 1992, Mary Jane took power of attorney over her father's

bank account, into which the pension payments were deposited. She contacted the pension company in 1999 about a change in the bank account number, but never mentioned that her father had been missing since 1993, the company noted in the lawsuit.

In total, Ed Fonder received $62,642.07 in pension payments. In its lawsuit, the pension company requested Mary Jane pay back all of her father's pension payments, plus interest, since his presumptive death in August 2000.

Applebaum told *The Intelligencer* he feared new media coverage from the lawsuit would further hamper his client's ability to get a fair trial in Bucks County.

"I'm sure it wasn't a calculated move (by prosecutors) to just keep heaping more and more information to the public to taint the jury pool. Hopefully, that won't be the effect," he told the newspaper.

Mary Jane's first-degree murder case was assigned to Judge Rea Boylan, which meant one thing for sure: Things were going to move very, very quickly.

In general, most murder cases were tried quickly in Bucks County. While in some surrounding counties it was not unusual for a trial to be delayed one or two years from the time of the arrest, in Bucks they tended to take place about six months following an arrest. But Boylan wanted this case on a particularly fast track, and scheduled an August 25 trial date.

Boylan had built up a strong reputation since taking her seat on the bench in 1999. She graduated from college at age nineteen and previously worked as a public defender and assistant district attorney before starting her own civil practice. She was the first woman president of the Bucks County Bar Association, and was only the fourth woman to take on the county judgeship.

During a discussion about a possible continuance for the original trial date, Boylan explained her simple philosophy to both Zellis and Applebaum regarding the need for a speedy trial: "If she's guilty, she belongs in the state penitentiary. If she's not guilty, she belongs back home. And we're going to make sure this happens, one way or the other."

Zellis didn't think Boylan understood exactly how complicated a case this was, and how difficult it would be to try it on such a tight schedule. Nevertheless, Zellis was excited to take on the case, which he believed could potentially be the crowning achievement of his career. He found it fascinating on so many levels: a murder in a rural community that in many ways was a throwback to a time that was long past.

And of course, there was the defendant herself. In his twenty-five-year career, he had never encountered a suspect as unusual as Mary Jane Fonder. If she were found guilty, she would be the oldest woman ever convicted of murder in Bucks County history.

As the months approached and Zellis prepared his case, Stumpo and Egan learned that Jim and Dorothy Smith had given Mary Jane two pairs of Rhonda's old shoes: a set of sneakers and a pair of dress shoes. The troopers visited Ed Fonder, who told them that he knew about the shoes, but had no idea they once belonged to Rhonda. Ed voluntarily handed over the dress shoes, but said he had brought Mary Jane the sneakers during a recent prison visit. If they wanted to get their hands on them, Stumpo and Egan would have to seek a warrant.

Meanwhile, Zellis was forced to respond to several court motions filed by Applebaum. First, he tried to have several of Mary Jane's statements from her February 25 police interview suppressed from the trial, particularly when she said "very sexual kind of feelings" and "warm feelings" about Shreaves. That motion was denied.

Applebaum also argued the trial should be moved outside of Bucks County altogether, because the media was making a "soap opera" out of the case. Indeed, the story had drawn particularly extensive media coverage, so much so that the NBC program *Dateline* had expressed interest in doing a piece about the case. Applebaum argued the stories—especially those about Mary Jane's romantic interest in Pastor Shreaves— would make it impossible to find an impartial jury in the county, and he feared a "whisper down the lane" effect would make it difficult for prospective jurors to differentiate the rumors from the facts.

It was a common defense tactic for a high-profile murder case, and it, too, was denied, but an unexpected development occurred during the pretrial hearing for that motion. As they waited for Mary Jane to be brought into the courtroom, Stumpo and Egan told Zellis about the warrant they were working on to get Rhonda's shoes back from Mary Jane.

"Wouldn't it be something if she wears them here?" Egan joked, resulting in a laugh from all three men.

A few minutes later, Mary Jane was led into the courtroom wearing the same red jumpsuit, handcuffs, and ankle shackles she had donned during her arraignment. The chains made a grating noise that echoed throughout the courtroom as they dragged along the ground, and Stumpo couldn't help but be reminded of the Ghost of Jacob Marley from Charles Dickens's *A Christmas Carol*.

Stumpo looked back at Mary Jane and the shackles around her ankles, and his eyes were immediately drawn to the dirty white sneakers on her feet.

"Bob," Stumpo whispered to Egan. "Are those the sneakers?"

Egan looked, as his eyes widened in surprise. "Yeah. Those are the sneakers."

"Holy cow," Stumpo said, in complete disbelief that Mary Jane would actually wear Rhonda's shoes to a court hearing about Rhonda's murder.

"Dave," Stumpo whispered to Zellis. "Those are the sneakers."

"What?" Zellis exclaimed.

"Yeah, she's wearing Rhonda's shoes!"

"Oh, you're kidding me . . ."

Zellis called for a county detective to come down to the courtroom and take a photo of the sneakers. If Jim and Dorothy Smith could look at those photos and identify them as Rhonda's shoes, it would make getting a search warrant that much easier. The detective, wearing khakis and a polo shirt, arrived just as the hearing was ending.

"Ms. Fonder, do you mind if I take a photograph of your sneakers?" he asked, without identifying himself, as Mary Jane was being escorted back to the jail.

"Oh no, go ahead," she said, smiling and nodding. "These are Rhonda's. Rhonda's parents gave them to me."

Zellis could have laughed out loud. *Well,* he thought, *now we don't even need the photographs.*

Indeed, a warrant was issued a week later, and Stumpo and Egan personally visited the Bucks County Correctional Facility to serve it to her. And, when a guard brought Mary Jane into the visitors' room with the detectives, she was wearing those same shoes once again.

Stumpo and Egan, seated in a chair directly across from the handcuffed Mary Jane, informed her that they had a warrant to take back Rhonda's shoes. An angry look came over her face similar to the one Egan saw back when they took her car. Once the detectives got the shoes, they informed a security guard standing by the door that Mary Jane could be brought back to her cell.

As they waited for the other guards to come and take Mary Jane away, she sat silently, staring at the detectives. Finally, she broke the silence by asking, "When am I going to get my dirty laundry back?"

The question struck Stumpo as so absurd that he was momentarily taken aback. Mary Jane was referring to the dirty laundry that was in her car back when they took it away, before she was arrested.

Here she is, Stumpo thought, *sitting in jail with the two men who are going to lock her up for the rest of her life for murder, and this is the only thing she can think to ask?*

After a few moments of silence, the security guard asked, "Aren't you going to answer her?"

"No," Stumpo said. "I'm not going to answer her. That's ridiculous."

And the four remained completely silent until the guards came back to take Mary Jane away.

CHAPTER 36

Mary Jane Fonder's trial for first-degree murder also would take place in the Bucks County Courthouse, located in the historic town of Doylestown. The 8,227-person borough was founded in 1745, and the quaint town retained much of its historic character through the preservation of many older buildings. Doylestown's postcard-perfect business district flourished through business from the courthouse and adjacent county offices, and also through weekend bed-and-breakfast-type tourism.

The start of Mary Jane's trial was scheduled for 9 o'clock the morning of Monday, October 20. A large crowd of reporters waited for Mary Jane to make her entrance into courtroom #1 at the Bucks County Courthouse, a large and historic room where portraits of retired judges line the walls. It's also often used for ceremonial gatherings.

At the courthouse, sheriff deputies escorted defendants from the adjacent jail, down a long public hallway and into the courtroom. The reporters waited for Mary Jane in the hallway. In addition to *The Intelligencer,* the trial also drew *The Philadelphia Inquirer,* and several of the Philadelphia news stations plus both daily newspapers in the Lehigh Valley—*The Express-Times* and *The Morning Call*—as well as the Lehigh Valley television news station, WFMZ.

As Mary Jane was brought into the hallway leading to

courtroom #1, the crowd of reporters swooped in on her. How was she doing? they asked. Did she have anything she wanted to say?

Mary Jane, dressed in a black-and-gray floral dress with a gray-checkered jacket on top, sure did.

"I'm a victim with Rhonda," she said. "I'm the second one from the church."

Pressed for any more words, Mary Jane continued: "All I can say is I'm innocent and I didn't do it.

"I did nothing," she concluded before she was escorted into the courtroom.

The trial hadn't even started yet, and already the media had a story.

The rest of the first day was far less exciting. Prospective jurors were called fifty at a time. They were asked question upon question, including whether they had read or listened to media reports of the highly publicized case. Thirty-two of the pool of fifty had. Judge Boylan also asked if any of the potential jurors attended or knew anyone who attended Trinity Evangelical Lutheran Church; none did.

First Assistant District Attorney Zellis asked whether knowing Rhonda was bipolar would affect any jurors' judgment. A few jurors said they knew people with the disorder, but it would not affect their objectivity. Defense attorney Michael Applebaum asked whether any of the jurors had strong opinions about gun ownership. About ten raised their hands indicating they did.

By 2:30 p.m., twenty-four of the pool of fifty had been dismissed. Another thirteen were kept after court was dismissed in the afternoon for private question sessions with Boylan, Zellis, and Applebaum.

The trial resumed at noon on October 21, when a second pool of fifty potential jurors were called in.

Zellis didn't take into consideration Mary Jane's age or religious beliefs during his jury selection, but rather just stuck to his general strategy when picking jurors. He generally tries to stay away from younger people, because he feels their threshold for what constitutes reasonable doubt is greater than that of older people. He also regularly passes on teachers and social workers, who he feels are more forgiving than most.

In the end, a jury of seven men and five women was selected, along with four alternates. The jury included a wide range of professions, including an educator, a nurse, and a law enforcement official. Once jury selection was completed, the trial was off to a late start, so there was only enough time left that day for Zellis's opening statement.

Zellis pointed out that there were many things Mary Jane wanted that Rhonda ultimately got, including financial assistance from the church and being asked to be the substitute church secretary.

"You'll see the root of this tragedy—this catastrophe— is the ego and the jealously of Mary Jane Fonder," he said.

Zellis laid out the timeline of the week before Rhonda's death, and how event after event increased Mary Jane's jealousy.

"There was only one person who had the malice in her heart. There was only one person with the motivation. There was only one person with a specific intent to premeditate and kill Rhonda Smith," he said.

In addition to being jealous, Zellis also portrayed Mary Jane as manipulative, pointing to the many sympathy cards she wrote and the visit to the Rhonda's parents where she came with an apple pie and left with some of Rhonda's shoes.

Zellis also laid out some of the physical evidence in the case. Law enforcement officials had proven a gun Mary Jane owns was the one used in Rhonda's fatal shooting, he said. Gunpowder residue was found in Mary Jane's car and bullet fragments found in her brother's car—which she borrowed— matched the bullets found inside Rhonda, Zellis said.

"You'll see the diligence of the hard work of law enforcement," he told the jurors.

With District Attorney Zellis closing out day two of the trial, defense attorney Applebaum got to open day three.

In his opening statement, he discussed possible alternate

theories in the case, including whether Rhonda's death was a suicide, as authorities initially considered.

"Initially they thought it could be a suicide, but the gun wasn't there," he told the jury. "Possibly somebody assisted a suicide and cleaned it all up."

Applebaum also brought up another avenue authorities looked into early in their investigation: whether Rhonda had been dating a married man.

"There's a possibility, somebody, a jealous wife, somebody, possibly the man she was dating," he said. "There was a reason she was killed."

But Mary Jane Fonder, on the other hand, had no reason to kill her, he argued.

"She wasn't jealous of Rhonda Smith," Applebaum said. "You won't hear anyone from the congregation say she said a bad word about Rhonda."

Applebaum alleged that the prosecution's case was weak, saying they had some evidence, but most of the case was based on speculation.

"They're going to give you a box with two hundred of the one thousand pieces you need to put it together," he said, comparing the case to a jigsaw puzzle.

After Applebaum's opening statement, the prosecution started on its lengthy list of witnesses, including eight alone who testified October 22. The young Garrett Sylsberry, who found Mary Jane's gun on the lakeshore, appeared at ease on the stand, and even got a few chuckles out of the crowd when Applebaum joked with him.

Garrett and his father, Doug, both testified that the gun was relatively rust-free when they found it.

"It was, like, perfect," Garrett said. "There was no rust or anything. It looked like it had just been tossed."

An avid scuba diver, Applebaum personally did not believe the lack of rust on the gun necessarily indicated it had been underwater for a short amount of time. Oxygen is required to produce rust, and Applebaum tried to argue the low levels of oxygen underwater could have kept the weapon relatively well preserved.

However, it would have been covered in moss and other plant growth. Applebaum argued that Doug Sylsberry, a gun collector, had cleaned off the revolver after discovering it in the lake with the intention of keeping it for himself. When he later decided to inform police instead, the attorney said, he lied about the condition in which it was found. Doug denied this when questioned on the stand.

The day's testimony also included the playing of Judy Zellner's emotional 911 call after she found Rhonda dead in the church.

Zellis asked Judy if she had helped Rhonda commit suicide, one of the theories raised by the defense.

"No, I didn't," Judy answered unequivocally.

The parade of prosecution witnesses continued on day four of the trial, with six giving testimony over the day-long hearing. The witnesses included several focusing on the scientific aspects of the case, including the forensic pathologist and the lead crime scene investigator.

Pathologist Sara Funke detailed her ruling that Rhonda's death was a homicide. She pointed to the spread-out gunpowder marks on her face and on the back of her right hand, which showed she was shot from about three feet away and raised her hand in front of her face when she was shot.

"There is no way, in my opinion, a person can hold a gun and have that stippling on their face and right hand," she said. "This is a homicide."

Applebaum suggested in his cross-examination a way in which it could have been a suicide. He asked whether someone could fire a gun three feet from his or her head and get stippling on their hands.

The pathologist discounted his theory.

"No," she answered. "It would be blowing forward or sideways, but not on the back of your hand."

Applebaum made greater headway with Trooper Louis Gober, the lead crime scene investigator who had to explain why Mary Jane Fonder's fingerprints weren't found at the crime scene.

"She could have been wearing gloves that day," he said. "Her hands could have been dry. . . . She could have touched something in the office and not left a latent fingerprint behind."

Several surfaces in the church were not very receptive to picking up fingerprints, including the side exterior door and the office door, Gober testified. Doors were frequently touched places so fingerprints were often removed when others touch the surface, he said.

Applebaum suggested maybe Mary Jane's fingerprints weren't at the church because she wasn't there the day Rhonda died.

Gober had an answer for that, too.

"I would say the simplest reason why her fingerprints weren't there is she didn't touch the items I tested," he countered.

Applebaum also grilled Gober on other aspects of his work. First, he questioned why the police didn't engage in "stringing," a practice of setting up a series of strings around at the crime scene to determine where the gun was fired from. Gober said the police believed taking still photographs of the scene was sufficient.

"In this instance we were not sure whether the person was standing," Gober said. "We were not sure initially if it was a homicide or not."

"Initially you thought it might be a suicide?" Applebaum asked, happy to emphasize that point.

"Initially, we did not understand what it was," Gober said. "We just knew we had a victim with possible gunshot wounds to her head and we were trying to keep an open mind as to what occurred. We attempted to treat the scene as a homicide, that being the most serious of offenses. But we weren't sure as far as to what exactly happened. Again, we were trying to let the physical evidence show us where to go next."

Applebaum also pressed him on his method of searching Mary Jane's car for gunpowder residue. He criticized Gober for searching the car while wearing his police uniform, which easily could have carried gunpowder residue.

What, Applebaum suggested, if the residue from their uniforms transferred into the car? Applebaum also questioned why police did not check her car service records, to see if a recent repairman who was a hunter could have transferred gunpowder residue into her car.

Then Applebaum brought up a two-minute phone call that took place at the church at precisely 12:07 p.m., according to phone records. That was more than an hour after Rhonda was supposedly shot at 10:55 in the morning. If Rhonda was still alive around noon, as Applebaum was trying to suggest, then Mary Jane couldn't have killed Rhonda because she was out at her hairdresser's appointment.

Zellis was blindsided. He prided himself on being extremely prepared for his cases, and he had no idea about this phone call. *How do I not know about this?* he thought.

Applebaum asked how Rhonda could have been on the phone for two minutes if that time of the shooting was correct. Gober had no sufficient answer to offer.

Applebaum also asked about a videotape that was filmed of the crime scene, which had gone mysteriously missing. Gober had misplaced the tape and, although Zellis knew it ultimately didn't make a difference for the investigation, he also knew it could look bad in the eyes of the jury.

"Now, I heard you testify that you took a video?" Applebaum asked.

"Yes," Gober said.

"So that people could get it right on the investigation?"

"Correct."

"I haven't seen that video and asked for it, and was told you lost it," Applebaum said. "Is that true?"

"That would be correct," Gober replied.

Later, during redirect questioning, Zellis tried to mitigate the damage. He emphasized that the still photographs were the primary way of documenting the scene, and asked Gober whether the video was simply an extra copy of those images. Gober happily responded in the affirmative.

The day's testimony greatly rattled Zellis. Applebaum was calling everything the investigators did into question, alleging they forgot to take crucial steps in some of the procedures they followed. They messed up, possibly contaminating the evidence, according to how Applebaum was portraying it. It was a page straight out of the O. J. Simpson defense.

But Zellis was particularly upset about the mysterious two-minute phone call that Applebaum brought up. During a break in the trial, he pulled Stumpo and Egan into his office and demanded an explanation. The troopers believed they understood perfectly well what the phone call was: Somebody had called the church and left a phone message.

Zellis, whose emotions had been building up all day, unleashed onto the two troopers. That explanation could very well be correct, he said angrily, but why didn't he know about it? That call was on the phone records the police reviewed, and the answering machine tape was available to take as evidence. It was an oversight that shouldn't have happened, and because it did, they were caught unprepared in trial.

Zellis didn't think the phone call was going to make or break the case, but that wasn't the point. Applebaum was trying to portray the authorities as bumbling idiots, a bunch of Keystone Kops who didn't know what they were doing. Even if Applebaum didn't have one big "gotcha" moment to prove his point, if he could present enough little setbacks like this, his defense could end up a success, Zellis said.

"A jury trial is no different than a boxing match," he told the troopers. "You hope you don't get knocked out in the first round, but here it's body blow after body blow. And if he keeps scoring these body blows, at one point we're going to go down if we don't fix this. So get your act together and let's get going here!"

CHAPTER 37

The fifth day of the trial was another difficult one for the prosecution. State police ballistics expert Mark Garrett was called in to demonstrate how Mary Jane's gun worked. But, after opening the cylinder and loading the bullets in, Garrett couldn't get the cylinder closed again.

"I, um, I can't get it to shut," Garrett said sheepishly.

Oh no, Zellis thought, the O. J. Simpson case flashing in his head again. He recalled the infamous moment when Simpson tried on the glove he allegedly wore the day of the murder, and it didn't fit. The moment that many felt directly led to Simpson's acquittal. *If the glove doesn't fit, you must acquit.*

Applebaum, of course, looked as if he had just been handed a newly wrapped Christmas present.

Sitting in the audience, Greg Stumpo shared Zellis's concerns, and he found it difficult to restrain himself from walking up and helping Garrett. Stumpo knew exactly what the problem was, and it had nothing to do with the gun being defective. Once the cylinder of the revolver pops open, a small rod pushes out slightly and, if not adjusted back into place, the cylinder won't close. All you have to do is push the rod a tiny bit with your thumb and it could snap shut, but Stumpo was all too aware how bad this looked to the jury.

Holy cow, Stumpo thought. *I don't believe this.*

After another minute or two, Garrett finally got the gun

shut. But that didn't stop Applebaum from pointing out the gun's failure during his cross-examination.

"If you can't close this, you can't fire the weapon?" he asked.

"Correct," Garrett said.

Applebaum also got the prosecution's gunpowder residue expert to admit that his theory about residue transferring from police uniforms onto other items was possible. After Elana Foster testified gunshot residue was found in three places within Mary Jane's car, Applebaum asked her if she had read studies naming police stations as one of the most prolific places to find gunshot residue. She said she was familiar with some tests showing residue in the backseat of police cars.

"Gunshot residue can be transferred," Foster said. "We can say the particles are present but how they got there, when, and from whom we can't say."

After a weekend off, the sixth day of the trial started with Ed Fonder testifying for the prosecution. Fonder, who was called because of the bullet fragments found in his car, was straightforward and precise in his testimony, unemotional in what must have been a difficult situation testifying against his sister.

He testified that he found two bullet fragments in his car on April 9, about two weeks after he lent the car to his sister. He turned the fragments over to state police after consulting an attorney, he said.

"I said, 'I have something that may be of evidentiary nature in my car,'" he said during his testimony.

The day's prosecution witnesses also included a chemist who testified about Mary Jane's assertion that she threw her gun in a lake fourteen years ago. It was impossible, he said, considering the very small amount of rust on the gun.

"My opinion was the weapon was submerged from between zero and two months," said David Rusak, a University of Scranton chemistry professor.

Applebaum asked whether it was possible the gun had been thrown in the lake, taken out and then thrown back again. Rusak said any scenario where the gun was underwater for less than two years was possible.

While Ed Fonder was unemotional on the stand, Rhonda's father, Jim, brought tears to the eyes of just about everyone in the courtroom with his testimony.

Jim had pneumonia that day and had to be brought into the courthouse in a wheelchair. But despite being physically weak, Jim was emotionally strong. He proudly told the jury how much he loved his daughter and how proud he and his wife were of everything she had overcome.

"We were very close," he said. "Her nickname for me was Dad-e-o."

Jim spoke about how her bipolar disorder negatively affected her life and kept her from her dream profession as a teacher, but that despite it all she kept persevering.

"She never gave up because of her bipolar and we are so proud of her," he said.

While Rhonda had her ups and downs, she was in a good mood when she called her father the morning she was killed.

"She said, 'Okay, Dad-e-o, I'm up and at 'em,'" Smith said. "And then we both started to laugh because she was in good spirits."

Applebaum pressed Smith on the theory that Rhonda could have committed suicide. But Smith, who remained collected throughout his testimony, strongly dismissed the suggestion.

"Never, never," he said. "She had every opportunity to commit suicide without anyone around. She had a vast amount of pills. Any night she could have taken too many."

Following the public disclosure that Mary Jane's motive for killing Rhonda was a perceived love triangle between him and the two women, Pastor Gregory Shreaves had repeatedly declined media interviews. But when he took the stand on the seventh day of the trial on October 28, he sought to clear up any and all the unanswered questions.

Mary Jane's infatuation with him was completely one-sided, he testified. He retold the story of the day Mary Jane confessed her feelings for him in his office and how he routinely ignored her frequent calls and rejected her presents to him for two years.

He firmly denied having a romantic relationship with either Mary Jane or Rhonda, though Applebaum pressed him on his feelings for Rhonda. At one point, Applebaum picked up a photo of Rhonda and held it in front of Shreaves.

"What do you see here?" Applebaum asked.

What's he getting at? Shreaves wondered. *Does he expect me to break down weeping and say, 'Oh, I miss my love Rhonda?' Or say something like, 'Boy, she's a hot chick?'*

"I see Rhonda," Shreaves said.

"You didn't notice she was a particularly attractive woman?" Applebaum asked.

"I didn't look at her in that way, no," Shreaves replied.

Applebaum believed he had made his point. In his opinion, Rhonda Smith was a very attractive woman. He felt Shreaves's claims that he did not notice were phony, and he hoped the jury would agree.

Applebaum had developed a genuine distrust of Shreaves. Part of it was the way the pastor had refused to allow him to visit the church and seek character witnesses for Mary Jane, which did not strike the defense attorney as very Christian behavior. It also had to do with Shreaves's background as a golf pro. Why, he wondered, would a man like that end up a minister in a little church in Bucks County, as if he was hiding from his past.

Although he never told the jury, Applebaum had even checked out Shreaves's alibi to make sure he was indeed at a convention when Rhonda Smith was shot. He thought it was perfectly possible that Shreaves had gotten mixed up in an illicit relationship with Rhonda, and then tried to silence her. But, of course, Shreaves's story had checked out, and there was no evidence the pastor had shown Rhonda any undue or extra attention.

The attorney pointed to previous testimony that Rhonda hadn't been talking to Shreaves as much as she usually did during the weeks before her death. Applebaum asked why that was, and why Rhonda wrote the words "pastor lied to me" in an entry in her diary?

"I can't think of any reason," he said.

Three other members of Trinity Evangelical Lutheran Church took the stand that day: Steve Wysocki, Sue Brunner, and Mary Brunner.

Steve Wysocki, the church choir director, testified about how Mary Jane didn't react when he called January 23 to tell her Rhonda had been found shot in the church.

"I didn't find there was any reaction about it or question about it like there had been with other choir members," he said.

During his cross-examination, Applebaum pointed out that Mary Jane had heard about Rhonda's shooting before the choir director called her. Steve Wysocki said she made no mention of that to him. Steve also admitted, under questioning from Applebaum, that he had never noticed any animosity between Mary Jane and Rhonda before her death, and that he never witnessed anything other than a congenial relationship between them.

"Did you ever have Mary Jane over to your house for tea and crumpets along with the rest of the choir?" Applebaum asked at one point.

Steve explained Mary Jane had been to his house before when he invited all the choir members over. But after further questioning from Applebaum, he admitted he had never invited Mary Jane alone over for a visit without the rest of the choir. Applebaum emphasized this point, and suggested that Steve, along with the rest of the congregation, never made Mary Jane feel welcome.

"Well, let's be candid," Applebaum said. "You didn't really *want* to have Mary Jane at your house, is that correct?"

"That's not true," Steve insisted.

"Well, she's highly talkative, right?" Applebaum asked.

"She's highly talkative."

"She's annoying?" Applebaum asked.

"I didn't find her to be annoying, I found her to be Mary

Jane," Steve said. "And no, as we all try to do at our church, we accept and involve and work with and love those people. I tried to find ways, as I do with a lot of folks at the church, for people to use their gifts and their talents and services to the church and into its mission."

Later, Sue Brunner and Mary Brunner testified about how Mary Jane seemed depressed during the days before Rhonda died. Sue Brunner said Mary Jane told her on January 21 that she wasn't going to be going to church for a while because she was depressed. Mary Brunner said Mary Jane told her on January 22 she was upset with the church's choir and Bible study group members.

"She said there's a group of people that whisper behind her back and don't include her and that made her sad," Mary Brunner said.

Applebaum used the Brunners' statements to add weight to his argument no one ever heard Mary Jane say anything bad about Rhonda.

"You weren't aware of any bad feelings Mary Jane Fonder had toward Rhonda?" he asked Sue Brunner.

"No, I wasn't," she responded. "I never saw them argue."

Also that day at trial, Trooper Gregg Dietz recalled Mary Jane's long, rambling rant after she had been arrested.

"Oh my God, they found my gun. It . . . is . . . threw away years ago," he read from his report. "Someone used that gun. . . . It doesn't look good for me."

Dietz also detailed the way Mary Jane lashed out at Pastor Shreaves after reading the arrest affidavit.

"I had no reason to attack that girl. He's a liar," the trooper read. "Somebody had my gun. That pastor . . . what a cad."

The prosecution wanted the jury to hear Mary Jane's jealousy directly from her own mouth. So, on the eighth day of the trial, almost three hours of her February 25 interview with police was broadcast throughout the courtroom.

"Lots of people think maybe my pastor was involved with that lady," Mary Jane said through the tape recorder. "I wonder if the poor pastor was in love with that lady."

Applebaum knew the interview was going to hurt his client in the eyes of the jury. He truly believed if she had simply declined to talk to police and kept her mouth shut, this could have been an open-and-closed not guilty verdict.

I always wonder why people who watch television don't understand the right to remain silent means the right to remain silent, Applebaum thought. *She had the right, but she just didn't have the ability, under any circumstance, to remain silent.*

But there was a flip side to the prosecution's strategy: The jurors also got to hear Mary Jane repeatedly deny killing Rhonda.

"I may have been upset. I have all kind of things to be upset about. But it had nothing to do with her," she said in the interview. "I didn't do anything to Rhonda."

The recording showed that Mary Jane was largely composed and forthcoming with police throughout the interview until they mentioned her wig was being tested for gunshot residue. Then her voice broke some as she asserted her innocence.

"I'm sure that nothing appeared in my wig because I don't have a gun and I didn't do anything," she said.

Nearing the end of its case, the prosecution also addressed timeline issues from the day of the alleged murder, including how Mary Jane could have shot Rhonda at about 10:54 a.m. and arrived at a Quakertown hair salon at 11:22 a.m.

The drive from Mary Jane's house to the Springfield Township church was about five minutes, Egan testified. The drive from the church to the Holiday Hair salon was about fourteen minutes, he said.

Stumpo testified how Mary Jane made a specific point to tell police she left her house for the hair salon at 11 o'clock, and arrived there at 11:30. The time of Rhonda's death wasn't public at the time of the interview, Stumpo said.

"Only the person who committed a crime in a case like this would know what time it occurred," he said.

Applebaum pressed Stumpo on how authorities could have known when Rhonda was shot. Stumpo responded that Rhonda's Internet activity abruptly stopped at 10:54 a.m.

"It could have been someone stopped using the computer because they answered the telephone . . . or someone went to the restroom," Applebaum said.

Stumpo said both those cases were possible. The time of Rhonda's shooting, then, was just a "guess," Applebaum concluded.

CHAPTER 38

After eight days of prosecution testimony and jury selection, it was finally the defense's turn to present their case. But as court resumed on the morning of October 30, it was announced the defense wouldn't be presenting a case, including that Mary Jane wouldn't testify.

With the jury kept out of the courtroom, Applebaum asked Mary Jane to explain why she didn't want to testify. He pointed to how the jury already had heard her say repeatedly in her taped interview with police that she had nothing to do with Rhonda's death.

"You would have repeated what you said before?" Applebaum asked.

"That is correct," Mary Jane answered.

In the back of his mind, Applebaum questioned whether keeping Mary Jane off the stand was the right decision. Although he knew her tendency to chatter would lengthen the trial by at least ninety minutes, he also felt there was a chance that she would come across as a warm, friendly, Christian woman to the jury. Thomas Joachim, on the other hand, insisted that keeping her off the stand was the right move. Mary Jane simply talked too much, and there was no telling what Zellis could persuade her to say on cross-examination.

And with that, both the defense and prosecution rested.

It was a surprise to many people that Applebaum didn't

present more of a case, but Zellis imagined Mary Jane didn't leave him a choice. He didn't know for sure, because attorney-client privilege prevented Applebaum from discussing it, but Zellis imagined that if it were up to him, Applebaum probably would have pursued an insanity defense. But to seek such a defense, Mary Jane would have to admit that she killed Rhonda Smith, even if she didn't realize what she was doing at the time.

In Zellis's opinion, Mary Jane would never do that. That church was her life, and she would rather go to prison for the rest of her life than admit to her fellow congregants that she did something like this. That's why Zellis was sure that Applebaum must have at least considered an insanity defense, but that Mary Jane ultimately tied his hands.

As was customary, Applebaum gave his closing statement first. But this time, his closing argument differed from that of his opening statement. Rather than pointing to the possibility of suicide or one of Rhonda's boyfriends committing the murder, Applebaum turned the spotlight on Ed Fonder, claiming he was a much more believable suspect than Mary Jane.

He pointed out how suspicious it was that Ed Fonder hired a lawyer after finding bullet fragments in his car.

"There's just as much evidence against Ed Fonder as there is Mary Jane," Applebaum said. "In fact, even more."

Applebaum's suspicions about his client's brother had been growing for some time. When he first met Mary Jane and Ed together, Ed was unequivocal in stating that Mary Jane left her house for her hair salon appointment at a time that would have made killing Rhonda impossible. Later, however, Ed seemed less confident about the timing and reluctant to go on the record about it, which made Applebaum suspicious.

The defense attorney also had his doubts about Ed's supposed discovery of bullet fragments in his car. Applebaum had been inside Ed's home before, and it was squalid. It was so filthy that Thomas Joachim couldn't even step foot in the place because of his allergies. Applebaum found it hard to believe that Ed's car would be sufficiently clean that he would notice tiny bullet fragments. And while Ed claimed he noticed it because of the sunlight reflecting off the metal, Applebaum felt their house was too deep into the woods for that to have been possible.

Ed Fonder could have found his sister's gun and used it to kill Rhonda, Applebaum argued. Rhonda had been helping Mary Jane find an apartment and that could have angered her brother, the defense attorney said. He might have grown upset at the prospect of losing her company or, perhaps more importantly, her Social Security income, so he murdered Rhonda for trying to take her away from him.

"The last time she tried to move, he got angry," Applebaum said. "Did he lose it and take the gun and shoot Rhonda? I don't know."

Now, he argued, Ed Fonder was letting his sister take the fall. Not only did this protect himself from prosecution for the murder, but also he now stood to inherit the entire house if his sister were imprisoned. Even Joachim, who was less confident in Mary Jane's innocence than Applebaum, had to admit it was strange that Ed would have so willingly come forward to police with the bullet fragments, something that could prove to be so damaging to his sister's case.

Zellis wasn't particularly surprised by this new tactic from Applebaum, which he regarded as smoke and mirrors to distract the jurors. Zellis wasn't even surprised Applebaum waited until the closing statement to spring it on the jury. He probably wanted to wait until the jurors heard testimony from Ed Fonder and got a sense for how strange he seemed, Zellis thought. The police had looked into Ed Fonder during their investigation, of course, but everything he told authorities checked out. In the end, they simply believed that he didn't have the motive, while his sister did.

As Zellis expected, Applebaum also pointed to the phone call to the church at 12:07 p.m. the day Rhonda was killed. The two-minute call, he argued, was evidence that Rhonda was still alive at that time.

"Sometime between 12:07 and 12:45 is when she was

shot, not 10:54," Applebaum said. "We know where Mary Jane Fonder was. She had signed in at Holiday Hair. . . . It was physically impossible for her to be at the church."

Zellis argued against some of Applebaum's assertions in his closing argument. He finally was able to refute Applebaum's claims about the phone call by pointing out that the church answering machine likely picked up the 12:07 p.m. phone call. Zellis also stressed that Ed Fonder did the right thing by turning in the bullet fragments found in his car and then getting an attorney.

Mary Jane Fonder had a motive to kill Rhonda and her brother did not, Zellis said. He again pointed out her jealously and how she did not feel accepted by the perceived clique at the church.

"She's a murderer and all the evidence points to it," Zellis concluded.

And with that, closing arguments concluded.

Around noon on the ninth day of the trial, after Judge Boylan gave the jury its direction, the twelve jurors started their deliberations.

Judy and Sue stepped into the court hallway as Judge Boylan cleared the courtroom. They had been present for all nine days of the trial, and their emotions were running especially high now that the jury was about to deliberate. As Judy excused herself to the restroom, Sue couldn't help but run through the defense attorney's arguments over and over in her head. All those things the police hadn't done, the sloppiness of the investigators, the carelessness in their search of Mary Jane's car.

Maybe the jury won't feel they have enough evidence, Sue thought. *Maybe she'll be found not guilty.* It was a horrifying notion. The seven months since Mary Jane was arrested had put a terrible strain on the Trinity Evangelical community, and people were terrified at the thought of Mary Jane coming back. If she were somehow acquitted, Sue knew the church couldn't possibly survive.

As Sue stood waiting for Judy to return, she glanced over

at three men talking among themselves. She recognized them as three of the four alternate jurors, who also had just been dismissed. Two of them in particular seemed to be very animated in their hand motions, and Sue couldn't help but eavesdrop on their conversation. The more she heard, however, the more the pit in her stomach tightened: It sounded like they believed Mary Jane was innocent!

One of the alternates noticed Sue standing alone. Recognizing her as one of the prosecution witnesses, he approached her and started discussing the case, confirming all of Sue's fears. The alternate indeed felt Mary Jane was innocent, and expressed confidence that she would be set free. The police didn't do their job, he said. They should have done more careful tests during the car search, should have been more extensive in their investigation.

"The facts aren't there," he said to a bewildered Sue.

Then, with an increasingly condemning tone, the alternate turned his accusations toward the church itself. The pastor hadn't done enough to help Mary Jane, he said. He had turned Mary Jane away, and so had the church community. Sue was floored. She didn't know what to say. Judy approached just as the alternate walked away, and found Sue even more anxious than when she left her.

"Oh, I'm really worried now," Sue said. "I'm just not sure."

Sue told Judy of the conversation she had just had with the alternate juror. *This is a man who was almost on the jury,* Sue thought. *If he was having these thoughts, what must they be thinking right now in their deliberations?*

Judy shared Sue's concern as she processed the new information. Although she had been worried when the trial came to a close, she mostly felt Mary Jane would ultimately be found guilty. *There was too much evidence against her,* Judy thought. *And she showed no emotion during the trial at all. She barely even moved.* But now, Judy didn't know what to think.

The two women found Zellis and shared their concerns with him. By now, the assistant district attorney was very accustomed to dealing with concerned church members in this case, having fielded calls almost every week from Pastor Shreaves after Mary Jane was arrested, checking on the status of the case, or expressing apprehension about the latest newspaper article about the murder.

Zellis felt a tremendous amount of sympathy for the church's parishoners. In some ways, he thought, this trial was harder for them than it was on Rhonda's family. For Jim and Dorothy, a guilty verdict would never bring their daughter back. Their lives had already been changed forever. But for the church, there was much riding on whether Mary Jane went free or not. *If she's found not guilty, they're putting their houses up for sale and moving on,* he thought. *Their whole lives would change forever.*

Zellis put on his best smile and assured Judy and Sue everything would be just fine. But by later that afternoon, he was starting to share their anxiety. More than four hours had passed and the jury was still deliberating. Every lawyer knows the quicker a jury comes out, the more likely they are to render a guilty verdict. But Zellis tried to reassure himself. *The trial was almost two weeks,* he thought. *There was a lot of evidence for them to go through. It's a serious job they have to do.*

Stumpo had a more difficult time rationalizing.

This is torture, he thought. Having attended only one or two trials in the past, and none for murder, Stumpo wasn't used to a jury taking longer than an hour or so. In Mary Jane's case, he couldn't believe the jury would need much more time than that. In order to find her not guilty, they would have to believe Applebaum's theory that somebody else had fished the gun out of Lake Nockamixon in 1994, kept it fourteen years, then shot Rhonda and discarded it.

What's to discuss? he thought.

Egan, as usual, appeared much calmer. Juries had surprised him in the past, of course. He had seen people go free when he felt the evidence was extremely strong. Sometimes, Egan felt, a defense attorney just came across better to a jury, or the police come away looking arrogant or incompetent.

Juries, he thought. *You never know what they're thinking.*

Nevertheless, Egan felt their case against Mary Jane was strong. *We have the murder weapon,* he thought. *It's her gun.*

Zellis was notified that the jury had come out with a question: They wanted to see the sign-in sheet from the Holiday Hair salon. The inquiry did little to reduce the attorney's anxiety.

Oh my God, why do they need to see that thing? Zellis thought. *They're going to buy into this timeline thing.* The defense had argued Mary Jane couldn't have possibly had enough time to kill Rhonda and make it to the salon by the time she did, but Zellis had been sure he discredited that argument in court. *Could I have been wrong?*

Meanwhile, Pastor Shreaves was at his parents' home in Virginia, although his thoughts were completely absorbed by what was going on back in Doylestown. He had been getting updates from Judy and Sue, but now, like everyone else, there was nothing he could do but wait. Shreaves chose not to attend that day for the same reason he avoided the rest of the trial when he wasn't testifying: He didn't want Mary Jane to see him there. He didn't want to give her twisted mind any indication whatsoever that he was there to support her, or that he harbored any emotional connection to her whatsoever.

He knew his congregation was worried about the possibility of Mary Jane going free, for their safety and the future of their church. Shreaves tried to keep up a brave front in the face of this possibility, but there was no doubt in his mind: If Mary Jane went free, Shreaves would never come back to Trinity Evangelical. He would immediately put in for a transfer and move far, far away from her, from the church, from this whole tragic chapter of his life. How could he ever feel safe there again if Mary Jane was free?

Back in Doylestown, Zellis was sitting at his desk suffering the agony of the wait. It had been about ninety minutes since the jury asked their first question, and there hadn't been a word since. But suddenly, his phone rang, and he quickly grabbed it. The jury had another question: They needed a clarification for the definition of murder in the first degree and murder in the third degree.

Zellis smiled as he hung up the phone. He turned to Stumpo and Egan and informed them about the question. All three immediately recognized what the question meant for their case: It was good news. The jury was no longer questioning whether Mary Jane did it, they were just discussing whether it was premeditated.

She's done, Zellis thought. *It's only a matter of time.*

CHAPTER 39

Only about a half hour later, the jury was back in the courtroom and Mary Jane was sitting beside Applebaum at the defense table, waiting to learn her fate. Judge Boylan asked the jury for its verdict and, after what felt like an impossibly long pause to everyone sitting in the courtroom, the foreman said the word: "Guilty."

Mary Jane stared straight ahead as the jury read their verdict, her face an expressionless mask, just as it had been throughout the majority of the trial. Slowly, she reached for a box of tissues on the table in front of her, but didn't take one out. Behind her, the rest of the courtroom remained silent, no gasps or murmurs of conversation following the verdict. Judy and Sue, both sitting in the front row behind Zellis, experienced a silent wave of relief. The two women both dabbed at their eyes with tissues as Judy clutched a framed photograph of Rhonda Smith with the inscription, "Always in our Hearts."

After deliberating for more than six hours, the jury had found Mary Jane Fonder guilty of murder in the first degree and possessing an instrument of crime. Although the verdict came with a mandatory sentence of life in prison, Judge Boylan said Mary Jane would be formally sentenced within thirty days, then ordered she be returned to county prison without bail before dismissing the court.

The sheriff's deputies directed Mary Jane away from the

defense table and led her down the middle of the rows of spectators through the courtroom doors. With her hands secured in cuffs in front of her and tears forming in her eyes behind her oversized spectacles, Mary Jane vigilantly stared straight ahead as she was led through the courthouse lobby, where almost a dozen journalists immediately scrambled behind her to catch up.

"Do you still say you're innocent?" one of them asked as the television and radio reporters shoved microphones into her face. Mary Jane nodded, moving a little slower than she had in the past few days, but her voice showing little sign of strain despite the tears in her eyes.

"That's the sad part about it," she said. "I'm innocent."

One of the reporters asked whether she had a message for the members of Trinity Evangelical. Mary Jane's response was immediate, "Good-bye. God bless you all. I'll miss you. God bless all my friends at the church."

As Mary Jane and her entourage approached the set of double doors leading back to the jail, one of the reporters asked how she felt about the prospect of spending the rest of her life in prison. With just the slightest hesitation, and with a faint touch of dryness in her voice, she replied, "It doesn't sound appealing." Before disappearing through the doors, she quickly added, "But I'll go wherever the Lord sends me."

With Mary Jane gone, the reporters turned their attention to the others leaving the courtroom. They first gathered around Zellis, surrounding him as he stood just outside the courtroom doors. Though not smiling, Zellis was visibly pleased with himself and the verdict. He expressed no surprise that Mary Jane continued to proclaim her innocence, and said he imagined she would continue to do so for the rest of her life.

"She's the most defiant person I've ever encountered in my twenty-five years as a prosecutor," he said. "She will never, ever acknowledge or take responsibility for this murder. You just know that this woman has a stone for a heart. She is a stone-cold-blooded murderer."

Stumpo and Egan, meanwhile, quietly slipped through the crowd, perfectly content to leave the media attention to Zellis. Both were relieved by the outcome, especially Stumpo, who had barely allowed himself to feel any true sense of relief even after Mary Jane was arrested seven months ago. After all those months of work, his first murder case had been brought to a close, and Stumpo finally felt at peace.

As he walked away, Stumpo remembered how he had sought homicide investigation courses over the years but was never approved for one. *Well, I feel like I've had one now,* he thought. *I've had absolutely the best course you could ask for in homicide investigations.*

Zellis, only too conscious of the berating their police work received from the defense during the trial, went out of his way to compliment the state police to the press.

"This is a testament to the excellent work they did," he said.

A few of the reporters asked whether he thought Mary Jane would have anything new to say about the disappearance of her father now that she was already facing life in prison. For Zellis, there wasn't a doubt in his mind: "I would never expect her to say anything about her father, except that he's still missing."

One of the reporters asked whether Zellis thought she had killed her father, but Zellis refused to take the bait, shaking his head and saying, "We're not going to get into that right now." But, he added, "I think everybody can draw their own conclusions."

Finished with Zellis, the press turned their attention to Applebaum as he exited the courtroom. He insisted he was not surprised by the verdict and hadn't decided yet whether there would be an appeal.

"She'll be all right," he said of his client. "She feels she's at peace and puts her faith in God."

After answering a few more questions, Applebaum expressed sadness that nobody from the church came forward to defend Mary Jane or speak on her behalf as a character witness. It was reflective, he once again claimed, of the disrespect she had received from the congregation for so many years.

"We attempted to talk to the people of that church on her behalf, but they had already closed her off," he said. "Written her off the books. It's sad."

Applebaum later learned that two alternate jurors, including the one who had spoken with Sue Brunner earlier in the day, had believed Mary Jane was not guilty. Given that, Applebaum was shocked that the jury managed to reach a unanimous decision. Every defense attorney knows that you only need to reach one juror, just one, to create that reasonable doubt and get a hung jury.

And we did reach two of them, Applebaum thought. *Just not the right two.*

Judy, sitting on one of the benches outside the courtroom, still grasping her photo of Rhonda, told an Associated Press reporter that, like Zellis, she was not surprised Mary Jane continued to maintain her innocence.

"She'll deny it till she goes to the Lord," she said. But it didn't make any difference, Judy said. She was just relieved for her church and community.

"I think justice has been done, but I hope she gets help," Judy said. "If she had asked for help, asked for compassion, anything, we were there. We were there for anybody."

Sue, standing just a few feet away from Judy, seemed to take particular offense to the remarks by Applebaum about the church failing to reach out to Mary Jane.

"She was always included," Sue said. "We'll pray for her. I still can't believe she did such a terrible thing. What drove her to commit this terrible act, I'll never understand."

With a sigh, she added, "Rhonda will be in our hearts forever. There was no reason for her to die. I know in Mary Jane's heart there was a reason, but I can't find it."

Back in Lower Saucon Township, Jim Smith was sitting quietly in his favorite living room chair when he picked up the ringing telephone. It was a reporter seeking a comment about the verdict. Jim and Dorothy had decided not to stay to hear it themselves due to Jim's poor health. Besides, he knew hearing the jury send Mary Jane to prison wouldn't have made a bit of difference to him anyway, and he said as much to the reporter.

"I just think it's a sad thing that happened," Jim said. "I don't feel any joy in my heart because a woman committed a violent act. We lost our daughter. There's no joy in my heart for something that should've never happened in the first place."

CHAPTER 40

It was already guaranteed that Mary Jane Fonder would be sentenced to life, but her sentencing on December 5, 2008, still drew a big crowd to the same Bucks County courtroom where her nearly two-week trial was held.

Judy Zellner and Sue Brunner had wanted to give victim impact statements, but the Smiths wanted them limited to family members only. Rhonda's beloved niece, Amber, read a poem about how much she missed her aunt and the fun they had together, including checking out men, having sleepovers, and eating hot wings.

"She was a fun-loving person who always gave me a shoulder to cry on," she said. "Just an all-around great person. I can feel her looking down on me today."

Amber also read a letter from her father, Rhonda's brother Gary, who was stationed in Afghanistan at the time of the sentencing.

"She touched many souls and had strong, enduring friendships," Amber read from her father's letter. "By the way, Rhon's passion was to teach; she never achieved that personal goal. Please, God, let her teach in heaven. After all, we both know she's certified to be in heaven!"

Jim and Dorothy Smith chose to read letters Rhonda had written about what her parents meant to her.

"I am very fortunate because she shows me the truth when

all I see is black," Dorothy Smith read. "My mother is the best gift of all."

Jim Smith read a letter in which his daughter thanked him for helping her through all her struggles.

"You taught me, even with my mental illness I can do anything anybody else can do," Jim read. "You always dealt with me logically and now that I am living in reality, I know how priceless that is. . . . Sometimes I think [giving up] would be easier, but I still fight because I know I'm on a good team."

Judge Boylan said it was the first time a family had ever read letters from a victim at one of her sentencings.

"I think that was the most eloquent and difficult thing you could have done," she told the Smiths. "You shared with us a little bit of what the loss has been—not only to you, but to all of us."

Then it was Mary Jane's turn to talk. She had declined to speak during the trial, but she wasn't going to pass up the opportunity again. She used her time to once again defiantly protest her innocence, as she had repeatedly to reporters.

"I did not kill Rhonda Smith," Mary Jane said before the judge. "I thought she was a lovely girl [and] I certainly wasn't jealous of this woman for any reason. I'm so sorry she's gone, but in the same respect, I will be gone, too. I'm the second person in the church to be murdered, by the system."

Boylan got the last word in the hearing. She said she felt a life sentence was appropriate in this case, considering the substantial amount of evidence against Mary Jane and the disturbing statements she made to police.

"I believe it is appropriate, the sentence of life without parole, because I believe there are significant issues that have to be addressed," the judge said.

Boylan agreed to Applebaum's request to have Mary Jane's sentence for weapons possession run concurrently with her murder sentence.

"Given your client's age . . . I see no benefit to a consecutive sentence," Boylan said.

The judge also granted Applebaum's request to step down

as Mary Jane's attorney. She could no longer afford a private attorney if she appealed the case, Applebaum said.

The Smiths, absent at the trial verdict because of Jim's health, were finally able to react publicly to the guilty verdict and Mary Jane's defiance. Speaking to reporters after the sentencing, Jim Smith said he took exception to Mary Jane calling herself the second murder victim.

"You're certainly not the second person that is injured," he said, his voice breaking. "Our family was injured very much."

Amber Smith said it had been very difficult for the Smith family to hear Mary Jane repeatedly maintain her innocence.

"I'm a little upset she can't be straightforward and admit to the crime she committed, but Rhonda is in a better place now," she said.

Dorothy Smith said Mary Jane's life sentence brought some satisfaction to their family.

"She'll pay the price in there just thinking about what she did," she said.

Bob Egan didn't make any statements to the press following Mary Jane's sentencing, but it made an impact on him, as well. He had attended many sentencings over his twenty-five-year career, but never saw a convict as defiant as Mary Jane Fonder.

Even after she was convicted and sentenced, she stood up in court and denied it, he thought as he left the courthouse. *You're tried, you're convicted, and sentenced to life in prison, and you still stand up in front of a judge and say you didn't do it.*

It's amazing, he thought, shaking his head. *The biggest denial I've ever seen.*

CHAPTER 41

On March 6, 2009, almost three months after Mary Jane's sentencing, the lawsuit over Mary Jane's alleged theft of her father's pension payments was resolved. Under a settlement agreed upon by both Mary Jane and the Pension Benefit Guaranty Corp.—and signed by Ed Fonder in his sister's place—the pension payments were discontinued and the Fonders agreed to repay all benefits paid after August 25, 2000, the seven-year anniversary of their father's disappearance, when he could be legally presumed dead.

As for Mary Jane Fonder herself, David Zellis later learned that life at the Bucks County Correctional Facility wasn't quite as difficult for her as one would expect. She had always been a woman who loved to talk and now she had a captive audience, one that couldn't easily slip away from her. Since the jail didn't have many elderly tenants, Mary Jane took on a kind of grandmotherly role to the other inmates. They liked having her around and listening to her, and Mary Jane reveled in the attention.

Once she moved to the State Correctional Institution at Muncy, however, it appeared that was all about to change. The maximum-security facility was much more restrictive than county jail. She said inmates were kept in their cells all but one hour a day and given limited time outside or opportunities for social interaction with the other prisoners. Mary

Jane found the atmosphere distressing, and complained about it during a hearing in late February 2009 to determine whether she was eligible for a public defender.

"It's terrible, just terrible. I don't like it," she said. "It's not like the Bucks County prison at all. Just a lot of restrictions."

The complaint was comical to some, and infuriating to others. As one reader wrote in a letter published in *The Express-Times,* "Since when is prison supposed to be fun? The last time I checked, you went to prison to be punished, not party."

But soon, Mary Jane appeared to adapt to life in Muncy as well. Just as in Bucks County, she developed a small network of friends among the inmates who listened to her stories, helped do her hair and treated her like their own grandmother. The strict routine of prison life, in a way, was healthy for Mary Jane. She lost more than fifty pounds over the next year, eliminating the need to take diabetes medicine and making her look like a different woman than from the television and newspaper images during the trial. Soon she was painting again, mostly birds and other images from nature.

This newly discovered sense of community was upsetting to some, including members of Rhonda Smith's family. Jim Smith, in particular, said on one occasion, "There she is, happy in prison, and here we are without our daughter."

Many members of Trinity Evangelical Lutheran Church felt the same way, but Pastor Shreaves looked at it a bit differently. He still harbored anger, of course, and meant in no way to belittle the loss that the Smiths had suffered. But he had long suspected, even hoped, that Mary Jane might find a niche for herself in prison the likes of which she never found in her own life. Now, it appeared she had indeed found a community that welcomed and embraced her, and Shreaves felt it was God's grace that allowed it to happen. Everybody deserved that feeling of comfort and belonging, he felt. Even Mary Jane Fonder.

But despite all of this, Mary Jane continued for months to

adamantly insist she did not kill Rhonda Smith. At every
court hearing, every reporter's inquiry, every given opportunity, she would lift her chin and assert her innocence, just as
she had throughout her arrest, trial, and sentencing. Stumpo,
Egan, Zellis, and practically everyone involved in the investigation believed Mary Jane would never take responsibility
for the crime, in part because it would mean admitting to the
church congregation—a congregation she still felt herself to
be a part of, even now—that she had lied to them.

"I'm convinced she convinced herself that she had nothing to do with this, and a lot of it is because of her relationship with the other church members," Zellis later said. "The
church was her only life. She doesn't want any of those people
to think badly of her. She wants them to remember her in a
good light and correspond with her, to pray for her. That
church is her lifeline, and if she admitted to doing this, that
lifeline would be cut off."

But before the first year of her prison sentence was complete, Mary Jane Fonder would come to a revelation that,
once again, would shock everyone.

Mary Jane Fonder awoke with a gasp one night in her cramped
Muncy prison cell. She had been having a nightmare, one of
several she had experienced in the last few months. In it, she
had been back at the Bucks County Courthouse, sitting next
to Michael Applebaum behind the defense table as the judge
and jury listened to David Zellis argue for her incarceration.
Dreams about her trial were not uncommon for Mary Jane.
In fact, she'd been experiencing them almost since the trial
first began. But lately, they had grown both in frequency and
intensity, and they shared a common element that her previous nightmares never had.

Rhonda Smith was there.

Rhonda never spoke in Mary Jane's dreams. She simply
stood there in the courtroom, unnoticed by anyone else,
staring at Mary Jane Fonder. It was as if everything else
around Rhonda was a blur: Zellis's arguments, the murmur-
ing of the audience, Applebaum shuffling his papers, Mary

Jane could barely hear or register any of it. All she took notice of was Rhonda Smith staring at her with a deadpan expression, one horrifying enough to jolt Mary Jane from her slumber.

As Mary Jane sat there on her prison bed, her mind still racing from having been jolted awake, she experienced an emotion she had never felt before. It wasn't guilt, not exactly, it was more of a sadness that Rhonda was gone. A feeling of grief. And suddenly Mary Jane realized that in all this time—the day Rhonda was killed, the difficult months at the church that followed, the interviews with the police, the arrest, the trial, the sentencing—she had never really mourned the loss of Rhonda Smith.

How could that be? Mary Jane asked herself. A member of her church was murdered, shot to death in cold blood right inside her own church, and she never even felt sorry for the woman? Mary Jane thought back to those horrible days in January 2008, but found her recollection a bit fuzzy. She couldn't even remember the day of Rhonda's death very well.

What she remembered, instead, was a choir practice at the church one Wednesday, one week before Rhonda was killed. Practice had ended and, as Mary Jane was getting her things together, suddenly everybody was gone. The choir room, the kitchen, the church office, they were all empty. She assumed everyone had gone home, but then she found Pastor Shreaves in the social hall. Mary Jane said hello and Shreaves looked back at her, an odd frown on his face. He looked at her for a few moments, continuing to frown, then left through one of the exits.

Mary Jane believed everybody from the choir had gone home, but when she went out to her car, she noticed a lot of cars in the parking lot. Then she remembered that it was January 16, the day before Rhonda Smith's birthday. *They must be having a birthday party for her,* Mary Jane decided at the time.

A party she wasn't invited to.

That must be why Shreaves was frowning at Mary Jane, she thought, although she couldn't quite pinpoint why. Maybe he was upset with the other choir ladies for not inviting Mary Jane? Or maybe Shreaves didn't want her at the party, and was frowning because he was worried she would find out about it?

The memory of this choir practice wasn't a new revelation for Mary Jane. In fact, she had even mentioned it to Stumpo and Egan during that four-hour police interview back in February, although the significance of it was lost at the time. Both Shreaves and the ladies of the choir would later tell police that there was no such birthday party, and they weren't sure why Mary Jane came to that conclusion.

But what shocked Mary Jane now wasn't the memory of that choir practice, but how poor her memory was in the week that followed it. Everything felt like a blur after that, all the way up to the day Rhonda died. She only remembered feeling like she was in a very frantic mood, like she could snap at any moment. A feeling like those she used to have in her past . . . during her breakdowns. . . .

Oh my God, Mary Jane thought. *I think I might have had something to do with it. With what happened to Rhonda.*

Mary Jane now believed that, at the time of Rhonda's death, she was having one of the emotional breakdowns she had been experiencing every seven years or so since she was eight years old. Like the one that had left her suicidal and institutionalized when she was sixteen. It all seemed to make sense to Mary Jane, it just seemed to fit. The stress and despair over not being invited to Rhonda's birthday party—a birthday party that never occurred in the first place—seemed to trigger a period of anxiety and hysterical emotions for Mary Jane.

When she suffered her breakdowns, those periods tended to last for about a week. The exact period of time between that choir practice and the day Rhonda Smith was murdered, on January 23.

Mary Jane still didn't remember killing Rhonda Smith—or at least that's what she would later tell people. She remembered calling the church two days before Rhonda's death and, upon hearing Rhonda's voice, hanging up in surprise.

She remembered growing jealous that Rhonda was asked to answer the phones instead of her, something the police had long insisted, but that Mary Jane claimed she didn't recall before. She still didn't remember going to the church on January 23 or speaking to Rhonda that day, but she suddenly had hazy memories of going that morning to Lake Towhee, a small lake and park in nearby Haycock Township. That was something she did not recall when the police interviewed her after the murder.

She claimed not to remember planning to kill Rhonda. She insisted she couldn't remember loading the gun, bringing it with her to the church, pulling the trigger. But with these nightmares, and the new memories and emotions that led them to her, coupled with all the evidence presented against her at trial, she now believed that she had killed Rhonda Smith.

"I'm thinking, all this evidence . . . It sounds like it to me. I have to be realistic about it," she would later say. "I can't believe I let everyone down. What an end this is."

Mary Jane continued to insist, however, that she had nothing to do with the disappearance and presumed death of her father.

By this point, Mary Jane was pursuing an appeal through a court-appointed attorney, having claimed her trial counsel from Michael Applebaum was ineffective. It was a fairly common tactic following a guilty verdict, and one Zellis and the police had little concern would prove effective. Zellis truly believed Applebaum provided the best possible defense he could have, especially considering that Mary Jane appeared to have tied his hands by forbidding him from pursuing an insanity defense.

But in February 2010, Mary Jane rendered the argument moot when she formally withdrew the ongoing appeal, something she had apparently planned to do for some time following her jailhouse revelations. Some, however, argued it was more related to money: She was eligible for a public defender, but would have had to put up for collateral the $400,000 Kintnersville home she co-owned with her brother.

Prior to officially withdrawing the appeal, Mary Jane Fonder shared with reporters the alleged realizations she came to in prison, first published in a December 2009 article in *The Express-Times,* then in a January 2010 article in *The Intelligencer.* Despite falling short of a full-blown confession, Mary Jane's partial admission of guilt came as a shock to practically everyone involved in the case, especially Stumpo, Egan, and Zellis.

"I never thought I would live to see the day when Mary Jane Fonder would take any responsibility for the murder of Rhonda Smith," Zellis told *The Express-Times,* adding, "Tragically, that doesn't bring Rhonda Smith back to life."

But as is usually the case with Mary Jane Fonder, the announcement did not leave the matter entirely clear.

Neither Zellis nor Stumpo and Egan believed Mary Jane's claim that she could not remember actually shooting and killing Rhonda. They believed she was too cunning and calculating, that the murder was obviously premeditated, and that Mary Jane took too many steps to cover her tracks for that to have been the case.

They recalled how, once suspicion fell upon her, she baked a pie to comfort the grieving Smith family, ordered a memorial statue in Rhonda's honor for the church, and sent sympathy cards to fellow congregants. Upon realizing the police were going to learn from phone records that she had called Rhonda two days before the murder, Mary Jane not only told police that information, but went out of her way to make sure others in the church knew it, too, in case police started asking them questions.

This was a woman who thought she could outsmart the police, the authorities believed, just like she thought she did when they were investigating the disappearance of her father. This was not the behavior of someone who could not remember what she had done.

Likewise, suspicion remained among members of the

church. Judy Zellner, for one, found little comfort in Mary Jane's partial confession.

"I don't like all this, 'I can't remember,' 'The evidence is against me,' all of this," she later said. "I wish she would just come out and say, 'Yes, I did it.'"

Michael Applebaum and Thomas Joachim were very surprised to read about Mary Jane's new admissions. She had never given them any indication she had shot Rhonda, nor did she ever tell them about these breakdowns from her past. If she had, Joachim believed they definitely would have pursued an insanity defense, or perhaps a plea bargain with the prosecution. If she had not tied their hands by insisting upon her innocence, Joachim wondered, what might the outcome of her trial had been?

For Jim and Dorothy Smith, Mary Jane's words brought no closure. But then again, there was no closure to be had. The arrest, the trial, the conviction, none of it was going to bring back their daughter. And, once the investigation and trial were no longer there to distract them, the pain of their loss only grew stronger as time passed.

But Jim said he did find at least a tiny bit of comfort in the fact that Mary Jane was starting to realize the pain she had inflicted on those who knew and loved Rhonda Smith.

"It makes us feel good, the fact that she's coming out in the open with this," Jim told *The Express-Times*. "I was asked by reporters at the court, and I said she has to think about what she did to Rhonda. That's what she did."

EPILOGUE

For his role in leading the Rhonda Smith murder investigation, Gregory Stumpo was named the 2009 Trooper of the Year for the Pennsylvania State Police's Troop M, which included the barracks for Dublin, Bethlehem, Belfast, Fogelsville, and Trevose.

"That case was a very, very complicated case," said Captain D. Michelle Turk, the troop's commanding officer, during a ceremony on May 1, 2009. "He was very tenacious."

Also honored at the same ceremony were Doug Sylsberry and his now-nine-year-old son Garrett, who received Meritorious Citizenship Awards for finding and turning in the murder weapon.

"They could have easily kept the gun or thrown it back in the lake," Turk said of the Sylsberrys at the ceremony. "They did what's right."

Stumpo continues to work for the criminal investigations unit at the Dublin barracks.

Robert Egan retired from the Pennsylvania State Police after twenty-five years of service in late 2008, almost immediately after Mary Jane was sentenced. The next May, he was selected by Northampton County District Attorney John Morganelli to spearhead a new task force investigating the county's cold cases. In October 2010, Egan and Trooper Raymond Judge, who also worked on the Mary Jane Fonder case, made their first cold case arrest with Lucinda Andrews, a fifty-five-year-old woman accused of shooting John Joseph Mayerchak to death in his Northampton County apartment in September 1985. Andrews pleaded guilty to third-degree murder in August 2011 and was sentenced to ten to twenty years in state prison.

Egan continues pursuing other cold cases, including the unsolved murder of Charlotte Fimiano, a real estate agent found shot and strangled to death in Lower Saucon Township on September 12, 1997. Egan had worked as an investigator on the Fimiano case and, out of more than seventy-five homicide cases over the course of his quarter-century career, it is the only one that has gone unsolved.

David Zellis made an unsuccessful bid for Bucks County judge in 2009. Since he was not an active politician throughout his career, he was not endorsed by either of the two major political parties, and his campaign lacked funding from local attorneys. In August 2011, Zellis departed from the Bucks Country District Attorney's office to start his own defense law practice, Zellis Law. He had been an assistant district attorney for twenty-six years, the longest tenure in the county's history."

The Mary Jane Fonder case marked the first time law enforcement authorities in Bucks County ever handled gunshot residue in the course of their investigation. They learned from the questions Michael Applebaum raised during the trial about how the state police searched for gunshot residue in Mary Jane's car. In response, Zellis set up a meeting between local law enforcement officials to develop a new search procedure that included far more precautions to limit any possible gunshot residue transfer from police uniforms and guns. In the future, Zellis believes, gunshot residue searches will be handled with a great deal more care.

Gregory Shreaves remains pastor of the Trinity Evangelical Lutheran Church, where the congregation membership has struggled to heal, but has for the most part remained intact. Mary Jane Fonder continues to contribute financially to the church from prison, and, to this day, she remains on the church prayer list.

Jim and Dorothy Smith continue to live in Lower Saucon Township and attend Trinity Evangelical Lutheran Church. On occasion, Jim feels some of his fellow parishioners do not feel comfortable having them around and would rather they find a new church, but that has only strengthened his resolve to remain. The Smiths started a memorial scholarship in Rhonda's name at her alma mater, Saucon Valley High School. The church has donated toward it.

The investigation into the disappearance of Edward Fonder III remains open and unsolved. Mary Jane Fonder is considered the prime suspect in the case, and the only suspect that has been publicly identified by authorities. However, as the police cannot divert resources from active cases with suspects not already incarcerated, the pace of the investigation has been slow.

Mary Jane Fonder remains incarcerated, serving a life sentence at the State Correctional Institution at Muncy, Pennsylvania.